LAWYERS IN TRANSITION

Planning a Life in the Law

Mark Byers, Ph.D.

Don Samuelson, Esq.

Gordon Williamson, Esq.

First Printing . . . . June 1988
Second Printing. . . January 1989

P. O. Box 9
W. Newton, Massachusetts 02165
ISBN 0-945736-00-2

". . . beware of what you want, for surely you will get it."

Ralph Waldo Emerson (1803—1882)

"Oh yeh?"

Fred "Butch" Emerson (1964—   )

CONTENTS

TABLE OF EXERCISES

SHORT BUT IMPORTANT PREFACE

"Oh that my words were now written!
Oh that they were printed in a book!"
Job 19:23

1. For many years now, poorly thought out job and career decisions have been epidemic among lawyers. The underlying reason for this is, we believe: The failure to have an articulated professional destination and a plan for getting there. Our thesis is this: No matter what choices are or are not open to you, planning a career in the law (or out of it after a tour of duty) is feasible, valuable, and rare.

2. With any work of non-fiction (in which category, we hope, this book will get placed) unanimity on the importance and ordering of contents is visionary. (The famous Casner and Leach Property casebook had a Preface and a Dissenting Preface. The order of materials in the book apparently tracked that used in class by Professor Casner. The Dissenting Preface listed the order preferred by Professor Leach.)

As the Table of Contents reflects, the guts of this book is in the second section which we have called the Foreground. For the impatient reader, our majority advice is to begin there. That is where tools assisting with the twin keys of assessment and planning are found. If your time is really (really, now) that valuable, go ahead and skip the Background chapters.

But there is much of value in the Background section. And that value is not just a vague, diffuse feel for the legal profession. The principal value is getting your subconscious thinking about realistic options and your real priorities, rather than those that the system imposes, so you will be better prepared for accurate, penetrating, and valuable assessment and planning. Even for busy attorneys, shortcuts don't always end up saving time.

3. As it progressed, our Bibliography began to take on a life of its own. When it got to be longer than any Chapter then extant, it demanded equal billing as Chapter 13, Resources. It also cried for a guide to its organization, which we have provided in the form of a Chapter Outline near the start of Chapter 13.

4. As children we are taught to revere books and treat them carefully. But in law school we learned to mark up books furiously in preparing for class. This is definitely a "mark up" book. Highlight any truths that leap off the page for you, do Exercises in the spaces provided (or do them elsewhere if more space is necessary), challenge the authors in marginal notes.

During the tumultuous Vietnam War years, a counterculture hero turned author urged bookstore browsers to "STEAL this book". We trust that your career concerns will not push you to that extreme in order to USE this book.

ACKNOWLEDGMENTS

Various Exercises and assessment ideas have been graciously provided by Maureen Provost, Assistant Dean and former Placement Director of Fordham Law School. Some have been modified and adapted for our audience and purposes.

The Resources Chapter was written and compiled by Elizabeth Debold, a consultant to law firms.

Discussions with, and criticisms by, various people have bettered this effort. Those people include, Gary A. Munneke, Esq., Roberta Ramo, Esq., Maureen Provost, Elizabeth Debold and the professional staff at Samuelson Associates.

"You dawdle, daydream. You make lists of things to do but can't get started. You seem to be restricted from doing what you know you should be doing. These problems will dissolve when you read Chapter Ten of my new book, at eight dollars and ninety-five cents."

Chapter 1

Transitions: Taking Turns

"I have been a stranger in a strange land."
Exodus 2:22

And now for the least startling disclosure since Potter Stewart on pornography: The legal profession is, in this last quarter of the twentieth century, in a period of rapid and extensive transition.

Transitions, really. Because every lawyer is affected by rapid change in various aspects of America's legal mechanism, including:

1. the way lawyers get trained;
2. the dissatisfaction and mobility of lawyers;
3. the enormous growth in young talent entering the practice of law;
4. the buyer/seller relationships between clients and lawyers;
5. the relationships among lawyers (especially within firms);
6. what a lawyer actually spends his or her day doing; and
7. the national perception of the value of lawyers and their work.

With all of these transitions, to which do we refer in our title? All of them are discussed, but for our purposes none of them is the crux.

The profession in transition is really a backdrop against which we address the individual transitions of individual lawyers as they travel direct and circuitous routes in their search for the financial and psychic rewards they seek from their profession. The moving metes and broken bounds of the legal profession form an increasingly fluid and frustrating map upon which each lawyer plots his or her career; consciously or otherwise. Unfortunately, in our estimation, the "otherwise" group of lawyers constitute a majority.

Historically, lawyers have haphazardly discovered these routes rather than truly planning them. In recent years, enterprising lawyers and thoughtful scholars alike have questioned such bizarre herd behavior by otherwise smart and independent thinkers. The authors have monitored and participated in this revisionist thinking from the perspectives of law school psychologist, legal career and legal search consultant, and practicing lawyer.

Wheel Inventors Anonymous

Career planning for lawyers has already been invented. Heretofore, however, aids to job change decisions and to actual career planning have been mostly verbal and anecdotal and available to the lawyers and law students who need them on a haphazard basis. It is our fervent, albeit fragile, belief that this book collects, organizes, and expands upon the information and tools needed by lawyers for informed career and job decision making.

Cliches would not become cliches without some important underlying truth. "Reinventing the wheel" must be said a million times a day . . . in Manhattan alone . . . usually without sufficient empathy for the important point it contains.

Unfortunately, every year large numbers of lawyers travel their career paths, and attempt to make turns in it, using wheels they have hurriedly jerry-built during a few precious spare hours.

You may improve upon the existing wheel, to be sure, but you need not start from scratch. If judges had to decide all cases without knowing what other judges had decided previously, not only would their job be unmanageably difficult, their decisions would inevitably become inconsistent with each other. In our experience, many lawyers must overcome a normally healthy skepticism of using the work product of others (even, shudder, non-lawyers) in order to profit from the ideas and tools we offer. We invite and encourage you to improve upon the wheels that you will find in following chapters. But, we urge you at least to try wheels that have smoothed some rough transition paths for other lawyers.

Bi-centricism

Each of us is likely a more or less integrated personality. But, like most major lifetime decisions, job and career decisions involve classes of factors that weigh more heavily either on a "strategic" or on a "psychological" scale. While the factors cannot be rigorously sorted into two bins, an awareness of this bi-centric character of the career planning dynamic is especially important since the weight of the factors inevitably change at various stages in your career. (For example, a psychological factor of "not living in New York" may be paramount for the long term but may be overcome by strategic considerations of the best training position for the first few years after law school.)

Systemic Issues

In recent years there has been much debate about the apparently growing glut of young attorneys. Such a glut raises philosophical and practical problems. In the practical area of competition for niches and clients, the lawyer with the well thought out plan will have a significant advantage.

The philosophical debate concerns the value of the profession's services to society. Any serious national rethinking of the place of attorneys should include an expansion of the spectrum of tasks that attorneys can valuably perform in our society. Lawyering is not the only job open to lawyers.

One way to view law school is as a graduate school of reading, writing, and thinking—using law simply as subject matter to teach skills of applicability far beyond the legal profession. Even if, as some suggest, America produces too many lawyers, it surely does not produce too many people skilled in critical analysis and careful communication.

Probably the most noteworthy of the thoughtful comments about the need for bright, creative people broadly across our society were articulated by Harvard President and former Harvard Law School Dean Derek C. Bok in a Report to the Harvard Board of Overseers for 1981-1982 entitled *A Flawed System.*

> " . . . I am constantly struck by how complicated many jobs have become, how difficult many institutions are to administer, how pressing are the demands for more creativity and intelligence. However aggressive our schools and colleges are in searching out able youths and giving them a good education, the supply of exceptional people is limited. Yet far too many of these rare individuals are becoming lawyers at a time when the country cries out for more talented business executives, more enlightened public servants, more inventive engineers, more able high-school principals and teachers."

Plainly, high priority ought to be given to a long, hard look at your intended, or merely inferred, professional destination and at the planned, or merely probable, path.

Two More Points

First, you must take personal responsibility for your career planning. Neither we nor anyone else can do it for you. If career planning strikes you as valuable, you might as well resolve right now to put some personal effort into it. Otherwise this or any other book will become a temporary amusement rather than a valuable set of self-help principles.

Second, any career analysis or plan must be hung on real-world pegs defined by the profession's real-world parameters. At times when the profession itself is in transition, those parameters and pegs ought not to slide in as unexpressed assumptions. We begin in the next Chapter, therefore, with a brief look at the state of the profession.

Chapter

2

The State of the Profession: Taking the Long View

"There is no remembrance of former things . . . "
Ecclesiastes 1:11

"We have a strange and wonderful partnership," A, of the firm of A & B, told us. "My partner is strange and I'm wonderful." While old A, Esq. was, presumably, practicing his wit, the practice of law itself is, indeed, strange and wonderful. At times more strange and at times more wonderful.

Most readers of this book will be at a time in their lives when the strangeness overshadows the wonderfulness, when they are unhappy or dissatisfied, when they are questioning their job or career choice. This is unfortunate. Even those in the euphoria of wonderfulness ought to be using their considerable intellect and expensive training to consider thoughtfully their own life's work and the path it is taking. More than practitioners of any other profession, calling, or trade, lawyers as a group seem to trust the fates rather than their own analytical skills in finding their life's work.

Awe And Scorn

Lawyers function in an environment of mixed awe and scorn. Mainstream America surely has a love/hate relationship with its lawyers. Popular topics of conversation at suburban cookouts and cocktail parties include how the lawyers are dragging out the divorce, how I had a great case that was lost from lawyer bungling, and how another lawyer recently got caught cheating on his taxes.

At the same time, lawyers are respected because of assumptions about their large incomes, because of the numbers of ex-lawyers who achieve political power, because of the ultimate authority of judges in our system, and because of the historical importance of lawyers in our country. (Lawyers got together and drafted two of the most important documents in modern history: the Declaration of Independence and the Constitution. One can become too arrogant on this point, however. A famous trial lawyer was once asked to speak to a medical convention about relations between the professions. He began, "When doctors were still applying leeches to their patients, a group of lawyers got together and wrote the Declaration of Independence." He was not invited back the next year.)

Lawyers' incomes are the subject of much misinformation both within and outside of the profession. Despite the attraction of public service to law students in the late 1960's and early 1970's, the rapid growth in the numbers of lawyers stems, fundamentally, from the general perceptions of the large incomes that can result from law practice.

Department of Labor statistics for 1985 place lawyers, at an average weekly income of $724, ahead of doctors and engineers in average compensation and more than twice the national average for all occupations. As with professional sports and the entertainment industry, however, averages of legal compensation may hide more than they reveal.

The range of legal incomes is enormous. Even larger is the range of total annual incomes (which can include large capital gains from transactions that a lawyer had access to because of his or her practice). With the 1985 median legal income at about $37,000, for every lawyer making $500,000 there had to be 27 making $20,000.

Part of the disparity is due to the relative youth of the profession. With the rapid growth in the number of lawyers in recent years, there are many more young lawyers (earning relatively less) than older lawyers. This can account for only part of the range, however. As with thespians. For every actor commanding seven figures per movie, there are thousands living hand-to-mouth as actor/waiters. (A leading Hollywood agent has estimated that in Southern California the average annual income of the 50,000 members of the Screen Actors Guild is about $5,000. Presumably that 50,000 includes folks named Cher and Dustin.)

The position of lawyers in North America is anomalous for additional reasons. For one, lawyers must serve various masters: The judicial system (as officers of the court), their clients (under the canons of ethics), and the financial interests of themselves and their families. Fortunately, the tri-headed master often speaks in unison. Nonetheless, there are many occasions in a legal career when soul searching not required in other jobs becomes, temporarily, a full-time and enervating task.

While juggling their obligations and loyalties, lawyers are held to higher intellectual and ethical standards than almost any other group in American society. As with judges and law enforcement professionals, society demands high standards in lawyers' conduct. Since *law*yers are presumed experts in, and devoted to, the law as a whole and in its specifics, any transgression by a lawyer is somehow more alarming than a similar peccadillo by another professional. Professional malpractice by a doctor and by a lawyer are viewed as more or less equivalent. But in a host of other violations of society's rules (e.g., tax shenanigans, motor vehicle violations), the transgression of the doctor is viewed as irrelevant to his professional oath and thus venial. For a lawyer, most believe there is no transgression that is not related to a lawyer's professional responsibilities.

The New Economics of the Legal Profession

The burdens of multiple masters and higher standards must be manageable. The profession, at least in numbers of practitioners and aspirants, is booming. While precise numbers are hard to come by, most sources indicate that the number of lawyers in the United States is between 600,000 and 700,000 in 1986 and that on the order of 35,000 new J.D.'s are granted each year. The number of American lawyers has doubled since 1970. It seems inevitable that by the early 1990's we will have 1,000,000 lawyers: one for every 250 Americans. (In 1965 it was about one in 630. In 1985 it was about one in 360; one in 64 in Washington, DC.)

The driving force behind such expansion of the profession in not hard to find. Between 1970 and 1980, when the number of lawyers doubled from about 300,000 to about 600,000, regulatory programs of the Great Society were funded and the dollars spent by corporations for legal services increased fourfold from about $7 billion to about $28 billion. Beginning around 1980, however, some thoughtful commentators have cautioned about unappreciated structural changes in the fundamental supply/demand relationships within the profession which were masked by the camouflage of continuing growth and superficial business-as-usual.

In this same mid-1960's to mid-1980's time frame, there has been simultaneous specialization and generalization. Individual attorneys within firms have tended more and more to specialize in ever more narrowly defined niches. The large firms themselves, however, were busy adding departments and specialties to their substantial repertoires in order to serve all the needs of multinational, multi-billion dollar corporate clients.

Not only were corporate clients mostly growing, but the needs of even static clients were increasing because of major expansions in government regulation. Commentators of all political leanings agree that, for better or for worse, corporate clients had dramatically increased counselling and litigation needs in the late 1970's as compared to, say, 1965.

A pendulum, as any patent attorney will tell you, reaches its maximum speed just before it begins to slow down. The torrid pace of growth in legal service consumption in the late 1970's has been somewhat quieted by the deregulation climate of the 1980's.

In addition to a sustained growth in lawyers accompanying a diminishing growth in legal work, another major change in the practice of law in the 1980's has been advertising by lawyers.

An initial tentative entry into this brave new world by sole practitioners in large metropolitan areas (usually having a tort plaintiff subspecialty—e.g., birth defect litigation) has grown into a major shift in lawyers' attitudes and actions. Former Chief Justice Burger, a supporter of lawyer advertising when the issue was before his court, has recently expressed shock at the nature and volume of such advertising.

Large national firms of impeccable reputation, while eschewing actual advertising, have been hiring public relations firms to assist in getting their names and successes before consumers. Even if hesitantly and with mixed success:

> ". . . most [major Boston firms] have taken what, for them, is a dramatic step by hiring public relations firms and consultants to plan and implement their marketing efforts and lobby the media outlets they once shunned.
>
> "The attempts by the law firms to publicize themselves are rudimentary by the standards of sophisticated public relations, and so far they have kept to basics like press releases and low-key brochures describing the various areas of their practices. They are also talking to reporters—on the record—and even inviting them to their offices . . .
>
> "But traditions are hard to break, and many firms that have embraced public relations companies are not totally comfortable with the relationships. Neither are the public relations people, who at times find the lawyers exceedingly hard to please and too tentative in their approach . . .
>
> "Mid-sized Boston law firms . . . have been particularly aggressive in using public relations to market themselves. [The partners of one firm] routinely write columns for newspapers and business publications and make guest appearances on radio talk shows to discuss legal issues. The firm experimented last year with its own regular half-hour show on a Boston area station."
> (*The Boston Globe*, May 13, 1986)

The business arrangements in which lawyers ply their trade are also evolving at a rate that would have dizzied a lawyer merely thirty years ago. While one and two person firms still account for the majority of all lawyers practicing in the United States, many of these individuals (and especially younger ones) are being lured into the relative security of the Jacoby & Myers or the Hyatt Legal Services type of firm. While the nature of their practice may change little and while they must remain very self reliant, in theory they have swapped a sole practice for membership in one of the largest law firms in the world.

The structural changes in medium sized and large firms in recent years are even greater. While exceptions remain, in many firms the dichotomy of associates and partners has all but disappeared. Senior associates may be treated more like partners than like junior associates, and partners come in various varieties. No longer can a lawyer or law student assume that the roles of associates and partners are approximately equivalent in externally similar firms.

In many major firms the important classification of lawyers does not appear on the letterhead or in law directories. That distinction is between the owners of the practice and the employees. A firm of a hundred partners may actually have but ten "Owners" who split the lion's share of the firm profits. All other partners may be "salaried profit centers" whose income is limited to fixed salaries and discretionary bonuses related to the overall economic performance of the firm.

A November 17, 1986 *Business Week* article, "Megafirms Are Taking Over Corporate Law", alludes to such structural changes:

> "The trend presents a host of management issues for the big firms. Critics worry about the quality of the legal work the profession will deliver to the corporate world. Lawyers can no longer count on a glittering partnership as a reward for years of toil. Many now find they are little more than career employees, even when they win the once-valued title. Some firms . . . have even created a class of junior lawyers who have no hope of partnership."

Other firms seem more like a co-op than a traditional law firm. In effect, groups of lawyers band together for convenience and efficiency, but with each "partner" essentially a sole practitioner for financial purposes.

The *Business Week* article pithily concludes:

> " . . . painful dislocation . . . is one of the inevitabilities in a profession that is busy reinventing itself."

The key point, of course, is that there is no longer a traditional or conventional firm structure and that each firm must be evaluated anew. Law students who, probably unrealistically, expect to spend their careers with the firm that they first join, as well as experienced lawyers considering a lateral move, can be surprised a few years downstream unless they investigate firm structure carefully in the beginning.

Personal Responsibility for Career Planning

In an earlier era, it was reasonable to hang out a shingle or to join a firm with the only requirement for advancement being the acceptance of assignments as they were given and the performance of work in a manner satisfactory to the firm. In an era of industry and firm predictability and stability, this was a satisfactory system. In these earlier years, the legal needs of clients were relatively stable and one's particular work content was not a particularly important component of long term success. For sole practitioners, there were fewer competitors per 100,000 of population. For attorneys in major firms, there were few sophisticated in-house lawyers in the picture at corporate clients, client relationships were stable, and the partnership decision was six to nine years in the future. One looked back on careers not forward. Planning was deemed unnecessary.

A major development of the 1970's that affected the way law firms organize and run themselves was the growth in size and importance of corporate law departments. In addition to other responsibilities, house counsel now must often decide whether to "make" or "buy" legal services. The decisions concerning the services that they buy are made more on the basis of individual attorneys' experience and credentials, rather than on that of a whole firm. The house counsel acts like a general contractor for his clients, the business managers of the company. Outside lawyers and firms resemble subcontractors with transactional rather than institutional relationships with the company. The key to success in this environment is for a lawyer in private practice serving large corporate clients to be on the list of preferred outside attorneys. This becomes an individual rather than a firm responsibility.

Career Implications

The new marketplace for legal services has important implications for lawyers trying to plan their careers. For example, it is increasingly unlikely that a first job will be permanent. Only 20% of lawyers starting with a sizable firm become partners of that firm. And, of those who eventually become partners, not all enjoy the privileges traditionally associated with partnership. Many partners are really employees of other partners.

There are two fundamental issues lawyers should confront in planning their careers. First, there is the "strategic" question of competence building. Where do I get trained? By whom? Doing what? Over what period of time? In what specialty area? With a view to developing what practice specialties?

The second issue is the "psychological" issue of life-style and choice of professional setting. Where and how do I want to live? How important is my profession to my whole life? What atmosphere and style suits me? What types of co-workers do I want around me? Do I need the freedom of a sole practice? Is it clear that I want to practice law for the rest of my life?

As important as the "life-style" matters are, they seem often overemphasized by younger lawyers and underemphasized by older lawyers. Indeed, lawyers generally do not distinguish very well between early, on-the-job-training positions and their ultimate practice. A closer attention to the training aspects of early, often temporary, jobs might lead one to select a superior short term training experience even if in a second choice city or with a culturally incompatible firm or organization.

Competence Building

A lawyer's training does not end with graduation from law school. Law schools, in general, teach research, reading, writing, and thinking, using law as the subject matter. Many legal educators, as well as the rest of us, assume that much of the practice of law will be learned when needed and that the practical skills needed to produce client services effectively will be learned after graduation; often in first and second jobs.

An ABA Task Force on Legal Competence has defined legal competence as encompassing three major themes:

1. Knowledge of substantive law and of the legal system—legal knowledge.
2. Ability to apply that knowledge to the diagnosis and solution of client problems, and to produce relevant products and services—legal skills.
3. Efficiency in the production of these solutions, products, and services—management.

The acquisition of this multiple function competence is essentially a nine year process, in some ways analogous to medical education. It can be thought of as successive three year training periods: Law school, an "internship," and a "residency." Law schools do a good job in training students to find and use law in preparing advisory opinions. They also introduce students to public policy and legislative considerations, and to the jurisdictional and procedural components of the legal system. Except for research and writing, there is little time to spend on teaching the "skills" of lawyering.

Skill training is emphasized during the internship. Young lawyers often join working teams involved in the diagnosis, design and production of legal services to provide real solutions to real problems for real clients. This experience emphasizes the differences between being a good law student and a good lawyer. Law school tends to be the "special event" of analysis. The practice of law, however, requires a decathlon of skills, most of which are not central to either the course instruction or the grading systems of law schools.

Evaluation of early job opportunities in terms of the acquisition of legal and management skills remains the exception among young lawyers. The opportunities for the development of legal and productivity skills available in government agencies, corporate law departments, and private firms can vary depending upon your eventual post-competence career goals.

So, how should a legal career be assessed and planned? There are some general principles. (Specific tactics are presented in subsequent chapters.)

First, a legal career should be particularized. It should meet the interests, abilities, capacities and priorities of the individual lawyer. Unfortunately, the hierarchical structure of the profession—oriented to the ranking of law students, law schools, and law firms—works against this relatively obvious thought. That structure produces institutional pressures on you to seek the "higher" paths of the practice rather than those most appropriate to your individual interests and values. In simple terms, you should not live out someone else's dream.

Second, legal careers are built out of credentials and increments that tend to define the alternatives presented at the next decision point. Without dwelling upon missed credential opportunities (why, oh why, didn't I apply myself more diligently and get that A in Torts?), you should choose from current opportunities recognizing the values to you of the credentials and skills you are accumulating.

Third, there is a major change in your marketability in seeking a second job. Your first job was based largely upon your law school's reputation, your grades, and your projection of a reasonable personality. Actual work experience adds a major new credential available to those evaluating you for a second position. You must learn to present that experience in the most effective way.

Fourth, the supply and demand for lawyers varies by geography, by practice area, and over time. Your bargaining power is not a simple matter, therefore, but needs careful assessment.

Fifth, during the competency building years you would do well to consider employment alternatives as if they were unpaid time investments. Think of the money you receive as a pleasant bonus. What long term returns will be generated by each alternative? What elements of competence will be obtained? How? What will your Resume look like after three years in each alternative position? And how will that advance your long term career interests?

Whither Your Life?

Historically, lawyers have lived by a double standard: A high standard for analyzing and addressing clients' affairs and a low one for thinking about their own careers. On the bright side, the situation is improving. One of the major themes in the practice of law over the last twenty years has been the increasing sensitivity of lawyers to the practical implications of their career goals. Every year sees ever larger numbers of young lawyers making career moves. Still, large numbers of lawyers in the middle and late years of their practices are amazed at the thicket of happenstance that has nudged them to their permanent geographical locations, firms, positions, and specialties.

The tortured, serendipitous career path is exciting, but so is Russian roulette. A major theme of this book is that a cold sober look at your own desires and talents, and at the realities of the evolving profession, ought to be undertaken early in your career and periodically along the way. We even presume to offer suggestions on the substance and procedure of such analyses.

Before you plan your own next step you should take a closer look at the influences that have contributed to the greatly enhanced lawyer mobility in recent years. At any give moment, about a quarter of all young lawyers are contemplating a transition to greener pastures. An analysis of why and where they go should assist your own analysis. It is to this that we now turn.

Chapter

3

Lawyer Dispersion and Dissatisfaction: Taking Flight

"I have spread you abroad as the four winds of the heaven."
Zechariah 2:6

The hardest thing for an experienced attorney (or any working person) to explain is the unpredictable, messy process by which people move from one job to the next. Even lawyers in a firm with noticeable turnover may have no idea of where people go; they just seem to disappear. Although the process of job change is not random, it is still difficult to understand without the experience of going through it all. The task of imagining change is difficult for lawyers because, until recently, the professional ideal was that of stability. According to one recent study, lawyers are "the most likely of those in any profession . . . to stay in their profession over the full course of the occupational career." (John P. Heinz and Edward O. Laumann, *Chicago Lawyers, The Social Structure of the Bar*, Russell Sage Foundation and the American Bar Association, New York, 1982.)

What then, are the facts about job mobility? Why do people change legal positions? How frequently do they do so? With what results? Those contemplating a move from a first to a second legal position often are concerned that their first job should be a lifetime commitment and whether the type of legal work they have done or would like to pursue will limit their future options. Those on their second or third jobs need to know the impact of further movement. All of these groups want to know how much movement is the norm for different kinds of positions; to know when people move, where they go, and how radical a shift they make. Perhaps most importantly, the job changer should know something about the dissatisfactions that impel lawyers to leave their jobs in order to compare those motivations and feelings with their own.

Fortunately, there is some hard data to address these questions. Some of it comes from a study that looked at the careers of nearly 7000 graduates, in four disparate age groups (law school classes of 1956, 1969, 1974, and 1981) and from seven varied law schools. (Leona Vogt, *From Law School to Career: Where Do Graduates Go and What Do They Do?*, President and Fellows of Harvard College, Cambridge, 1986. The "Career Paths Study".) From it, we obtain a picture of career patterns over many years.

Looking at Career Paths

The Study gathered information by class year and by size and type of employer. Looking at the classes of '56, '69 and '74, fewer than one quarter of them were still in the same organization they entered upon leaving law school. This might not be so startling, but consider that in 1984, at the time of the study, one half of the class of '81 had already changed jobs. Moreover, although two is the average number of jobs held by all classes since graduation from law school, approximately forty percent of the classes of '74 and '81 have already had two jobs. This Study thus suggests growing mobility among the younger classes.

The impression of increased mobility is reinforced by the data on the class of 1974. It made no difference if a lawyer started out in a firm of over eighty-five attorneys, in a small firm, or in legal services. After eleven years lawyers in all employment categories had experienced a median of two job changes. Those at least sixteen years out in large law firms tended to settle down in their careers and make few changes after the first one or two. At the other extreme, nonlegal business settings yielded the most movement.

The Study showed that big firms have provided relatively stable employment settings. Big firm lawyers in the older classes—generally partners—started and stayed with their first type of employer more than other categories of attorneys while today the volume of job changes into and out of big firms is much larger.

Obviously, the choice of a big firm does not guarantee stability. Rather, stability is increasingly a matter of employee choice. Voluntary turnover has been a matter of concern to many firms, some of which have responded by taking a hard look at their working conditions. Other large firms, although anxious to retain associates, are actually beginning to accept that turnover may be a normal fact of life as it is in other businesses.

Certainly, turnover in the big firms doesn't mean wholesale defection from that type of firm. Indeed, a look at Table 1, "Type of First Position After Law School By Current Position," reveals that 67 percent of the class of '81 who started in large law firms remained in that category even if they had changed jobs. (Note that the Table shows percentages still working in the same practice setting as their first job.) Yet, the percentage shrank to 47 percent for those eleven years out, suggesting that over time the big firms do see attrition. Moreover, the Study indicated that in recent years nearly half of those leaving first jobs in private practice (in firms of all sizes) leave private practice entirely. Turnover results from *career* changes as well as from *job* changes.

We should emphasize that the data covers only *classes* of employers. For example, the data does not speak to mobility of lawyers from one large firm to another—a type of movement on the rise as young lawyers begin to realize the training value of temporary "intern" and "residency" positions.

Leaving aside the question of mobility from the large firms (which, after all, comprise but a small segment of the total lawyer population), to what extent does the first job out of law school determine future employment? Table 1 begins to answer this question.

For each category of employment, Table 1 shows the percentage of each class still in that category and in other organizations where sizeable numbers of lawyers are currently working. Thus, it is possible to get a picture of the limits of dispersion of lawyers who started out in different practice settings.

Recognizing that the rapid transitions in the legal marketplace in the last decade complicate the data, some conclusions can still be drawn from these data:

1. People who start in very small firms tend to remain in small firms or go into solo practice, government, or business. If they have been in practice for about fifteen years, they may have moved into, or expanded into, a 9 to 35 lawyer firm.

2. Those starting in small firms (9 to 35) appear to have access, by movement or expansion, to medium sized firms (35 to 84) or to smaller firms. Those graduating in '56 seem to have moved into a somewhat wider range of firms, either because there has been more time for the firms to grow with them or because their firms were perceived to be larger and more impressive than they would be today. In interpreting this data it is important to keep in mind that the definition of a large firm has changed dramatically in the last twenty years. Chicago's Sidley and Austin, now in excess of 400 lawyers, had a population of 79 in 1970. In any case, all Table 1 persons in the Study entering small

Table 1

TYPE OF FIRST POSITION AFTER LAW SCHOOL BY CURRENT POSITION
("Effect of First Job on Future Employment")

Organization	Class	% Still in Type of Organization as of 1984	Significant Other Organizations	Average Retention Rate as of 1984
Firm (2-8)	'81	59%	solo, government	41.50%
	'74	47	solo, business	
	'69	36	9-35, government	
	'56	24	9-35, solo	
Firm (9-35)	'81	37	36-84, 2-8	43.00%
	'74	22	36-84, 2-8	
	'69	17	36-84, business	
	'56	5	85+, 36-84, 2-8	
Firm (36-84)	'81	42	85+, business	31.00%
	'74	11	85+, business	
	'69	3	9-35, business	
	'56	4	85+, business	
Firm (85+)	'81	67	36-84, 9-35	51.50%
	'74	47	business, education	
	'69	27	2-8, business	
	'56	65	business	
Firm (solo)	'81	47	2-8	45.25%
	'74	33	2-8	
	'69	33	2-8	
	'56	68	2-8	
Government*	'81	60	2-8, solo	40.00%
	'74	45	85+, businesss	
	'69	31	85+, 2-8	
	'56	24		
Business**	'81	71	9-35	67.25%
	'74	74	solo	
	'69	63	solo, 2-8	
	'56	61	solo, 85+	
Legal Services	'81	55	85+, solo	25.00%
	'74	32	2-8, business	
	'69	13	education, government	
	'56	0		

* Includes legal and non legal; prosecutors, federal, state and local employees.

** Includes legal and non legal.

From: *From Law School to Career: Where Do Graduates Go and What Do They Do?*, Leona Vogt.

firms since 1969 have not been inside a firm larger than 85.

3. People starting out in medium sized firms (36 to 84) since 1974 have had access, by firm growth or lateral movement, to large firms or business. The class of 1969, in a pattern we shall see repeated, seems to have gone the other way toward smaller organizations. Note that very few of any of the classes studied are currently working in firms of of 36 to 84; even the class of '81 shows only 42% working in this category. One explanation is that the medium sized firm is a dynamic, unstable entity. Like entrepreneurial individuals, the middle sized firm seems to "keep its options open." It is often on its way to becoming something else, most often a big firm but occasionally a small firm, a specialty boutique, a merger candidate, or a dissolution. Consequently, the middle sized firm should represent the environment from which there is the most fluid movement in all directions.

4. The figures for people starting out in large firms demonstrate the trickiness of the question "to what extent does a first position determine future employment?" On the one hand, very high percentages of most classes starting with big firms remain there, whether voluntarily or involuntarily. For many lawyers today the combination of narrow specialties and high salaries has effectively limited their alternative employment opportunities. On the other hand, those who leave the large firm environment in a timely fashion appear to have access to middle sized and small firms and business. We emphasize timeliness because delay may be limiting. As the managing partner of one small firm said in a recent careers seminar, "If you've been too long at a big firm I wouldn't touch you with a ten foot pole. You'd be unfit for our practice."

Of course, the figures in Table 1 do not tell us whether, and to what extent, turnover is out of choice or externally imposed. We merely learn what percentages of people were still working in the kinds of position they first entered after law school. And by that standard, turnover is greater in some types of organizations than in others. Although the data doesn't address it specifically, evidently some types of organizations retain larger numbers by a combination of commitment and the loss of access to other kinds of jobs. In other words, many people stay in sectors of the legal world by choice *and* necessity.

The Career Paths Study looked at the variety of occupations held by the subjects during the course of their careers, with the following results:

> "approximately one-third of the respondents have worked for the government since law school (compared to 14 percent starting in, and 15 percent currently in, government).
>
> "one-fourth have been in business (compared to 11 percent starting and 18 percent currently in business).
>
> "approximately three-fourths of all respondents have worked in law firms (compared to 58 percent starting in law firms and 50 percent currently in law firms).
>
> "15 percent have been in solo practice (compared to 4 percent starting and 8 percent currently in solo practice).
>
> "10 percent have worked for legal services programs (compared to 6 percent who started in legal services and 3 percent currently in those programs).
>
> "8 percent have been in education (compared to 2 percent who started and 3 percent who are currently in education)."

If there is a significant moral to be derived from these findings, it should be that substantial mobility has always been present in the legal profession. As was pointed out by Lynn Miller in a 1986 article in *The Student Lawyer*, the current focus on the increase in mobility in a previously petrified sector of the profession (the larger firms) can obscure the long time mobility in other sectors.

Yet, whether you are employed in a large firm or elsewhere, you may still have no clear idea of where people go. Reasons for this in a large firm include the sheer size of the organization, which allows stragglers to disappear from the periphery of the herd almost unnoticed. In all forms of legal employment it is easy to become isolated in your own specialized world, losing touch with what others are doing.

One of the more methodical examinations of the destinations and motivations of those leaving large firms is a 1986 survey of transfers out of the 40 largest Chicago firms over a three-year period conducted by one of us (Samuelson). The survey found that the moves were into the following categories of jobs:

Law Firms: Moves were made from large firms to other firms with national practices, to regional and local practices and to firms in other parts of the country. The motivations were to find better experiences, a more pleasing atmosphere, and more probable partnership prospects. Moves were of all types: From large firms to small firms; from medium firms to large firms; from generalist experiences to specialty practices; and the reverse.

Corporations: Some individuals with business and legal generalist orientations moved into senior or 'first' lawyer positions. Others moved into an expanding variety of staff lawyer positions. These positions appealed to lawyers wanting to concentrate on sophisticated legal problems in a less pressured, more predictable work environment.

Financial, Professional and Consulting Legal Positions: A number of lawyers moved into commercial banks, investment banks and other financial institutions. There were also moves into other professional firms: accounting, real estate, brokerage, insurance, construction, design, and venture capital.

Nonlegal Positions: Lawyers also moved into nonlegal positions building upon their prior education and the subject matter of their legal experience: administration and management, finance, money management, strategic and financial planning, insurance, lobbying and legislation, communications, mergers and acquisitions, risk assessment, real estate, benefits, personnel and special project situations requiring the intellectual independence and rigorous approach of a lawyer.

To these findings the Career Paths Survey would add transfers into government, public service, and teaching.

Few who haven't studied the matter are familiar with the range of positions available to lawyers in these various organizations. Thus, a quick perusal of Appendix A may yield some revelations. Appendix A lists the legal job titles from the Samuelson survey and from the table of contents of the invaluable study by the National Association for Law Placement, "Legal Careers, Choices and Options". Merely considering these alternatives of lawyer work should broaden the horizons of even the most tentative job changer.

Limitations

The discussion of dissatisfaction and options would not be complete, however, without some reference to factors which limit access to different kinds of positions. We have already touched upon this subject in asking how first jobs influence future employment. What of factors such as gender, race, financial burdens, school attended, and geographical constraints?

Since women have been represented in substantial numbers only since the seventies, the available statistical information on gender is mostly from recent classes. For those classes, however, the job pattern differences are significant. The Career Paths Study discovered, for instance, that women are underrepresented in senior positions in large firms and in non-legal business roles, while a larger proportion are to be found in legal positions in business, legal services and law-related positions. Women eleven years out of law school were twice as likely as men to be in government legal positions. In the class of '74, women were underrepresented in law firms of all sizes.

Similar patterns prevail for persons who are older when they graduate from law school, according to a recent survey of the class of 1985 conducted by the National Association for Law Placement ("Employment of Recent Law School Graduates", press release from NALP, January 24, 1987). According to this report, "the largest number of graduates over 30 [years old] found employment in government (26.6%), in very small firms of 2 to 10 attorneys (21.6%) and in business and industry (13.9%)."

The Career Paths Study data on the experience of ethnic minorities is somewhat "soft" because of the smaller sample sizes involved. However, from some very preliminary analysis of the data, it appears that for blacks the patterns are similar to those for women, showing a concentration not in private law firms but in business, government, and public interest organizations. Other evidence suggests that in more narrowly defined circumstances these patterns may not hold true, and that in some of the big firms minorities may be retained and promoted on a par with other associates, assuming that they have been hired in the first place. Even with the large firms, however, progress has been slow. A *National Law Journal* survey concluded that blacks accounted for 2.9% of the attorneys at firms of over 200 lawyers.

With recent law students graduating with an average debt of $15,000, sometimes reaching as much as $20,000, the effect of financial considerations on job choice and mobility is obvious. This is especially so since the disparity between salaries in the public and private sectors has been growing, as it has between large and small firms. Little has occurred to offset this situation, with one exception.

A few law schools with the resources have instituted low income protection plans to help those graduates who have taken lower paying jobs in the public sector. References to those schools are to be found in Chapter 13, Resources. Because this is a rapidly evolving situation, the list will quickly become incomplete. You should also consult your own school to see if such a program exists.

There is no question that the law school one has attended has major impact on opportunities to which one has access, or that employers have a fascination with schools and grades which is hard to shake. Lest job seekers doubt their own judgement in this matter, there are several studies which have underscored the importance of academic credentials. Frances Zemans and Victor Rosenblum in their study *The Making of a Public Profession* (American Bar Association, Chicago, Illinois, 1981) were able to show "quite clearly that the nature of the law school attended is the most important of the predictors of both size of organizational context of practice and the prestige of the specialty practiced."

The Career Paths Study also found that which of the seven law schools in the survey was attended influenced whether the graduates worked in large firms, in small firms or in solo practice. About twice as many graduates of the "national, prestige" schools were to be found in large firms as graduates from other schools. The schools also varied in the percentage of graduates in the public sector, with one school having a high of 30 percent of each class in that area, and another having less than 18 percent.

On the other hand, it is important to realize that there are ways in which the products of the various schools are apt to have increasingly homogeneous career paths. For instance, about 30% of the classes of all seven schools in the Career Paths Study were in small and medium sized firms. Perhaps more importantly, a larger proportion of recent graduates went to work with large firms. The National Association for Law Placement employment survey for 1985 also indicates that 25.8% of law school graduates from the 175 schools surveyed started work in firms of 25 or more (19% of them in firms of over 50 persons).

Indeed, it is easy to overemphasize the constraints of not having attended a "prestige" school. As the authors of *The Making of a Public Profession* point out:

> "attempts . . . to establish rankings of law schools nationwide are . . . destined to be of limited validity . . . it is practicing lawyers who hire new lawyers and largely deter-

mine their distribution within the bar. With the exception of perhaps the half-dozen schools typically designated as the 'elite,' the lawyer market takes little cognizance of 'national' reputations. Rather, there appears to be a well-established hierarchy relevant to the local area with rather fine distinctions drawn among those law schools from which local lawyers are traditionally hired."

Progressive employers are increasingly happy to reduce their recruiting expenses by looking closer to home for new associates and lateral hires.

The importance of local legal employment markets raises an interesting point concerning the magnitude of the constraint that credentials place on mobility. Many young lawyers would be surprised to learn that the location of the first job could have a greater impact on subsequent mobility than the school attended. Among respondents to the Career Paths Study 70% are still residing in the cities of their first jobs. Thus one's range of opportunity is often bounded by one's familiarity with the job market in the region, by one's familiarity with the substance and procedure of local law, by the familiarity of employers and clients with the educational and work background of individual lawyer, or by one's willingness to uproot. The constraints on job choice may derive not so much from credentials as from decisions, like choice of city or specialty, that can carry unanticipated consequences.

Data on lawyer mobility, of course, tell us nothing about why lawyers move to new jobs or careers. The increasing mobility is undoubtedly a complex function of two disparate variables: Better career planning and greater dissatisfaction with a particular job or with law as a career.

Trends in Lawyer Dissatisfaction

We have paused to discuss the objective factors, some beyond anyone's control, which might affect the mobility of lawyers without reference to their subjective dissatisfactions. However, the objective factors only serve to increase a lawyer's vulnerability to the negatives that plague the work of all lawyers and to decrease the potential for satisfaction that exists for all.

The migration of lawyers to other jobs is driven by complex drives and dissatisfactions involving psychological, economic, and strategic considerations. These can range from fundamental clash with basic values of the profession to career stage-specific concerns such as the need for competency building; from strategic considerations such as the need to become familiar with certain businesses to purely personal considerations such as the desire to live in a different community or to find the time to raise children.

What is known about the problems lawyers have with their work, and what is the relationship of job dissatisfaction to the reasons usually given for leaving jobs? How much do others in the profession share any doubts and discontents you may have?

Lawyers are not always very insightful or communicative about such things, and when they are, their rhetorical tendencies may lead them to exaggerate or minimize their true feelings. You often hear fashionable foxhole-griping which sounds intense, but is actually part of the bitter sweet, ritual agonizing that accompanies thankless tasks such as spending all night at the printer proofreading galleys of an important brief. At the other extreme of questionable sincerity there is the *Doonesbury* cartoon in which a law student buries her face in her hands as another student exclaims with glossy enthusiasm, "God, I love the law!"

In general, lawyers do not lead lives of quiet desperation. A 1983 ABA study by Rosslyn S. Smith on lawyer life-styles revealed that only 6 percent of a sample of 2000 lawyers reported being moderately to totally unhappy with their career choice. Those most inclined to such feelings were lawyers thirty years old or younger, but the dissatisfied segment for even this group remained small (15%). According to this study, the level of contentment was greater among older lawyers, although it is not clear whether this reflected accumulated experience (or wealth!), generational differences in how lawyers view their careers, or a departure of the dissatisfied to other pastures.

The most detailed and sophisticated study of lawyer satisfaction was done by Ron Hirsch for the ABA Young Lawyers Section, (partially reported in "Are You on Target", in the Winter 1985 edition of *Barrister* magazine). Hirsch found the level of dissatisfaction with current jobs (16%) to be somewhat higher than dissatisfaction with career. Younger lawyers were again the most discontented, with 25 percent of junior associates and staff attorneys reporting job dissatisfaction.

As the authors of the above studies point out, this is, on the whole, good news suggesting a high level of satisfaction. However, other aspects of their findings are puzzling and less optimistic. For instance, Smith's study found that 43 percent of her sample were by no means certain that they would select law again as a career, even when they were reporting satisfaction with their career choice. And Hirsch's study disclosed a great many specific dissatisfactions even among those who described themselves as contented overall. It is hard to know if many basically satisfied individuals are simply indulging in the all-too-human penchant for picking at nits or if many basically dissatisfied individuals haven't the introspective powers necessary to admit that fact to themselves, much less an investigator.

In truth, work satisfaction is too complex to be wholly assessed by asking a few simple questions about contentment, even in those occupations whose satisfactions are assumed to be simple. Where law is concerned, definitions of work satisfaction become multifaceted in the extreme.

Note, for instance, that while Smith surveyed dissatisfaction with career choice, Hirsch examined dissatisfaction with current job, i.e. the kinds of feelings that make people want to change *jobs* rather than *careers*. This distinction between long term values and immediate needs is not always clear in the individual situation, and is only one of the ambiguities attached to feelings about life in the law.

Elements of Dissatisfaction

At least nine separate factors seem, logically, to bear upon job satisfaction or dissatisfaction. Some elaboration of them should make the research results more meaningful.

1. The first factor, *historical change*, affects all the others. We have seen that even very recent classes of law school graduates have faced rapid changes in society and the profession. The practice of law that they discover is not the work that they assumed when they decided to go to law school. We'll allude to some of these changes as we discuss the other determinants of job and career satisfaction.

2. The nature of the work itself is paramount; especially the *intellectual challenge*. Whether you are doing anything to keep the mind alive is critical in any of the professions. Of course, there are fashions in intellectual challenge, too, which partly reflect changes in practice. Thus you find an older lawyer reminiscing how in the thirties litigation was far more prone to technicalities, and how "technical motions addressed to the pleadings were resorted to with great enthusiasm." Or you find a partner, in a recent article on young lawyers and the lure of investment banking, bemoaning that his lawyer son cannot see the challenge in the father's work.

3. The *status of the specialties* within the profession can weigh heavily on self-image. Whatever your convictions, your status still affects your compensation, how you are treated by fellow lawyers, and how you are perceived by society. For example, in the aforementioned study of Chicago area lawyers by Heinz and Laumann, practicing lawyers ranked the various specialties as follows:

1. Securities
2. Tax
3. Antitrust (defendant)
4. Patents
5. Antitrust (plaintiff)
6. Banking
7. Public Utilities
8. General Corporate
9. Probate
10. Municipal
11. Admiralty
12. Civil Litigation

13. Labor (management)
14. Real Estate
15. Commercial
16. Labor (unions)
17. Environmental (defendants)
18. Personal Injury (defendants)
19. Environmental (plaintiffs)
20. Civil Rights/Civil Liberties
21. Criminal (prosecution)
22. General Family (paying)
23. Criminal (defense)
24. Consumer (creditor)
25. Personal Injury (plaintiffs)
26. Consumer (debtor)
27. Condemnations
28. Landlord/Tenant
29. Divorce
30. General Family (poverty)

Appendix B contains a further table from the Heinz and Laumann study showing how these specialties were evaluated in terms of intellectual challenge, rapidity of change, public service, ethical conduct, and freedom of action. The subjects of the study approached unanimity in these rankings regardless of their own specialty.

The list obviously reflects a current professional bias toward complex, business-oriented practice—the work of highly paid specialists in large law firms—at the expense of what one law professor arrogantly described as "the petty problems of ordinary people." The list also says something about the nature of challenge and intellectual satisfaction in the profession, as the top three specialties in this area were also highly rated for rapidity of change.

The ramifications of any stratification of prestige within the profession are too numerous for detailed exploration here. Two, however, stand out for our purposes: (1) stratification forces many lawyers to wonder whether they are perceived as "real lawyers" because both their clients and their skills rank low in the current professional pecking order. And, in some instances, (2) stratification also imposes too stark a contrast between doing good and doing well. The amount of support, financial and moral, for legal services work in the late sixties and seventies, now woefully missing, is an example of how the prestige of a specialty can vary with the times.

4. *Feedback*, in the form of compensation and evaluation, obviously shapes self-image and the sense of competence. To some extent, this factor is more critical to satisfaction in the early stages of a legal career, but it is never absent. Opportunities for getting feedback are much shaped by economic and organizational change. For example, the competition for "good" associates and inflated starting salaries creates an inflated sense of well-being. Yet growth in firm size also creates an environment which can be deflating to an associate's ego. Informal feedback is as essential as the most meticulous formal review, which, in fact, it may completely undercut.

5. *Level of expectation* and 6. *realism of planning* can cause two individuals to have widely differing reactions to the same experience. Psychological studies on decision making have shown that adequate consideration of the "down side" of any decision greatly increases the probability of satisfaction with the outcome. A realistic grasp of the trade-offs involved in the choice of career, positions, and individual tasks depends upon good sources of information and the willingness to use them. Acceptable trade-offs obviously vary with the times, as evidenced by the very senior partner who remarked that in his day "a young associate was happy to to carry his boss's brief case and listen to the conversation of his betters."

7. It might be accurate to say that level of expectation is actually a product of the *relationship of one's work to other goals in life.* This factor is highly personal. Lawyers of different ages are variously insistent on the importance of their personal lives. Those raised through the Depression and World War II have been more familiar with notions of sacrifice. Those coming into the profession in the sixties felt the overriding priorities of politics. The eighties are supposed to have ushered in a new age of self-interest and the promotion of personal—as opposed to work—motivations. All of these attitudes coexist today, with many people exhibiting great

creativity in how they orient their work to more personal goals never suspected by their co-workers and sometimes not even by themselves.

8. The variety of attitudes concerning the relationship of work to other, personal goals is itself increased by a lawyer's *age, sex and race.* The rewards and liabilities of the legal profession can be very different to those arriving with differing agendas. In some cases sex and race appear to be *the* major determinant of job satisfaction. It is not unusual for minorities to arrive at the banquet table as the feast is winding down.

9. In discussing the two studies cited above we have suggested that *stage of practice* seriously affects job and career satisfaction, as in the case of lawyers approaching partnerships in times of declining profitability, or the associate "coming of age" just in time to see his or her firm institute a two-tiered partnership.

Hirsch's research, reported in the Winter, 1985 issue of *Barrister,* suggests all these factors are present in his findings. Hirsch not only discovered that 25 percent of all lawyers were planning to change jobs within the next two years, but he found that of those planning to change, more than half were ready to abandon private practice all together. (There is some independent validation of these intentions in the Career Paths Study, which found that of those in the class of '81 who had already left their first jobs, half were no longer employed by law firms.)

Hirsch went on to ask what sorts of people in what settings were most prone to dissatisfaction. In this regard he found that "junior associates in most firms and lawyers in general in 2-3 man firms are far more dissatisfied than those in other positions and settings. And women are far more dissatisfied generally, regardless of position." However, he goes on to say that being a junior associate or woman is not an absolute guarantee of dissatisfaction. Nor can middle-aged white males be confident of enjoying their work. Rather, people in the dissatisfaction-prone categories are often more vulnerable to certain negative job factors which seriously affect any lawyer's capability to enjoy his or her work.

Hirsch was interested in a variety of these motivational factors which included:

- general opportunity for advancement
- warm and personal atmosphere
- merit-based advancement
- political intrigue
- control of one's work
- intellectual challenge
- training
- time for self
- financial reward

He discovered that there were two clusters of factors, one positive, one negative, which were most important. The optimum combination of these factors would virtually assure satisfaction with one's job.

For the sample overall, Hirsch found that their high level of satisfaction was due to the "overwhelmingly satisfying presence of intellectual challenge [which was] enough to overcome the various negative aspects of their jobs. If a warm and personal work atmosphere is combined with intellectual challenge, you have the most potent combination of positive factors."

These positives can be offset by political intrigue and backbiting and, nearly as detrimental, an extreme lack of time for oneself.

The high negative potential of "extreme lack of time for oneself" is not surprising. Forty percent of Hirsch's sample worked more than 200 hours a month and reported an inability to use their vacation time. As a consequence, 64 percent of the sample cited fatigue and exhaustion at the end of the day.

Smith's study obtained similar results, in that time demands were the single most negative element of practice reported by her respondents.

One of us (Byers), in a study of stress among recent graduates of law school, also found that long hours was the most frequently cited cause of stress. It is thus safe to assume that this is an issue from the outset and, judging from Hirsch's data on the hours put in by partners and associates, that it never ceases to be a major cross borne by large numbers of lawyers. Given the almost exclusively hourly rate method of selling legal services, this problem appears structural in the profession.

These four factors (warm atmosphere, intellectual challenge, intrigue, and time pressure) accounted for most of the variance in satisfaction. Other factors, however, played significant roles; notably opportunity to advance, treatment by superiors as a professional colleague, and control over one's work.

Hirsch's data on the combination of positive and negative factors in firms of different size is highly interesting to anyone trying to determine his or her optimum work environment. Table 2 summarizes his data. From this Table you can see that probably the optimum size firm with respect to the four factors are firms in the 20 to 60 person range. This group, especially, seems to exemplify the positive factors and somewhat escapes the negative, although "time for self" is clearly an issue in firms of all sizes.

Table 2 does not include non-firm settings, but we can augment it with results from the Career Paths Study, which confirms the commonly held view that hours are less in business, the public sector, and education.

Hirsch's data on the experiences of women is disturbing. Despite evidence that they find their work as intellectually stimulating as do men, they are far more susceptible to dissatisfaction with their jobs because their work environments are more susceptible to negative factors. "More women," he says, "report that their job atmosphere is not warm and personal, that advancement is not determined by the quality of the work, that they have no control of the cases they handle, that tension is high, and that they have virtually no time for themselves. Finally, the income of women lawyers is far below that of their male counterparts in most situations."

Once again, the Career Paths Study reinforces these findings, reporting that "with the exception of the large law firms, the average male graduate makes more annually than a woman graduating in the same year and working in a similar organization . . . the smaller the firm size, the greater the income gap between women and men; and the difference is more pronounced" the longer they are out of school. Smith's study describes similar conditions.

Although, according to Hirsch, dissatisfaction with income is *not* a significant determinant of overall job dissatisfaction, we may assume that in the case of women it is perceived as a reflection of the other inequalities.

Careful consideration of these results for women are applicable to anyone contemplating a job change. Average results from broadly-based studies are no doubt useful. But everyone has their own priorities, needs, and agendas. Anyone having a background or goals different from the norm must weigh the job factors differently in determining the level of dissatisfaction and in devising remedies. A woman looking at Hirsch's Job Factors table and the other studies we have mentioned, might attach more importance than a man to the fact that women are likely to obtain salary equity in the large firms. Other minorities might make a similar calculation. Again, if personal time is as much an issue to you, as it evidently is to many women, you may be even more inclined than the average lawyer to view the working hours as a serious problem.

Thus, the data on why lawyers change jobs may not wholly explain why you might change yours. On the one hand, people move even before they become deeply dissatisfied or out of highly personal reasons. On the other, their departures may be quite involuntary or, at any rate, shaped by outside forces having little to do with their preferences.

Why Lawyers Change Jobs

The Career Paths Study questionnaire did not give respondents a chance to directly cite hours or political intrigue as reasons for departure so its results must be related to Hirsch's data by inference. Many of the reasons offered in the questionnaire, however, are closely connected with the motivational factors investigated in Hirsch's dissatisfaction study.

Respondents' reasons for leaving their jobs were classified into five groups, four of which were job related. Those four were:

Table 2

JOB FACTORS: PERCENT WITH NEGATIVE SCORES

Firm Size	Opportunity to Advance	Warm and Personal Atmosphere	Advancement Determined by Work	Political Intrigue	Control of Work	Intellectual Challenge	Training	Time for Self	Financial Reward
Solo	25%	5%	25%	0	14%	17%	0	39%	52%
2-3	22%	5%	22%	12%	22%	15%	62%	43%	32%
4-9	18%	6%	15%	17%	24%	12%	60%	45%	26%
10-20	14%	11%	14%	26%	40%	4%	58%	50%	26%
21-30	7%	7%	9%	27%	37%	4%	58%	50%	26%
31-60	10%	13%	8%	39%	34%	8%	42%	58%	11%
61-90	24%	16%	15%	40%	54%	12%	63%	65%	22%
91 +	13%	27%	8%	40%	41%	13%	58%	47%	6%

From: *"Are You On Target"*, Ronald L. Hirsch, in *Barrister,* Vol. 12, No. 1, Winter 1985.

Growth: Wanted to be own boss, start organization; increased responsibilities; growth potential; increase in salary or income.

Negative: Job dissatisfaction; limited/no advancement potential; to reduce job pressures; disliked way skills being used; not challenged to potential; didn't like colleagues; was bored; felt burnt out; was fired.

Neutral: Wanted to use different skills; wanted to do different work; position was abolished; completed temporary assignment; wanted to change organization.

Personal: Wanted to change location; pregnancy/child rearing; spouse/family concerns; health problems.

As may be seen, some of the factors are rather specific and others are more general. "Job dissatisfaction" is so broad that no one should be surprised that it tops the list of reasons for departure. The reasons were grouped so that the numbers would allow patterns to emerge. The results do suggest that many of Hirsch's motivational factors were involved.

For instance, looking at the entire sample ranging from the classes of '56 to '81, of those who left their first jobs, one-third left for negative reasons, one-fourth for growth reasons, one-fourth for neutral reasons, and 11 percent for personal reasons. Thus, the largest category included those reasons probably based on the key Hirsch factors—intellectual satisfaction, warm working environment, hours, and political intrigue. The most frequently cited of the "growth" reasons was "wanted to be my own boss."

As the authors of the Career Paths Study point out, it makes sense that many people left their first jobs for negative reasons, since the first step of any career is likely to be tentative and directed toward finding the "best fit." In most occupations, presumably, one's aim improves with time and experience.

It is striking, however, that the two most recent classes studied had a greater proportion of people leaving for negative and personal reasons. Here again is the suggestion that the recent generation of lawyers are experiencing a clash of values and goals with the expectations of their employers. There is also the suggestion of structural changes in the legal marketplace—increased firm overhead as a percentage of revenue, revenues tied to lawyer hours—creating additional pressures that tend to get transferred to the younger lawyers.

Consider two examples, each constructed from various interviews of the authors:

> Linda was in her second year at a medium/large firm. Her vague feelings of dissatisfaction with her career became more focused in counseling. Despite all of the indicia of success—large salary, compliments from partners, etc.—she finds great pressure in the firm's billable hours requirements. The time pressure itself is then exacerbated by subtle feelings that anyone's time can't be worth what some client is paying for hers and feelings that some of her assignments are almost make-work—of marginal value to any client and given more to produce hours and revenue.
>
> Franklin, a forty year old parner, never had any of Linda's misgivings. He adored his career and his job with a medium-sized firm from day one. He would be perfectly content to spend the rest of his life doing exactly what he has been doing for the last 14 years. However, his firm recently adopted new partnership rules that will jeopardize his income and his authority if he cannot generate clients for the firm. The drumming up of business is both unsuited and distasteful to Franklin's demeanor and talents. His idyllic life is threatened and he never saw the problems on the horizon.

***

John L. Holland, a well known occupational psychologist and author (*Making Vocational Choices,* Prentice Hall, 1973) has explained that job dissatisfaction is usually resolved by one of three responses: changing ourselves, changing our environment, or leaving the environment.

For an adult, changing yourself substantially is surely problematic and probably painful. Changing your environment is usually only somewhat less difficult than changing yourself, unless it is but a minor matter in your environment that annoys you. Changing a large entity, like a law firm or educational institution, is a problem similar to turning the Queen Mary around in the narrow confines of the Chicago River. There is little room to maneuver and great energy is required to change its course even a bit.

Thus, in the real world of lawyering, dissatisfaction is usually dealt with in two ways: stoicism and changing jobs.

Whether your job is truly a lost cause is not always apparent. An annoying quality of dissatisfaction is its often ephemeral nature. While specific gripes can usually be produced on demand, they often are microcosms of more global irritants. Although precise quantification of dissatisfaction is unattainable, a rule or scale for comparison of key employment features often helps focus free-floating job dissatisfaction. To this end we have provided a Job Criteria Evaluation Scale as our Exercise 1.

In a surprising proportion of instances, filling out this Scale is revealing. Sources of job dissatisfaction may be highlighted for the first time. You may even discover that your dissatisfaction is not with your job, but with some other source that you have been unwilling to acknowledge (e.g., in-laws asking for free legal advice).

EXERCISE 1: Job Criteria Evaluation Scale

The twenty numbered phrases will be descriptive of your current position to a greater or lesser extent. For each phrase circle the number that best corresponds to your feelings about the application of the phrase to your job. The number scale goes from zero ("Not at all") to 5 ("Very much").

Adding the scores for each of the 20 items will give a "score" for the job. The highest possible score (probably never reached by any real job) is 100.

1. Draws on my strengths.

   0 1 2 3 4 5 ...._____

2. Provides me with the training/experience I need.

   0 1 2 3 4 5 ...._____

3. Doesn't clash with the "real me".

   0 1 2 3 4 5 ...._____

4. Will not impede my long range development.

   0 1 2 3 4 5 ...._____

5. Provides my kind of intellectual stimulation.

   0 1 2 3 4 5 ...._____

6. Allows me to work in appealing areas of the law.

   0 1 2 3 4 5 ...._____

7. Meets my definition of social value.

   0 1 2 3 4 5 ...._____

8. Gives me the means to feel effective.

   0 1 2 3 4 5 ...._____

9. Makes me feel good when I tell others what I do.

   0 1 2 3 4 5 ...._____

10. Provides necessary and appropriate compensation.

    0 1 2 3 4 5 ...._____

11. Allows sufficient time and energy for a personal life.

    0 1 2 3 4 5 ...._____

12. Provides the company of people I enjoy.

    0 1 2 3 4 5 ...._____

13. Provides the right mix of formality and congeniality.

    0 1 2 3 4 5 . . . . _____

14. Meets my requirements for comfort and aesthetics.

    0 1 2 3 4 5 . . . . _____

15. Provides acceptable work facilities and staff support.

    0 1 2 3 4 5 . . . . _____

16. Provides reliable evaluation and review.

    0 1 2 3 4 5 . . . . _____

17. Is in the right geographical location.

    0 1 2 3 4 5 . . . . _____

18. Transportation to work is not a problem.

    0 1 2 3 4 5 . . . . _____

19. Provides a good mix of responsibility and supervision.

    0 1 2 3 4 5 . . . . _____

20. Provides participation in goal setting/ management.

    0 1 2 3 4 5 . . . . _____

TOTAL SCORE _____

Logically, if you take deep issue with some aspect of your job, even if that aspect is not one of the traditional sources of dissatisfaction, it will still prompt a strong desire to escape. According to Hirsch, 30 percent of his "satisfied" subjects were nonetheless contemplating a job change within the next few years. In other words, even relatively happy people can be motivated for change. As a colleague of ours is fond of saying, "every four years or so I turn into something else just for the hell of it."

After filling out the Job Criteria Evaluation Scale you may find that the basic preconditions for contentment grace your job in large measure but one or two characteristics made the position seem intolerable. Sometimes a single issue can become a work "deal breaker". In Hirsch's study, many people claiming to like their jobs still reported high strain and fatigue in their hours. Often, they found training and supervision inadequate. They looked for more variety and client contact in their jobs. Or, basic political or religious values might be offended by a job nonetheless highly enjoyable as a pure activity.

Know Thyself

In truth no job checklist or research summary will substitute for self-knowledge in discovering the wellsprings of your own motivation. None of the reasons cited above or advanced in job counseling interviews may capture discontent you feel in your work.

Perhaps, like some lawyers, you are facing a crisis of belief, as suggested by Lee Smith, Dean of Students and the Director of the Law, Ethics, and Religion Program at Cornell Law School. In a recent article in *Student Lawyer,* Dean Smith suggests that the crisis occurs because the work of many associates [and partners] doesn't relate to their lives.

> "When I talk to young people about a calling or profession, they don't know what I'm talking about. Until they are able to articulate the source of their problems, not just that they're unhappy or overworked, they can't begin to deal with their problems."

Further complicating matters, as those young people age they will face additional problems and pressures at relatively predictable points in their careers, as Chapter 5, Adult Development, explores. But first, in Chapter 4, we offer a closer look at the job and career opportunities that have attracted the majority of lawyers. Here we revert to the lawyer's favorite dictum: Know Thy Options.

Chapter

4

The Main Alternatives: Taking Refuge

"Even a child is known by his doings, whether his work be pure, and whether it be right."
Proverbs 20:11

I. OPPORTUNITIES IN PRIVATE PRACTICE

The Spring, 1987 description of recent faculty publications of the University of Chicago Law School listed the following: "The Constitution as Architecture: Legislative and Administrative Courts Under Article III"; "Story and Language in American Law: Comparative Perspectives on Abortion, Divorce and Dependency"; "Comparative Civil Procedure and the Style of Complex Contracts"; "Torture and Plea Bargaining"; and "Serial Polygamy and the Spouse's Forced Share".

Plainly, American legal education continues to be preoccupied with arcane scholarship and with its intellectual standing in the University hierarchy. Law school faculties pride themselves on "not being trade schools". If it is clear what they are not, it is less clear what they are.

With internship and residency still ahead on the road to legal competence, graduation from law school is but a milestone and not a finish line. Young lawyers who have passed the bar exam are thought by outsiders to be ready to undertake any legal matter that walks in the door. In reality, of course, this is not the case.

Most young lawyers receive clinical training in the skills and productivity talents that they need in order to progress. In private practice in firms of substantial size a significant source of this training are the first and second jobs of the young attorney. Governmental employers usually have formal or informal on-the-job training programs. Sole practitioners' on-the-job training is often in the form of unbilled or reduced-billed hours while sorting through the law and the logistics of a first-impression situation. Continuing legal education seminars, and the like, are available to all.

The majority of law school graduates are in private practice at any given time. Some are there temporarily, whether or not they realize it, on their way to corporations, government, law school teaching, business, or the judiciary. More precisely, about two-thirds of the 650,000 active law school graduates in 1986 were in private practice:

Private Practice	420,000
Corporations	90,000
Government	60,000
Teaching, Misc.	80,000
	650,000

Among the lawyers in private practice, the greatest number are in sole proprietorships:

Sole proprietorships	210,000
2-3 Lawyer firms	70,000
4-10 Lawyer firms	70,000
Over 11 Lawyer firms	70,000
	420,000

(All numbers are approximations derived from 1980 U.S. Census figures and extrapolations.)

The rapid growth of the largest firms has received much publicity. The total number of additional lawyers employed in these firms, however, is a very small percentage in the universe of law school graduates.

National Practice

Although it is still customary to describe law firms in terms of their size ("very large", "small", "mid-sized," "more than 100 lawyers," etc.), a more meaningful description focuses upon the size and types of markets that the firms serve. While size and market-type are somewhat parallel, the market-centered description is usually more meaningful in explaining a firm to potential new employees.

In general, the very large law firms (more than 300 lawyers) tend to be serving the needs of the national financial community and Fortune 500 corporations. These clients have national and international businesses. They have periodic needs for large groups of lawyers to work on deals and multi-location law suits involving millions of dollars. The firms serving these national corporate clients must be national law firms. The firms themselves are often headquartered in cities that have major financial communities as well as clusters of Fortune 500 clients (e.g., New York, Chicago, Los Angeles, Washington, D.C.). Firms with national practices usually have offices in more than one of these major cities.

These national practice firms hire far more associates than can possibly be expected to become partners. A 1983 report from Columbia University Law School stated that of 246 lawyers from its class of 1972 who entered the very large firms in New York City only 33 had become partners. (For example, at Cravath, Swaine & Moore, 10 of 27 made partner; at Sullivan & Cromwell, 2 of 22; and at Davis, Polk & Wardwell, 2 of 23.) These partnership statistics are not necessarily bad news for the young lawyers. Even though the firms hire squads of young lawyers to deploy against major legal matters, the young attorneys get good compensation and, more importantly, the training and credentials that enable them to move on to other opportunities.

The nature of the legal work in the very large, national firms is often highly sophisticated because the needs of the clients are often highly complex. The sheer numbers of lawyers in these firms usually restrict a young lawyer's contacts to only a small, structured group within the firm. Compensation is top dollar, but the work load is demanding—both intellectually and in the hours required. National law practices can be thought of as the equivalent of teaching hospitals in the medical profession. They handle cutting edge questions of first impression when cost is seldom a major consideration.

National practice firms are beginning to resemble corporations in form of governance. Executive and management functions are delegated to lawyer committees or to professional management staffs. Most partners are content to practice law.

Regional Practice

A second type of law practice serves regional corporations, the regional needs of some of the larger corporations, and private families and individuals accustomed to a high level of professional service. The clients of regional law firms usually don't have a staff of internal lawyers and sometimes not even a General Counsel or CFO. In such situations, the law firm can function as both a business and a legal advisor.

In size, the regional firms are usually in between the large national firms and the "small" firms, offering some of the benefits of each. They often offer more sophisticated and challenging work than the typical small firm. Client contact, on the other hand, usually does not come as quickly as in a small office, nor is it as delayed as in a very large firm. And chances of being relegated to the library with long law or fact research projects are less than in the larger firms.

Although the work of the regional firms may be more sophisticated than that of the smaller firms, it does not always bring exciting intellectual challenges. A part of the process of learning to practice law involves some routine and essentially unimaginative tasks, whatever the size or character of the firm. For example, a stock offering in the abstract may be exciting and challenging, but somebody still has to proofread filings, often well into the night and often at the financial printing establishment. That somebody is likely to be the junior associate.

The regional practices continue to resemble law as it was practiced in the 1960's. The partners actively manage the practice. Staff functions are often minimal. The firm usually has one office.

Boutiques or Specialty Firms

There are certain law firms that specialize in defined practice areas or specific industries. They are often competitors not only of each other but of the specialty practice groups in the larger (national or regional) firms. They are usually the equal of the prestige firms in the quality of their work, but simply limit themselves to a narrow specialty and thus limit their required size.

Areas of law practice that seem to best accommodate these specialty firms are plaintiff's litigation, criminal law, divorce, tax, intellectual property, bankruptcy, and labor. In Washington, D.C., there are a host of specialty practices related to the work of particular administrative agencies of the federal government: energy, communications, transportation, international trade, and environmental protection.

The practice areas of the boutiques are those that can be more or less "self contained". They can be practiced without large numbers of general corporate lawyers and litigators. The economic value of the legal advice in these fields is sufficient to warrant the development of the specialty.

These practice areas (e.g., bankruptcy, divorce, plaintiffs' litigation, criminal law, labor law) are also those that were formerly not seen as desirable by the large national and regional practices. Labor, specifically the representation of plaintiffs and unions, was considered inconsistent with the firms' customary position as corporate defendants' counsel. The intellectual property practice (patents, trademarks, copyrights) often required lawyers with degrees in science or engineering. The practice was hard to understand and integrate with other areas of a general practice. It was easier to refer these matters out.

The referral systems of the large firms tended to support the specialty practices. In most cities, matters involving divorce, criminal law, labor or bankruptcy could be farmed out on a transactional basis to very competent specialty firms. The Washington, D.C. specialty firms could be retained when matters arose involving the administrative, regulatory, or legislative requirements of governmental agencies.

This referral system appears to be eroding. Bankruptcy has become profitable and is often seen as a hedge against reduced work in other areas in bad economic times. Larger firms have also discovered the profitability of the various specialties. They also are trying harder to offer "one stop shopping" as they try to keep "institutional" clients from drifting into "transactional" clients.

Local Practice

Practices that are purely local are usually the smaller firms and sole proprietorships. The markets served may differ widely within this group. Some lawyers are general practitioners, handling the normal problems of the suburban family (e.g., estate planning, real estate, investments, domestic relations, and simple litigation). Others function as corporate counsel to smaller corporations. Still others have distinct specialties—perhaps comparable to those in larger firms—but which don't require any significant professional staff support.

In general, the smaller the firm, the more local its practice and the more likely it is to be providing generalist legal advice; an attractive feature to many who choose this practice. The less wealthy and sophisticated the clientele, of course, the more likely the lawyer is to be providing more general "coping with the world" advice as opposed to the strict professional advice of the lawyer.

A small firm may be a true partnership with a written agreement or a handshake partnership often resting on a long-standing and well-understood relationship. It may be a group of sole practitioners sharing offices and expenses such as secretarial assistance, library, and legal assistants, with each practitioner having his or her own clients and retaining all fees on an individual basis. The subtle variations on any of these themes are limited only by the cumulative imaginations of these 300,000+ lawyers.

A true sole practitioner practices entirely alone with only secretarial or legal assistants in the office. The numbers presented earlier in this chapter show that over 40% of all lawyers are sole practitioners. The increased need for specialization and capital investments required in private practice has resulted in a drop in the percentage of sole practitioners over the last thirty years. There is reason to believe that this percentage may shrink even further in coming years and that more lawyers will at least share space and equipment.

One reason for this is the growing need of lawyers to invest in equipment (e.g., computers, copiers, fax machines, etc.) to remain competitive. It is difficult for a true sole practitioner to justify expensive equipment that may be in use only a small fraction of each day.

Another reason is the preservation of a client base. Even though each lawyer in a group practice may be acting independently, each may become more skilled in particular matters. Referrals take place even though there is no true firm structure, much like medical specialists with offices in the same building. Of course, there is usually the understanding that the client will be returned to the originating attorney when the special matter is completed. Working cooperatively with others also simplifies an attorney's life with regard to vacations, bar association work, and the like.

* * *

The Three Opportunities In Private Practice

There are essentially three types of opportunities for lawyers in the current world of private practice.

1. Law Firms As Training Facilities. First, private practice can be a training ground whatever your ultimate career goal. It is conventional wisdom that lawyers can achieve competence by learning within a governmental setting and later going into private practice. (Such as, working for the Justice Department for a few years and then joining a firm to practice Antitrust law.) But, many people overlook the feasibility and value of the reverse situation.

Clients don't buy the technical legal knowledge of wills, trusts, and taxation . . . they buy estate plans that fit their needs and desires. Clients don't buy the individualized knowledge of corporate law, securities, or the Codes' Subchapter C . . . they buy binding and satisfactory mergers, acquisitions, and financings. The practical, clinical aspects of law could be taught as cases or problems in a law school that sought to make them a major part of the curriculum. Law schools, however, tend to teach single subject matter courses by studying appellate opinions or statutes, rather than by reference to the practical problems or business objectives of clients.

Most larger firms function, de facto, as "training hospitals" for inexperienced lawyers, paying substantial salaries while the young lawyer gains legal competence. Those substantial salaries, in fact, may be an impediment to seeing the training value of such a situation. In every decade of this century, young lawyers have listened with mixed awe and amusement to the stories of how hard their elders had it when they were young. ("They gave me a desk and the opportunity to watch good lawyers at work.") Ignoring the disparity in starting compensation for young lawyers between the 1930's and the 1980's, the important fact of "free" training should not be obscured by either awe or amusement.

Most young lawyers will work for some entity initially, be it a law firm from one to several hundred attorneys, a corporation, an association, or a governmental entity. All such employers offer, formally or de facto, training opportunities. The types of opportunities, experiences and resume-building values of these situations, however, vary enormously. Furthermore, the scale of desirableness/undesirableness of the possible situations will be different for each young lawyer depending on his or her career goals. Opportunities will always be there. As suggested in Chapters 6-8, the hard part is a careful and honest self-assessment. One lawyer's opportunity may well be another's disaster. Someone else's ranking of desirable firms is necessarily suspect . . . unless, perhaps, it is that of your identical twin.

2. Owners of Law Practices. Second is the longer term opportunity to be an "owner" of a law practice. This can mean anything from practicing alone to being a joint owner of a multi-hundred attorney, national law business having gross receipts of nine figures.

Any member of the bar can be a law practice owner by simply hanging out his or her shingle. Introspection of the kind suggested in Chapters 6-8 is advisable to determine whether the benefits and burdens of ownership match your career goals, life-style desires, and temperament needs.

Attaining ownership status in a pre-existing firm of substantial size is more problematic. It is far from a sure thing and ought to be pursued only vigorously and only after a clear determination, for each individual, that the monetary and psychic rewards are worth the effort to achieve them.

Those rewards can be substantial. The financial reward is enhanced by leveraging the difference between the sales price and the cost of younger lawyer and paralegal labor into firm profits. Typically, these profits are distributed among owners of the firm on the basis of some combination of seniority, productivity, business development, and firm management. Founders and heads of traditional businesses (e.g., manufacturing) have become wealthy because they make a little off of the labor of each of many employees. Sole proprietors (whether druggists or lawyers) can only charge for their own time and effort. No matter how good they are, and thus how pricy becomes their labor, they can never match the dollars generated incrementally by large groups.

It used to be said that bringing in clients to a firm was neither a requirement of becoming a partner nor of advancing within a partnership hierarchy. Whether this was ever really true, it pretty clearly isn't today. Indeed, as suggested above, these days advancement to law firm partnership is much more the celebration of the completion of training or the acquisition of competence than it is the beginning of firm ownership. The owners of law practices today are those that are critical to a firm's professional and economic capacities, and to the management and leadership of the firm. Just as with a sole practitioner, owners of firms today are required to possess all of the skills and characteristics of an entrepreneur or business owner in any other service occupation.

Especially practice owners, but even non-owner partners and senior associates, must wrestle with the realities of building a practice. In today's competitive environment, circulating at suburban cocktail parties is probably not enough to do the job. Some thoughts on the business of building a law practice are collected in Appendix G.

3. Non-Owner Partners (Salaried Profit Centers). A third opportunity in private practice is to produce the services in which you have gained competence as an employee or "salaried profit center." Although this type of position is at variance with traditional rigid divisions between partners and associates, with "up or out" policies, simple economics and practice realities are rapidly turning most firms in these directions. Rather than the self-defeating practice of disposing of now-trained lawyers whose contributions to new business, etc. do not merit an ownership position, firms are recognizing the value of non-owner-partners to the productivity and economic well-being of the firm. Clients pay firms about $150,000 per year to "rent" the use of the firms' associates. After six years, or $900,000 in "rental" fees, firms are realizing the value in retaining that trained asset to generate further returns, rather than throwing this asset, free of charge, into the marketplace.

This is far from a second class citizenship. Many lawyers with clearer self-views and well-defined professional and personal goals and needs prefer the more predictable, the less risky, and the more traditional profession of lawyering (rather than entrepreneuring). This trend is augmented by the rapidly increasing numbers of women lawyers who, often, decide to combine a career with child bearing and raising responsibilities.

The growth in desirability of non-ownership positions is mirrored in the great increase in demand by younger lawyers for corporate positions that, increasingly, combine sophisticated practices with more moderate working conditions.

Various firms are experimenting with special status attorneys within the firm but outside of the classical career path. These positions can be structured to serve the needs of both the firm (large numbers of non-owner lawyers to work on major legal matters for large clients) and the attorney (interesting work and good compensation without the competitive tension normal among younger lawyers within a large firm). Jones, Day, for example, has introduced the concept of a special class of associates to augment its normal associate ranks to accommodate specific client projects. Other firms have even brought in lawyers from outside of their normal hiring criteria on a contract basis to staff certain unusual projects.

It seems inevitable, then, that there will be increasing opportunities, increasing rewards, and increasing flexibility in non-owner legal positions as the firm owners and less driven individuals, alike, find mutually beneficial arrangements within which to practice their profession.

II. OTHER OPPORTUNITIES IN LAW

Corporate Counsel

Opportunities in corporate law departments are often unappreciated or misunderstood by young lawyers, even those who find the idea generally appealing. Yet, 90,000 lawyers currently practice in corporations—a fourfold increase over those in 1960—and their ranks are constantly replenished by those leaving private practice. Although obviously outnumbered by the 420,000 in private practice, corporate attorneys have achieved increasing influence in the profession and have shaken off many of the stereotypes of the past. The old view of corporate legal departments as a haven for defrocked private practitioners has long since lost any credibility it may ever have had and is kept alive mainly by insecure detractors.

We described some of the changes in corporate counsel activities in our overview of the profession. Here we focus on the features of corporate legal departments which should interest the individual lawyer considering alternatives to private practice. Obviously, for such a person the important question is whether corporate legal departments differ enough from private practice to offer real solutions to particular job dissatisfactions. What can they offer in organizational variety, intellectual challenge, compensation, training and life style?

All of the types of private practice catalogued earlier in this Chapter—national, regional, local, and specialized—have their counterparts among corporate counsel. Beyond these, there are organizational variants seemingly limited only by the idiosyncrasies of industry and corporate culture.

The average corporate legal department is reported to have 17 attorneys, two paralegals, two non-attorney professionals, and 14 legal support personnel. Many departments are substantially larger. A corporation like Exxon which employs over 400 attorneys from coast to coast is as "national" as the most expansionist law firm, and generates a range of legal problems to rival that encountered in private practice.

This range is reflected in Table 3 which reproduces a recent organizational chart of Columbia Broadcasting System's law department. The variety is mind-boggling. Perhaps the most striking feature of this chart is the revelation that attorneys at CBS can do more than immediately comes to mind when thinking of broadcasting. Such is often the case in large industries in the era of diversification. For instance, both the wood products and insurance industries provide opportunities in real estate development, which makes sense after a moment's reflection on the spin-off implications of their main activities. Corporations such as United Technologies, which encompass several industries, have virtually a federal system of legal departments engaged in national and local affairs for the corporation.

Table 3

CBS LEGAL ORGANIZATIONAL CHART

GENERAL COUNSEL SECTION

General Counsel
Associate General Counsel
Managing Counsel
Manager, Administration
Systems Administrator
Manager, Law Files
Information Retrieval Specialist

Areas of Responsibility. Counsel to senior management; internal investigations; Law Department management and supervision; responsibility for Department policy and for compliance with Company policy; coordination of support services for the Department.

BROADCAST

BROADCAST (LICENSING/GOVERNMENTAL AFFAIRS)

Assistant General Counsel
General Attorney
General Attorney
Broadcast Counsel
Broadcast Counsel
Broadcast Counsel
Broadcast Counsel
Broadcast Counsel

Areas of Responsibility. Counsel to CBS Broadcast Group divisions (principally, News, Television Stations, and Radio Divisions) in the following matters: Communications Act & FCC matters; network/affiliate relations; political broadcasting; review of proposed news reports for potential legal or regulatory concerns; program, talent & miscellaneous contracts; subpoenas seeking news material; Freedom of Information Act claims; commercial clearance issues (excluding contests).

CONTRACTS, RIGHTS & DEVELOPMENT

Assistant General Counsel
Broadcast Counsel
Broadcast Counsel
Broadcast Counsel
Broadcast Counsel
Broadcast Counsel
Manager, Registry Office
Legal Assistant

Areas of Responsibility. Counsel to CBS Broadcast Group divisions (principally, Television Network, Sports, Operations and Engineering, Radio, International, Entertainment, and News divisions) in the following areas: Contracts; sweepstakes & title clearances; music rights; property rights; copyrights; new broadcast technologies; script reviews for potential legal matters; FCC "must carry" proceedings; and Consent Decree compliance. Section also does contract work for CBS Management Information Systems.

CORPORATE

Secretary & Associate General Counsel
Associate General Counsel
General Attorney
Assistant Secretary

Areas of Responsibility. Corporate Secretarial: Board, Board Committees, Annual Meeting matters; maintenance of corporate subsidiaries and corporate records; conflicts of interest matters. Corporate: Securities law filings and compliance; financing matters; benefit plan matters; acquisitions and dispositions; intellectual property matters; general corporate matters.

INDUSTRIAL RELATIONS & ADMINISTRATION

Associate General Counsel

EMPLOYEE RELATIONS

Assistant General Counsel
Labor Counsel
Labor Counsel
Labor Counsel

Areas of Responsibility. Unions: Labor contracts; negotiations; drafting. Labor Dispute Resolution: Grievances; arbitration; litigation. NLRB Litigation: Unfair labor practice & representation. EEO/FEP Discrimination Complaints and Litigation: Race, sex, age, etc. Employee Grievances (Union & Non-Union): Personnel actions, policies, benefits; supervision of labor and EEO/FEP litigation.

REAL ESTATE

Senior Real Estate Counsel
Real Estate Counsel

Areas of Responsibility. Real Estate: Acquisition; sale; lease; partnerships; regulation; zoning; financing; easements; agreements; mortgages. Facilities: Construction; maintenance; repair; equipment; closing; operations; contracts; supervisions of real estate litigation.

LITIGATION

Associate General Counsel
Assistant General Counsel
General Attorney
Litigation Counsel
Litigation Counsel
Litigation Counsel
Manager, Litigation Support Services
Litigation Assistant
Litigation Assistant
Litigation Assistant

Areas of Responsibility. Supervision of litigation instituted by or against the Company; attorneys of record on cases handled in-house; liaison with CBS Risk Management with respect to insurance acquisition and claims handling; liaison with Corporate Security and corporate auditors. Assistance and advice to other Law Sections as requested.

LITIGATION—SPECIAL UNIT

General Attorney
Litigation Counsel
Litigation Assistant
Litigation Assistant

Areas of Responsibility. Unit created primarily to handle Ziff-Davis lawsuit in conjunction with outside counsel.

PUBLISHING

Associate General Counsel
General Attorney
Publishing Counsel

Areas of Responsibility. Legal work (including libel, copyright, invasion of privacy, contract review and drafting) for the CBS Magazine Division and the Columbia House Division. Also, antitrust advice, antitrust litigation supervision and Hart-Scott-Rodino filings for all parts of the Company.

RECORDS
Associate General Counsel
General Attorney
General Attorney
Records Counsel
Records Counsel
Records Counsel
Records Counsel
Records Counsel
Records Counsel
Manager, Records Section Administration

RECORDS—WEST COAST
Records Counsel
Records Counsel

LONDON LAW
London Counsel

Areas of Responsibility. Preparation, review and/or negotiation of agreements for CBS Records, CBS Records International, CBS Records Group, CBS Music Video Enterprises, Masterworks, and CBS Records Operations (U.S.); related legal matters affecting CBS Records Group; review of CBS Records album cover artwork; London office counsels CBS Records International, CBS Broadcast International and CBS, Inc. regarding European matters.

WASHINGTON
Washington Counsel
Associate Washington Counsel

Areas of Responsibility. Federal law, regulatory and legislative matters affecting CBS's businesses.

WEST COAST
West Coast Counsel
Litigation Counsel
Litigation Counsel
Broadcast Counsel
Broadcast Counsel
Broadcast Counsel
Broadcast Counsel
Broadcast Counsel
Broadcast Counsel
Manager, Administrative Services
Legal Assistant
Legal Assistant

Areas of Responsibility. Represents CBS's West Coast operations, primarily in the following matters: Litigation; contracts for the Publishing Group's Magazine division and the Broadcast Group and its Entertainment, Operations and Engineering, Television Stations and Radio divisions; FCC matters; Consent Decree issues; and script reviews for potential legal problems.

At the other end of the scale from the main headquarters at CBS would be the general counsel of a local TV station, standing in somewhat the same relation to the parent company as St. Helena to the British Empire. The general counsel of the local TV station is like the postmaster of the smallest imperial outpost, running the general store and driving the only taxi. Listen to how one such lawyer describes her relationship to the TV station:

> "I function as 'country lawyer, in-house psychologist, good listener, and designated objective observer with confidentiality.' As sole counsel, I report directly to the general manager of the station and am often able to advise on business policy and to practice 'preventative' law. In some ways, I feel that I am doing what used to be considered 'general practice,' but the specialized nature of my one client also gives my work a 'boutique' flavor."

This perception of being in general practice in smaller legal departments is shared by counsel in a wide range of settings. Consider these two excerpts from a recent survey of alumni career paths (*Graduates at Work,* Office of Career Planning and Placement, Yale Law School, 1987):

From a medium-sized, diversified manufacturing company:

"With only two lawyers on the legal staff I find myself handling an incredible variety of work. I am doing things I never would have done in my entire career if I had stayed at the law firm. A list of the things I have been involved with during my short stay here would include mergers and acquisitions, patent and antitrust counseling, employment law, trade secret law and confidentiality agreements, litigation coordination, leasing of real and personal property, Article 2 work, product liability prevention, international licensing of intellectual property, real estate purchases and sales and environmental law. I am certainly not an expert in all of these areas, but the opportunity to learn about these new areas keeps the job interesting and challenging."

And, from a University legal department:

"College law, then, is . . . a setting for the practice of a diverse grouping of legal specialties . . . A representative day might include a meeting a with a group of administrators to develop a charter for a new high technology center on campus, then a phone call to an outside law firm for some advice on an environmental matter. A call might come in from a dean's office concerning a student's claim of unfair treatment . . . An inquiry from our development office might concern the interpretation of a Will in which land is left to the University . . . Other typical work would include the review of a lease of University land or of a research contract with a corporate partner . . . Our work is as varied as the University itself. It is truly a generalist's law practice."

On the other side of the coin, in the largest of corporate legal departments the opportunity for extreme specialization exists, often without the penalties attached to specialization in the law firm. This is true whether we are talking about substantive specialties, such as ERISA work, or functional specialities, such as supervision or management. A prominent advantage of the corporate setting is that with a guaranteed client, or clients, in the company, the in-house specialist does not have to worry about losing ground to rainmakers, a constant concern of "technical" or managing lawyers in private practice. Of course, once your corporate ship has come in, it can go out . . . and down . . . with all hands on board. A single client is to be chosen with care.

Compensation and advancement obviously vary with the size and complexity of the legal departments. Those in the larger corporations, or in the more affluent industries, offer salaries generally competitive with their counterparts in private practice—although large law firm partners arguably do somewhat better at the top end of the salary scale than their peers in corporations. Bonuses, stock options, pension plans and other fringe benefits can make the income discrepancy more apparent than real. Such benefits also help offset the fact that general counsel positions are relatively scarce.

The paucity of general counsel positions in larger corporations simply reflects the pyramidal structure of the legal departments, which does not mimic the hierarchy of law firms—although some departments have created pseudo "partner" designations to satisfy the nostalgic. More middle management positions and fewer top level positions are available in corporate law departments than in private practice. Position definitions can give a flavor of this structure:

General Counsel—not only directs company legal policy and activities, but is often a Vice President or corporation secretary involved in general management.

Chief Assistant or Associate General Counsel—may be General Counsel's managing attorney or have responsibility for major company divisions.

Assistant General Counsel—usually heads a major section of a division, e.g. the CBS Assistant General counsel in charge of the Contracts, Rights and Development section of the Broadcast Department.

Senior Attorney—generally a specialist in some phase of legal operations.

Junior Attorney—entry level person corresponding to new associates.

These categories reflect a greater variety of advancement possibilities than exists at many law firms. Even so, the list is typical of the more codified structure of the larger, traditional corporate departments. Smaller, newer, or more entrepreneurial corporations may involve hybrid or innovative versions of these categories suiting their own needs. The following cases illustrate typical situations where companies have hired new in-house counsel to facilitate the achievement of their business objectives.

Profile #1—The "Turnaround" General Counsel. A new management team was installed in a $600 million consumer products company to clarify business objectives, and to expand the company through the development of an acquisition and disposition program.

The company's existing three-person law department performed traditional Corporate Secretary, regulatory compliance, contract drafting, and counseling functions. Acquisitions, financings, and other complicated legal matters were routinely "packaged" and sent to outside counsel.

The company's aggressive acquisition program called for a business-oriented General Counsel who could work with management at the front end of deals, structure the appropriate financing, resolve impediments along the way, and move quickly to closing.

The General Counsel hired was a former partner in a private law firm who had served as outside counsel to variety of mid-sized OTC companies and had specialized in venture deals and financings. As part of the management team, he organized the existing lawyers into a lean, quality law department capable of broader representation.

Profile #2—The Finance Company General Counsel. A rapidly growing $80 million finance company had developed a large portfolio of delinquent loans. Loan officers originated the loans, outside counsel documented them, and a separate department serviced them.

The company concluded that increasing litigation costs necessitated an inside lawyer with a credit background who could develop an integrated system for approving, documenting, and monitoring loans and for processing delinquencies.

The company hired a lawyer with eight years of banking and bankruptcy experience—four years with a law firm and four years with a commercial bank. He was a CPA with an undergraduate business degree. His loan workout experience was substantial.

He promptly set up an automated system for documenting and monitoring loans and for litigating defaults. As a result, the company collected $1.1 million in delinquent loans during the first year and sales tripled within two years.

Profile #3—The R&D Corporate Lawyer. A $50 million manufacturer of electronic components was spending in excess of $100,000 a year on patent reviews and applications. Given the company's plans for new product development, its legal costs would clearly increase. The company decided to employ its first in-house lawyer to function both as patent and corporate counsel.

The lawyer would work with R&D and new product teams to provide protection through patents, trademarks, licensing, and distribution agreements. In addition, the lawyer would act as Corporate Secretary and develop operations. He would work with outside counsel on acquisitions, financings, and litigation.

The company hired a six-year associate with four years of private practice experience and two years in a company law department. After five years, the lawyer assumed the full role of General Counsel. Within ten years, sales reached $200 million and the General Counsel was performing $500,000 in legal work. Outside counsel legal fees were limited to approximately $40,000.

Profile #4—The Hybrid General Counsel. A $30 million manufacturer and distributor of personal electronic equipment decided to bring the legal function inside before it was clearly cost-effective to do so. Outside legal expenses at that point were $100,000.

The company structured a first-lawyer position combining the additional functions of credit manager, export manager, customer and public relations, and special assistant to the CEO. In the latter role, the lawyer functioned as a general problem solver, a corporate planner, and as one of the three members of the company's business planning team.

The position was filled by a lawyer with eight years of experience, four years as a corporate associate in a major firm and four years as a mid-level staff attorney in a high quality corporate law department. The lawyer is now the Executive Vice President of the company. A second lawyer has been hired as General Counsel.

Profile #5—The Real Estate Development Lawyer. A real estate development company that structured and syndicated six real estate deals during the preceding year decided to add a lawyer to its team. The company was spending about $250,000 a year in legal fees.

There were two problems. First, excessive developer time was devoted to processing financial and legal details rather than in finding and structuring new projects. Second, too much expensive lawyer time was consumed in meetings with financial agencies, designers and contractors, and in the public approval process.

To expedite the development process, the company hired a six year associate from a prominent real estate law firm with experience representing developers, lenders, investors, and contractors. After two years of effectively moving deals from conception to closing, the lawyer assumed additional responsibility for investor relations and syndications. A second lawyer was hired from the same law firm and the company eliminated virtually all of its outside legal costs.

Profile #6—The Business Initiative Lawyer Specialist. A $300 million publishing company with leading brand products in mature markets was interested in expanding into new markets through joint ventures with smaller entrepreneurial companies. A new Executive Vice President was hired to spearhead this initiative in which the Chairman planned to be personally involved.

Recognizing that this deal-oriented new initiative was out of character with the traditional role of the existing three-lawyer law department, the company retained a new breed General Counsel. He had six years of law firm experience representing emerging technology companies and six years as Associate General Counsel of a communications conglomerate. As a key member of the "deal" team, his responsibilities included structuring joint ventures and their financings and expanding the work being performed by the existing law department.

These job profiles portray some striking differences between private practitioners and corporate counsel. Some of these differences are only a matter of degree, but others are qualitative.

For instance, the productivity and value of an in-house lawyer is assessed somewhat differently. There is less emphasis on billable hours per se, partly because of corporate preoccupation with attorney efficiency, and partly because of the corporate bias towards "management by objective". In other words, people are expected to work exactly as hard as it takes to get the job done. This approach to work often permits something resembling a nine-to-five work day. It may also require killing hours equal to the worst that private practice has to offer, and dedication to client goals exceeding that in private practice.

This identification with corporate goals

demands a broader awareness of business conditions than is always necessary in private practice. Moreover, as seen in the examples above, corporate work often creates the opportunity or necessity of participating in management. Not surprisingly, the lawyers who enjoy these conditions often have actual experience in business or an attraction to business problems. In the extreme case, many of them describe their experience in private practice as frustrating because they often wished they "could be" their clients.

With empathy for managerial issues comes a general sensitivity to interpersonal and organizational matters. John Sciamanda, vice president of legal affairs for Control Data Corporation, has said of corporation lawyers, "We are dealing in an organization context and in order to do our job we are dependent on a lot of other people who we may need to influence and/or whose help we may need." Despite the growing complexity of large law firms, most lawyers may be unused to the organizational politics and social interdependencies that are a given in the work of corporate counsel.

From the profiles above, you can see how corporate counsel might be a cross roads for many career paths. In the speech just quoted, Sciamanda also describes the varied careers of the attorneys in his company, a variety virtually enforced by internal developments characteristic of corporate counsel departments in recent years:

> "We have gone from a time 15 years ago where we started out with no inside lawyers, where all the work was done outside, to today where virtually everything is done inside. For years we had no turnover whatsoever. But for the last five years we have not only not grown in terms of total attorneys, but we have reduced the total number of attorneys while continuing to bring more of the work inside, including setting up a litigation group this past year. The result of this, over the last two years, was a large rate of turnover.
>
> "The turnover consisted in large part of many of the attorneys taking on executive responsibilities on the business side; two attorneys left to become general counsels of affiliated organizations which we had acquired a minority interest in or had spun off from our parent organization. Our General Counsel became head of a major business unit, one of our Assistant General Counsels became head of our consumer loan company, an attorney who was servicing a group of venture capital companies left to become president of one of them, another organizational attorney left to become sales manager of our litigation support services group which serves the legal profession, another attorney became a computer system salesman, and finally, just recently, one of our Associate General Counsels accepted a position as dean of the William Mitchel Law School."

This is great variety indeed, and is certainly a distinctive feature of in-house career paths. However, the distinction may become less marked as time goes by. As law firms take their first tottering steps toward diversification the possibility of corporate counsel careers within law firms emerges. As a *National Law Journal* article (Vol. 10, No. 6, October 19, 1987) reminds us, many firms are presently billing clients for non-legal services, often to complement the legal services:

> "Subsidiaries, joint ventures, sister corporations and partnerships—all to provide a diversity of services beyond the traditional law practice—are the hot items on the law firm horizon in the search of new profit centers . . . More often now, as the lure of these offshoot businesses catches on, firm partners are moving from an oversight role to actually running the new business in conjunction with non-lawyer professionals whose skills are complementary."

A distinguished pioneer in such joint ventures is Washington D.C.'s Arnold and Porter. The firm has established subsidiaries which provide a wide range of services in banking and real estate development. Several Arnold and Porter partners have assumed management responsibilities for these subsidiaries. Eventually, descriptions of the career paths of Arnold and Porter partners may sound strikingly similar to the destinies of the the Control Data attorneys. Who would deny that lawyers are in transition?

* * *

Government and Public Interest Law

If you are leaving private practice and are not going in-house, then odds are you are thinking about the public sector. According to the 1983 management statistics from the United States' Office of Personnel, 17,796 attorneys work for the federal government (excluding hearings examiners and administrative law judges.) Adding the attorneys working for state and local government, the percentages of the profession working for government and for corporations are roughly equivalent. This equivalence probably reflects the often antagonistic, always interdependent relationship between government and business—when one side increases its troops the other must respond.

A truly adequate picture of opportunities in government lies well beyond the scope of this book or the expertise of its authors. Considering that federal government attorneys ply their trade in settings as diverse as the Panama Canal Commission, the Legal Services Corporation, and the Comptroller of the Currency, it is difficult to be succinct about the variety or generalize greatly about the satisfactions. Fortunately, there are a number of excellent guides to government and public interest employment, listed in our Resources Chapter, which map the sometimes tortuous paths to government positions. Once again we limit our treatment to those features which might interest someone looking beyond the law firm. Curiously, there are parallels between government and corporate careers when both are regarded as alternatives to private practice.

Organizational variety is one such parallel, with government offering even more varied conditions of employment. The national, regional, and local categories of practice described above obviously have their counterpart in federal, state, and local government. The same functions are found at each level of government, and include prosecution; regulation and enforcement; house counsel; public advocacy; policy analysis and consultation; and working for executive and legislative branches as part of the political process. In addition to these functions there are many which do not require a law degree but may be suited to lawyers. (See Appendix C.)

Probably the broadest distinction to be made between types of government attorneys is between the litigators and non-litigators. If you are a litigator in private practice, it is arguable that only variations of your present work are found in government. The variation need not be insignificant since the side of the table on which you find yourself may be the most important shift you can make. The basic litigation process is, of course, familiar and transferable. Adversaries such as NLRB attorneys and labor lawyers in private practice may feel a basic kinship, however ambivalent.

Non-litigating attorneys, on the other hand, perform tasks that may seem appealing precisely because they have no exact analog in private practice: Writing as well as interpreting agency regulations, supporting an agency's position in legislative bodies, giving advice to agency program administrators. These are functions equally characteristic of the non-litigating public interest organizations. These tasks may indeed lead to public administration in much the same way that the work of corporation counsel may lead to management.

This distinction between litigators and non-litigators might be more important to your career path than the distinction between levels of government or substantive areas of practice. On the other hand, if you have a burning aspiration for a career in local politics, the level of government may be more important to you than it's function or substance. Your aim in this instance might be to gain broad experience of roles and substantive knowledge all at one level of government. Your interests and strategies would be similar, therefore, whether you were a George Bush toiling through a variety of elected and appointed federal jobs towards the highest office in the land or a local figure progressing through the school committee and the board of aldermen toward mayor.

To yet others, the opportunity to gain specific experience in every conceivable subject, from educational disabilities to military procurements, constitutes one of the greatest appeals of government. Thus your main motive in seeking a government job might be to learn as much as you could, say about toxic hazards to the environment, regardless of level or function.

Most careers in government will be chosen to balance all three factors, function, specialty, and setting. You might, for instance, begin as a civil rights litigator in a state legal services agency. Specific cases might give you a secondary specialization in housing and educational disabilities. Contacts with state and municipal attorneys familiar with your work might lead to job offers and subsequent positions in municipal commissions and state agencies where litigation was not the primary activity. Thus your career would be defined by a moderate degree of subject specialization, based on litigation, in state government.

Opportunities in the public sector may be diverse, but the satisfactions and drawbacks are strikingly uniform, judging from the comments of practitioners. A strong sense of direct involvement in socially meaningful activity is the common denominator of most kinds of government work. It is similar to the sense of direct participation in other people's affairs felt by corporate counsel, but is obviously more openly political. Once more, the first person accounts from *Graduates at Work* nicely convey this feeling:

> "Satisfactions include: worthwhile, often exciting substantive work; unusually close contact with a Cabinet officer; the intimacy of a lean/mean cadre within the executive Office of the President . . . newsworthy issues; great opportunities for learning . . . about salmon, semiconductors and . . . how the European Community relates to its member states . . . and government service."
>
> —Office of the U.S. Trade Representative

> "Representing the government before the Supreme Court and helping make legal decisions within government, is for me, both exciting and educational . . . Helping to make such judgments and crafting good legal papers . . . many with significant impact, are among the greatest satisfactions of my job."
>
> —Assistant to the Solicitor General

> "The most satisfying aspect of the job evolves from the constant immersion in issues — constitutional, statutory and ethical — with significant public importance."
>
> —Assistant U.S. Attorney

> "It is the ability to see and to respect as individuals people who are merely processed by the other actors in the criminal justice system which keeps lawyers going . . . Public defender work, as opposed to 'public interest' representation is above all about the needs and desires of individual human beings."
>
> —Staff Attorney, Public Defender Service

> "In advising a state agency, lawyers obviously use their traditional legal skills of analysis and persuasion. But because most every 'legal' decision in the public sector has public impact, there is a great deal of satisfaction, excitement and involvement which does not always exist in private practice."
>
> —Assistant Secretary of Consumer Affairs and Business Regulation

These quotes play interesting variations on the same theme. For some the significance of the participation is deeply personal, for others it is broadly political, and for still others it is intellectual. These elements are present to some degree in all the descriptions, but setting and specialty tip the balance in one direction or the other.

Of course, every peculiar virtue has its own down side. The price tag of participation is the possibility of getting mired in situations for which legal training and the independence of private practice are poor preparation. Identifying with institutional goals means political battles, bureaucratic struggles, and getting caught in the crossfire of conflicting social agendas.

Some lawyers enjoy these problems as much as others enjoy the passions and conflicts of business, but some just find them frustrating. They speak of "limits, which arise mostly from the limits of criminal prosecution in solving the social ills of the society and the nation," or "the need to take into account the larger political context within which government litigation takes place," or "the inability to make the trade deficit go away because its caused largely by macroeconomic factors irrelevant to trade policy," or "a judicial system stacked against the poor."

An important satisfaction peculiar to government is greater social diversity, particularly with regard to women and minorities. In some instances there is also less of a social hierarchy and a greater sense of informality than exists within large law firm practice. (Bureaucratic hierarchy is another matter.) Add an official commitment to affirmative action, it is no wonder that larger percentages of women and minorities leave private practice for government and business.

Related to social diversity is the life style satisfaction of lower hours and/or greater autonomy, which allow greater compatibility with family life. This benefit may be discovered at all levels of government. In federal agencies, municipal counsel offices, or state attorneys general may be found niches which allow trade-offs between personal and professional life. This may be true even in hotbeds of frantic litigation, if you pick your spot. An assistant D.A. who works in the appeals division of her office says:

> "On a more personal level, my time commitments are relatively limited and predictable, so that I am able to maintain a stable and satisfying home life. This kind of position lends itself very well to part-time work, which I did for several months after the birth of my second child. Even on a full time basis, I can count on leaving the office at a regular time nearly every day, and I can occasionally read transcripts and work on briefs at home if family obligations require."

Along with small law firm practice and some corporate counsel work, government legal work often offers the satisfaction of early responsibility. The public defender, the State Department legal advisor, the assistant U.S. attorney, all may find themselves with major assignments while attorneys in private practice are standing in line at the copying machine. Some would argue that a greater range of competence or ambition in government creates opportunity responsibility not to be found in private practice. Others point out that one formula for early responsibility is "stretched staff and minimal supervision."

Indeed, early responsibility, like political participation, has its negative side. This negative usually emerges in the charge that government offers poor training and calls it "responsibility." Government counters that it trains best for what it does, that early experience is the best trainer, and that the larger agencies have resources for training comparable to those of the larger law firms. In some ways the debate is irrelevant. The best way for you to be trained depends on the best way you learn. Some learn best by viewing, others by doing. Increased responsibility can be a liability at one stage of your career and an asset at the next. As we shall see, only a good understanding of career development and a careful self-assessment will tell you when you are ready to turn a negative into a positive.

Alas, not much positive can be said of government and public interest salaries. Your government paycheck is a sow's ear that resists being turned into a silk purse. On the other hand, although our society seems to have decided that those who serve the poor shall be compensated accordingly, it is possible to do good and do well . . . or well enough. This is particularly true of government, which seems to represent the middle path between those two values.

The Federal government hires experienced attorneys at about the GS-12 level or higher, which means a 1987 starting salary of $33,000 up to $72,000. (A special category called the senior executive service permits negotiated salaries, and is aimed at attracting attorneys from the private sector.) A recent look at the government attorneys from the Harvard Law School class of '69 suggested that their incomes ranged between $44,000 and $100,000. By any standard in our society, aside from the inflated world view of large law firm practice, these incomes may be considered "doing well." One assistant D.A. captured the essence of the issue when he said:

> "My wife and children not only wear shoes, we eat at restaurants with table cloths, cook in a microwave and take vacation trips to places people have heard of! And, my children can understand what I do and think I am one of the good guys; this means the world to me."

Those who can adapt to public sector salaries may find it harder to deal with the lack of structure and predictability in government career opportunities. This problem takes many forms, among them an official lack of centralized information about job vacancies for lawyers in the federal government, and often in state government as well. As Abbie Willard Thorner writes in her invaluable *Now Hiring: Government Jobs for Lawyers:*

> "Every agency establishes its own application procedures, based on Office of Personnel Management guidelines. Lawyers who want government positions must file the proper forms with every agency that interests them, and in many cases with individual divisions or bureaus within an agency."

This problem exists not only for entry level jobs but for lateral movement within government as well. According to Thorner, "Lawyers who wish to move to another government agency rely entirely on their own initiative." Such a move is apt to be the result of personal contacts made through a close working relationship between agencies, just as an attorney might leave private practice to work for a client.

Even within agencies there is wide variation in attitudes toward in-house transfers and requirements to specialize or remain in assigned areas. To complicate matters, job mobility and stability are both affected by political instability. As one lawyer wryly remarks, "the usual government dilemma (is) that if you're a political appointee, you must leave at some point; and if you're a career appointee, you can't get promoted beyond a certain level." On the other hand, there are many pockets of "permanent civil service" employment safely sheltered from the winds of politics.

A good example of sheltered civil service is the office which provides legislative drafting services to the U.S. House of Representatives. Attorneys in the office work with members and staff of both parties. The non-partisan, objective manner in which they perform their task is very much in accord with the classic view of neutral legal services. Their jobs are relatively safe from the political change around them, and their longevity often makes them the "institutional memory" of the legislative body.

The ebb and flow of political life also affects opportunities to return to private practice. Although substantive knowledge and experience acquired in government are often negotiable assets in returning to private practice or going into business, they can also be millstones around your neck. What is "hot" in government today may become a dead issue with a change of administration or the march of time.

For instance, when Congress enacted the Immigration Reform and Control Act of 1986, the new law created a large number of new attorney positions in both the Immigration and Naturalization Service and in the Justice Department's new office of the Special Counsel for Immigration Related Unfair Employment Practices. To spend too long in government following those opportunities could lead to overspecialization and the danger that if one should eventually leave government, the problems in immigration would no longer be numerous or current. On the other hand, an immigration attorney with experience who left government to work privately in this field would have had interesting topical opportunities in the Cuban prisoners' crisis of late 1987.

Whether you leave government to work in private practice, business, or a public interest advocacy group, timing and a creative willingness to take risks are always critical. The absence of predictable career paths in the public sector is a curse or an opportunity depending upon your temperament and needs. Those who are able to take risks may, in fact, encompass all the satisfactions of private practice and its alternatives in the course of one career. We end this section with the example of one lawyer's creative use of timing to effect several transitions through government, public interest and private practice:

> "My career pattern has been somewhat unorthodox. After I graduated in 1972 . . . I went to Washington D.C. where I had taken what I regarded as a public interest job as a lawyer in the Federal Trade Commission's Bureau of Consumer Protection.
>
> "I stayed at the FTC for 5 1/2 years and while there headed industry-wide investigations of funeral abuses (which produced the FTC's Funeral Practices Trade Regulation Rule . . .) and condominium abuses and worked on a variety of other consumer protection projects.
>
> "While in D.C. I got admitted to the D.C. bar and did a couple of pro bono racial discrimination cases and some pro bono work for the ACLU, in addition to my FTC work.
>
> "When I was getting ready to leave the FTC in 1978 I read about the case of the Estate of Karen Silkwood v. Kerr McGee (the radiation contamination case upon which the movie 'Silkwood' was based) and offered to help out 'for a couple of months'.
>
> "My offer was gratefully accepted, and I resigned from the FTC and came to Oklahoma in June of 1978. Two months later I was put in charge of preparing the case seeking recovery for Silkwood's contamination, and I later second-chaired (to Gerry Spence) the 11-week trial, which led to a $10 million verdict and have been lead counsel for the Estate in the appellate proceedings, which are still going on.
>
> "Along the way, I served as special counsel to the estate with regard to the Silkwood movie, publication rights negotiations, a slander action against an exploitative paperback publisher, and related off-shoots of the litigation.
>
> "I got admitted to the Oklahoma bar in 1979 and have been in private practice here since then. My practice is somewhat varied but primarily involves civil litigation in different areas including some 'commercial' public interest litigation . . .
>
> "I also presently have a couple of sex discrimination cases, 'toxic tort', and whistleblower cases. I also do some civil rights/due process litigation; I have represented a group of reporters in a public records access case, and have done some plaintiff's environmental litigation. I also handle some plaintiff's personal injury, products liability, and medical practice cases.
>
> "Handling a variety of different types of cases is very appealing to me. The mixture allows me to handle some cases for little or no fee and others on a contingent fee basis where there may well be a substantial recovery ultimately down the road.
>
> "I believe it is important for students to realize that public interest work does not necessarily have to be uncompensated work. To me, it is important to be able to work on what is interesting and worthwhile . . . and to be able to work on what you want to, whether or not a big fee, or any fee, will come out of it."

(Letter from Arthur R. Angel, published in *Public Interest Director,* Ronald W. Fox editor, Harvard Law School Placement Office, 1986.)

This man's career shows clever use of setting, experience, and timing to exploit the satisfactions of both public and private practice while avoiding their traps and liabilities. Like all inspirational examples it is perhaps inimitable in some respects. However, the most powerful moral to be derived from the trail is that alternatives to private practice, and within private practice, are as much in your state of mind as in any particular sector of the profession. It is very much a question of risk, imagination and a relish for change.

* * *

III. OPPORTUNITIES IN NON-LEGAL SETTINGS

If, as we have suggested earlier, law schools can be viewed as graduate schools of reading, writing, and thinking, the training ought to be useful beyond the practice of law. And clearly it is.

In fact, many people opt for a non-legal career right out of law school and many others enter non-legal careers after practicing law. Few, however, enter private practice after careers in non-legal settings. In entities other than private law firms, the line between what is legal and what is non-legal is becoming increasingly blurred. Indeed, the blending of legal and non-legal aspects makes certain jobs all the more attractive to some law school graduates.

Law school alumni records, the Career Paths Study mentioned in Chapter 3, and books devoted to the issue all speak eloquently to the large and growing melange of careers successfully being pursued by ex-law students and ex-lawyers. This portion of law school graduates can be expected to increase in coming years in response to increased competition for limited legal business by ever-increasing numbers of lawyers; in response to the increased ambivalence of many young lawyers to the intrusive time and energy demands of the practice of law; and, perhaps, in response to a growing recognition of the need for talented young men and women in so many other areas of human endeavor.

Beyond these economic and psychic motivations for pursuing a non-legal career, there are at least three "content factors" that pave the way for relatively easy transitions from legal to non-legal careers.

First, law schools develop process and generalist skills more than a technical knowledge of law. Students arrive in law school from every conceivable type of college and university with every conceivable undergraduate major. Proven superior academic performance is the basic admission standard; a standard relevant far beyond the law. First year law school courses tend to teach basic rights and relationships and the structure of the legal system. The emphasis is on reading carefully, thinking logically, expressing oneself in a hostile environment, and seeing a variety of perspectives—skills that are pertinent to a broad spectrum of positions (door-to-door salesperson to CEO). Second and third year courses introduce the problems of business: Tax, corporations, securities, trade regulation, commercial code, etc. While there are exceptions (e.g., estate planning), most second and third year courses are taught using business transactions and scenarios as a basis for discussion and analysis.

Second, the practices of an enormous number of lawyers are centered on the problems of business. Lawyers typically learn far more about business management than business executives learn about law. Switching from the legal seat to the business seat is not as drastic as many, lawyers included, believe.

Third, as legal careers advance there tends to be less emphasis on technical knowledge and more on the value of general counseling. This is evident in the descriptions of the stages of a legal career offered in the introduction to Exercise 11 of Chapter 7. In this respect, senior lawyers resemble senior accountants, consultants, or business executives—perhaps even more than they resemble younger lawyers. Their function evolves into providing corporate clients with vision and judgment, grounded in an understanding of the legal system.

This is not to say that all styles and specialties in the practice are equally adaptive to a subsequent career outside of law. For example, it is far more common for young litigators to get caught up in their art (procedural niceties, emotional oratory, etc.) and learn less about the underlying businesses they represent and business issues than it is for young corporate attorneys. There is, however, no fundamental impediment to any reasonably thoughtful attorney seeking a second career. Litigators do learn investigative and organizational skills and techniques of persuasion, no matter what else they learn. Many also learn something of the regulation of the business community via antitrust, trade regulation, securities, international trade and the more specific industry-regulating agencies: transportation, energy, environmental protection, etc.

Although non-litigation specialties seem, and in fact are, more pertinent to subsequent business careers, that pertinence is often more due to peripheral learning situations than to the primary lawyering activities. The primary role of young corporate lawyers is usually to "manage" a transaction along a partner-described production system using forms, documents, and checklists. The young lawyer deals with document production, coordination, proofing, and printing and with managing the closing. By being responsible for the "zero defect" standard of documenting and managing transactions, however, they learn many business considerations by merely "being there" and interacting with the panoply of actors in major transactions—investment bankers, bankers, developers, accountants, market researchers, top corporate management, etc. To the extent that the young attorney is interested in and understands these various other roles and functions, he or she is in a perfect position to learn much of the economics, the risks and rewards, of a wide variety of business transactions. It does, of course, require that interest and sensitivity on the part of the lawyer for a good business sense to develop over time. It also requires that a lawyer recognize the skills and experiences necessary for the non-lawyer to play his role in the transaction. There is more to real estate development than legal forms.

Transition to a non-legal career is also a function of when in a lawyer's life the change is to be attempted. Later in a career the lawyer's knowledge and judgment should be more extensive and refined. But, later in a career the financial rewards of lawyering may have become so substantial that non-legal positions of comparable compensation are scarce.

Then there is the special case of senior lawyers in large firms who are already acting as business executives. They are the owners and/or managers of large ($50 to $200 million) businesses called National Law Firms. As such they allocate resources, set policy, provide institutional direction, prioritize, and decide the major issues of the enterprise. No wonder it is seemingly effortless for senior lawyers to move in and out of law firms, appointive government positions, and industry. At the top of any large organization, the functions are essentially the same.

The movement from a legal to a non-legal position requires the very same assessment and planning activities to be discussed in the legal setting in the next portion of this book. You must learn the skills and experiences required of the position you would like, assess which of those you already possess, and then find intermediate positions that will beef up your experience, and your resume, in the deficient areas. Here, of course, those intermediate positions may be legal or non-legal. But the process of analyzing and articulating the desired experience is the same.

There have always been a variety of non-legal positions that have attracted lawyers. The 1980's, however, have seen a growth both in the spectrum of positions deemed suitable and in the numbers of lawyers seeking such positions. In 1980 such opportunities were discussed in Frances Utley's ABA monograph *Nonlegal Careers: New Opportunities for Lawyers* (ABA Standing Committee on Professional Utilization and Career Development). A second edition of this work by Utley and Gary A. Munneke was published in 1984 under the title, *Nonlegal Careers For Lawyers In The Private Sector.*

As early as 1980, the Standing Committee, after a survey of sixty of the nation's largest corporations, concluded that:

> "In most large corporations the number of legally trained persons employed in administration and management posts far exceeds that of the legal department."

It then categorized the corporate nonlegal opportunities in the following groups:

- Taxes
- Employee Relations
- Finance
- Real Estate
- Government Relations/Public Relations
- Consumer Relations/Public Relations
- Traffic
- Insurance
- Regulatory Compliance
- Corporate Secretarial
- Purchasing and Contract Administration
- Marketing
- Industrial Development
- Exports/Imports
- Strategic Planning
- Administration and Management

Various surveys of the National Association of Law Placement have revealed over a hundred specific job types accepted by new law graduates.

Non-legal career paths, of course, can defy any effort at classification, no matter how inclusive. Recently, a Boston attorney forsook his vocation and turned to an avocation to support himself while his wife completed law school and, presumably, thereafter. He is now a Bonsai Master, advises owners on the care of their valuable little trees, and is referred to as "Doctor Bonsai".

Clearly, the opportunities are manifold for the restless lawyer. The strategies of preparing for these positions and careers are basically those of Chapters 6 through 8. The tactics of finding and winning the job you want are basically those of Chapter 9 through 11. Chapter 13, Resources, includes discussions of reference materials that will help you to gather and dissect non-legal opportunities that may currently be unfamiliar to you.

Articulating priorities, needs, and sources of problems with job or career requires a probing self-assessment to get to the heart of it all. That self-assessment, however, will be more comprehensible when displayed against a background comprising the predictable phase transitions in adult life . . . the subject of Chapter 5. As Pascal would have it, "the heart has its reasons the mind never knows."

Chapter

5

Adult Development: Taking Time

"To every thing there is a season, and a time to every purpose under heaven."
Ecclesiastes 3:1

Before getting to the specifics of the person that is you, we turn to some accumulated wisdom that can form a backdrop against which your own life and career may make more sense. It is useful to have a scheme or framework for thinking about these problems in your life. The vocational self-assessment of the next three Chapters will be incomplete without such perspective.

In the last few years much has been written about the adult life cycle, much of it based on the psychological theories of Erik Erikson (inventor of the identity crisis), Daniel J. Levinson and Roger Gould. Reasonably accessible in its own right, the work of these men has been very ably expanded and popularized in the works of Gail Sheehy. All are listed in Chapter 13, Resources. Relying on Sheehy's work, we present here a summary of adult development to be used in your self-assessment. The summary does not include all stages, but rather begins with the stage corresponding to early career development.

Important Stages of Adult Development

The *first stage* covers the years roughly from 22 to 29 and is called "Provisional Adulthood." Or one might call it "Entry-Level Adulthood," because every decision is an entry-level decision: What career to enter, what relationships to enter, what social reference groups are important, and so forth. The stage is characterized by a great deal of tentativeness and exploration even as it imposes great pressure for commitment. "How do I know?" and "What if I make the wrong decision?" hover over every commitment. Because young adults believe strongly, or at least struggle to, they fear every step is momentous and irrevocable.

The specific tasks of this stage (and each stage has tasks to ensure continued growth) are to find work and a mentor at work, to achieve intimate relationships with friends and lovers, and to form a vision of oneself in the world which can become the basis for life goals. The greatest challenge of this period is to throw oneself into life wholeheartedly while retaining enough judgement not to get trapped or hurt. As Sheehy says, "people who do not invest much of themselves in the choices of their twenties will not get much out that allows them to change and grow."

For people with the normal college-at-18, law-school-at-22 lives, this stage corresponds roughly to law school and internship.

The *second stage* covers the years roughly from 29 to 32, and is called "The Age Thirty Transition." A motto for this stage could be Emerson's dictum, "young man, beware of what you want, for surely you will get it."

In residency and having achieved some competence and acceptance at work, one is on the verge of becoming a junior member of the "occupational tribe." Having achieved some ability at entering into intimate relationships, one is faced with the deepening and broadening of those relationships. For those yet unmarried, the pressure to commit has increased; for the married, the issue of children has intensified.

At work and in relationships the realization that life is a long-haul proposition grows. It will be necessary, one realizes, to focus energies, to specialize, to make long term plans. As Matthew Arnold once said, "there must be some closing of the gates of the mind before thirty if one is to accomplish anything in life." Training is over, production has begun. Anxiety mounts in the face of this challenge, resisting the narrowing, re-examining options. Having satisfied the expectations of society, family, and one's own early dreams, one asks with new urgency, "What are my real needs?"

The *third stage* covers the years roughly from 32 to 39, and is appropriately called "Rooting." Now, one gets a new, firmer grip on life. Having rededicated to early goals or shifted to new ones, persons at thirty-five burst into a highly energetic, productive phase at work, or else settle into a resigned pace, depending upon the value they place upon work. Levinson calls this the "BOOM" phase, "Becoming One's Own Man."

Autonomy, from one's peers especially, assumes great importance at this stage. The feeling comes, "it's now or never" to reach that platform from which one may achieve some higher level of financial or professional eminence. At home, this stage may be symbolized by such decisions as whether to have more children, whether add a wing to the house, whether a spouse will return to school, or whether to run for local office. In the midst of all these increasing involvements, one takes another look at favorite old dreams, deciding which to hang onto at all costs.

The *fourth stage* occurs in the vicinity of age 40, and is the famed "Mid-life Transition," second only to the "Identity Crisis" in popularity among novelists and screen writers. The momentum of "becoming one's own man" is slowing down and it has become possible to glimpse the probable limits of one's achievements in life. For that matter, the end of life is foreseeable. Though still distant, it no longer seems so abstract.

Even success, if it becomes repetitive, feels like stagnation and ways to elaborate and vary work become important. If success has been illusive, there seems to be just enough energy left for one more try, as in the Jack London story in which an aging prize fighter's last title attempt depends upon his eating a piece of steak. In the first instance, one feels free to start a new life; in the second, one feels compelled to do so. Whether feeling restless or depleted, one is apt to put a strain on marriage and family while attempting to break out of a rut.

The *final stage,* in our condensed version of this scheme, becomes "Restabilization and Flowering," which takes place at around ages 43 to 50. Having readjusted expectations downward or broadened interests outward, one often arrives at a new plateau of satisfaction.

This scheme should immediately strike you as a relative of the internship-residency-partnership model of professional development. Indeed, the latter may be seen as a kind of subplot of the former. However, it is not always easily integrated with the whole story of one's life.

Delayed Starting

With the more flexible educational attitudes of recent years, more people are interrupting their educations to sample other experiences. Others are deciding rather late that a law degree will assist with a life's plan discovered only in their thirties or beyond.

The correspondence of the classic adult stages with one's legal career, obviously, will be markedly different for such individuals. They must make suitable shifts in the above discussion and the following Exercise.

Exercise 2 provides compartments for specifying Goals for your stages of professional development and the corresponding stages in the life cycle. Between the Goal compartments are corresponding Conflicts & Trade-offs compartments where you should describe what one part

Exercise 2: INTERACTIONS AT CORRESPONDING STAGES OF PROFESSIONAL AND PERSONAL LIVES

PROFESSIONAL: LAW SCHOOL & INTERNSHIP		PROFESSIONAL/ PERSONAL	PERSONAL: PROVISIONAL ADULTHOOD	
RELATIONSHIPS Supervisors Mentors Colleagues Clients Subordinates	GOALS	CONFLICTS & TRADEOFFS	GOALS	**RELATIONSHIPS** Lovers Spouse Friends Parents Children
MEANINGS Meaning of Profession Choosing Training Jobs Discovering Specialties Participation in Employer Goals				**MEANINGS** Religious Values Political Participation Physical Development Intellectual Interests Artistic Interests Social Organizations Projects
ECONOMICS Salary Benefits Paying off Debt Hours				**ECONOMICS** Housing Transportation Finances Vacations Possessions

Exercise 2: INTERACTIONS AT CORRESPONDING STAGES OF PROFESSIONAL AND PERSONAL LIVES

PROFESSIONAL: RESIDENCY		PROFESSIONAL/ PERSONAL	PERSONAL: AGE 30 TRANSITION/"BOOM" PHASE/ROOTING	
RELATIONSHIPS Stay in this job? Senior colleagues Partnership Own clients	GOALS	CONFLICTS & TRADEOFFS	GOALS	RELATIONSHIPS Become a parent? Become a parent again? Spouse's career or ed. Children's ed. Social needs Keeping old friends
MEANINGS Stay in law? Deepen specialization Change specialization More participation in management?				MEANINGS Are values same? Can you maintain important activities and interests
ECONOMICS "BOOM" income phase More discretionary income Investments? What?				ECONOMICS Expand present lifestyle or change it? Possessions or experiences?

Exercise 2: INTERACTIONS AT CORRESPONDING STAGES OF PROFESSIONAL AND PERSONAL LIVES

<table>
<tr><th colspan="2">PROFESSIONAL: PROFESSIONAL ESTABLISHMENT</th><th>PROFESSIONAL/
PERSONAL</th><th colspan="2">PERSONAL: MID-LIFE TRANSITION/
RESTABILIZING/FLOWERING</th></tr>
<tr><td>RELATIONSHIPS
“Owner” at work
Obligations to partners, subordinates</td><td rowspan="3">GOALS</td><td rowspan="3">CONFLICTS & TRADEOFFS</td><td rowspan="3">GOALS</td><td>RELATIONSHIPS
Welfare of 2 generations
Preserve freshness of relationship with spouse</td></tr>
<tr><td>MEANINGS
Train employees
Direct organization
Rainmaking
Strategizing</td><td>MEANINGS
Peak participation in political or community life
Achievement of “wisdom”
Preservation of health
Conservation of energy</td></tr>
<tr><td>ECONOMICS
Extracting major benefit from gains of last decade</td><td>ECONOMICS
Funding provisional adulthood of your children
Maintaining lifestyle
Planning retirement</td></tr>
</table>

(personal/professional) of your life requires from the other—thus making overt conflicts and trade-offs that would otherwise slip by unbidden. For instance, "If I am to acquire more responsibility for litigation management, my children must learn to take greater responsibility for household management." Or, "If I am ever to meet someone I like enough to marry, I've got to be out of the office by ten o'clock."

This Exercise should convince you, if you haven't been protesting already, that the above scheme of adult development really describes a monstrous juggling act. Under the best of circumstances synchronizing personal and professional life is a perpetual challenge, which is why Freud said that mental health could be reduced to success at love and work.

Convoluted Stages

At this juncture in our society, the whole sequence of the life cycle has been distorted, delayed, and protracted for many people, among them professionals. The tasks of various stages are deferred and carried over into the next stage. As a result the tidiness and universality of the model breaks down. It states the tasks and issues well, but individuals must struggle with forging their own version. For instance, there are at least three contemporary discontinuities in adult development which might apply to you and which serve as good examples of the sychronizing problem.

1. With protracted schooling, it is not uncommon for young adults to arrive at graduate school with such delayed social development that they are ready for a college social life just when they are required to spend ungodly hours plowing through the rules of evidence. This problem continues into the internship and provisional adulthood stage which helps account for the deserved popularity of fellowships, clerkships, and other moratoriums that allow people to catch up with themselves.

2. Another case of work and personal development getting out of phase is the delayed parenting common with many of the baby boomers who find their energies taxed on two fronts in a manner atypical of previous generations. Here is how one lawyer describes life in his college class's twentieth anniversary report:

> "The past five years have been a period of consolidation and personal development for me. Professionally, I continue to specialize in corporate and securities law at __________, having been there over ten years now. One of the rewards of growing older is participating in the training and development of young attorneys. Ten years' experience also gives you a better perspective on the role of law . . . There is a great deal more to the practice of law than the technical legal issues that we deal with every day . . . Personally, our family life has been enriched — and complicated, and occasionally exasperated — by the arrival of our younger daughter . . . It is interesting how many members of my college class . . . are raising very small children while entering their early forties. On the whole, I believe that the advantages of doing so outweigh the drawbacks. Stay tuned to our 35th report, however, to see how some of us in our late fifties will be coping with our then teenaged children!"

In this man's perceptive account we sense how, in true-to-life fashion these days, his stages have all jumbled together. Continuing the process of becoming his own man, he is consolidating his specialties at work while as a partner and mentor to young adults he is putting down roots. Yet, he is also anticipating his wise elder statesmen stage by beginning to reflect on the larger role of his profession. Then, to complicate things further, there arrives a daughter, forever altering the relationship between his past, present and future.

Special Phase Shifts for Women Lawyers

3. Perhaps the best example of disjointed and overlapping stages in the adult life cycle is the saga of women committed to careers. This is a

subject which, rightfully, has stimulated some excellent research, including Sheehy's. Chapter 13, Resources contains some other works dealing specifically with the experiences of women in law. What follows is a mere sketch of typical tensions women lawyers may experience at different moments in their career.

In the provisional adulthood phase, the young woman lawyer may feel conflict between throwing herself into the still predominantly male culture of law firms and retaining her own style of doing things. This tension begins early in law school, as in the case of the first year student trying to decide between participating in an all male study group, which she perceives as a bunch of competing egos uninterested in learning, or an all female study group, which she perceives as a cooperative learning environment unable to teach her intellectual competition.

In the law firm, issues of belonging may become more acute. Our research into stress on the first year of the job suggests that women may feel more anxiety about "learning the ropes" of internal procedures than do male attorneys. Reasons for this may include natural ambivalence about participating in all the informal values and interests which help social induction into the firm. A good example of this is the woman who failed to learn about an important procedural change in her department because it was informally communicated at a basketball game to which she was not invited.

Finally, if the young woman lawyer has postponed achieving intimacy while completing her education, she must rush to catch up so she can get to the next stage and beat the biological time clock. All of these problems may throw into question her ability, or desire, to immerse herself in the world of her profession.

These pressures are exacerbated by the Age Thirty Transition. Reassessing whether one wants to become "a junior member of the occupational tribe" is harder with the realization that rededication to career for a woman may require harsher trade-offs than for a man. The decision to have children may present itself as a more radical career shift because, at present, women pay a higher price for this decision than do men. Similarly, they pay a higher price at work if they are still committed to finding a mate.

In the rooting phase, between ages 32 and 39, women may feel compelled to withdraw from full commitment at work, just when men are settling in. If, after ushering their progeny through early childhood they are hastening to catch up at work, they may have a spouse whose own crisis is driving him to make some risky career change. Thus one spouse is looking for belated involvement while the other is seeking detachment. Then again, perhaps the woman wishes to make her own radical change by deciding to work less, but financial pressure produced by her husband's job change requires her to redouble her work.

At forty, the woman attorney may be entering her own BOOM(W) phase. Her "now or never" feeling comes with the increasing independence of her children, and she is ready to begin a new, productive stage of her life when at last she will come into her own. Her husband, on the other hand, may be somewhat preoccupied with his mid-life crisis, feeling his life constrict around him.

These limited examples should indicate how, at present, women may have a less regular schedule of personal and professional development. Their developmental tasks are those in the general model, but, by necessity or nature, the sequence is different.

According to the National Association of Law Schools, in 1985 twice as many women as men entered law school after the age of thirty-nine. These older women have not always received as much support from their spouses as the older men students do from theirs. This disparity well reflects the differences in developmental schedules.

Lack of correspondence between the requirements of spouses leads to classic lapses in empathy and communication for which the only cure is a great deal of good will and deliberate planning. *Married readers had better, therefore, draw their spouses into the self-assessment process from the very beginning.*

And now to the nitty-gritty of that self-assessment.

Chapter

6

Self-Assessment I: Taking Stock

"He discovereth deep things out of darkness . . . "
Job 12:22

A mass produced career plan is about as valuable to you as someone else's false teeth.

This Chapter will help you find the foundation upon which any personal career plan must be based: Your own needs and desires. Unless you take responsibility for your own assessment, you run the danger of drifting into someone else's future. Your epitaph could be like that on the eighteenth century gravestone: "Here lies John Jones, born a man, died a grocer."

In this Chapter you will review systematically some of your life experiences and career decisions to find revealing interests, skills, and values. Aided by several Exercises, you will rummage through your past looking for patterns and themes to guide your next steps.

The benefit? Through these Exercises you should get a better idea of what you have been doing and of what you would like to be doing, and for whom and at what level of responsibility. You should be able to fit these thoughts into a broader perspective of your personal development and life-style requirements. At the least, you should be able to talk about your experiences in a more organized and persuasive fashion in an interview situation.

In doing all of the above, you will be acting as your own career counselor. To be effective in this role you need to overcome the customary lethargy most feel in the face of self confrontation. But, as W.C. Fields once said, "there comes a time in a man's life when he has to seize the bull by the tail and face the situation." (This sensitive philosopher undoubtedly knew that women would do something far more sensible.)

Read this Chapter and do the Exercises with the care and deliberation that you would apply to your work for an important client. Vague musings will not do the job. As someone, (not W.C. Fields) once said, "you can't plow a field by turning it over in your mind." Not only should you read and write, you should converse with friends, colleagues, and family about what you are doing. Talking to others is important because voicing your concerns and plans gives them a weight and importance they don't have as private meditations.

Ideally, assessment should become a process that is done systematically and annually—like strategic planning in business. It is an opportunity to evaluate performance, to review the marketplace, and to guide professional development strategies for the future.

On the other hand, as you proceed through your self-assessment try to exclude from your mind an obsession with what you presently perceive to be your opportunities.

Shifting your goals to conform to available opportunities causes you to lose sight of who you are and what you truly need. It is premature strategic thinking. So, keep an open mind and see what will come of it.

The materials in this Chapter deal with both personal and professional assessments of the integrated person that is you. While we recognize that these are not neat, mutually exclusive categories, separating the materials along these lines simplifies the presentation and has some logic to recommend it.

Will you get some guidance during this odyssey? To be sure. These Exercises will be generously interspersed with commentary and questions. For some of the more involved exercises we have collected, in the Appendices, completed samples by people of varied backgrounds. The various elements of the assessment process have been clearly marked so that you may pursue them selectively if you so choose. So let us begin. You need only a pencil and an open mind.

ANALYZING BACKGROUND, TRAITS AND STYLE

Work Style Preferences

A person's "vocational orientation" is part of what occupational psychologist John Holland calls a character type, or a "particular personal disposition that leads one to think, perceive and act in special ways."

Different character types tend to seek out work environments that match their skills, interests, and values, thus expressing their work style preferences. Knowing your type or combination of types can, of course, assist with career and job decisions. Even within the law, different specialties and types of jobs may be best suited for certain types and type combinations.

The character types, and their work style preferences, are described in the famous Strong-Campbell Vocational Interest materials as follows:

The Realistic Types: "are rugged, robust, practical, physically strong; they usually have good physical skills but sometimes have trouble expressing themselves or in communicating their feelings to others . . . . They prefer to deal with things rather than with ideas or people. They enjoy creating things with their hands and prefer occupations such as mechanic, construction worker or . . . skilled trades."

The Investigative Types: " . . . are task oriented; they are not particularly interested in working around other people. They enjoy solving abstract problems, and they have a great need to understand the physical world. They prefer to think through problems rather than act them out. Such people enjoy ambiguous challenges and do not like highly structured situations with many rules. They prefer occupations such as design engineer, biologist or . . . social scientist."

The Artistic Types: have "little interest in problems that are highly structured or require gross physical strength, preferring those that can be solved through self-expression in artistic media. They resemble Investigative types in preferring to work alone, but have a greater need for individualistic expression, and are usually less assertive about their own opinions and capabilities . . . Vocational choices include artist, composer . . . and symphony conductor."

The Social Types: are "humanistic, concerned with the welfare of others. These people usually express themselves well and get along well with others . . . . They prefer to solve problems by discussions with others, or by arranging or rearranging relationships between others . . . . Such people describe themselves as cheerful, popular, and achieving and as good leaders. They prefer occupations such as school superintendent, social worker . . . or vocational counselor."

The Enterprising Types: have a "great facility with words, especially in selling, dominating, and leading . . . They see themselves as energetic, enthusiastic, adventurous, self-confident, and dominant, and they prefer social tasks where they can assume leadership. They enjoy persuading others to their viewpoints .... They like power, status and material wealth .... Vocational preferences include business executive ... industrial relations consultant ... and political campaigner .... "

Lawyers are usually assigned to the last type. However, like most of us, you may have recognized something of yourself in all the above descriptions, and feel that your work draws on the traits of several character types. In fact, Holland's theory goes on to posit that most people and occupations must be characterized as combined types, and in his scheme the law is considered an enterprising/investigative profession. Sub-specialties in law may attract yet other variants—a fact important to keep in mind when assessing your own potential. (Litigators may have a greater dose of the Enterprising Type and Labor Negotiators a dash of the Social Type.)

An off-the-cuff selection by you of your "type" would probably be overly simplistic and relatively unrevealing. Of more benefit, we believe, is Exercise 3, a thoughtful attempt to see what aspects of your professional and personal lives may include each of the various character types of Holland's. You may be surprised to find activity types you never suspected and that are important to you for the interest and diversity they afford.

EXERCISE 3: Workstyle Preferences

The Realistic Type

You may not think that there is much opportunity for this type in the legal profession. But realistic activities may occur at a mundane level. For instance, yesterday you may have repaired a typewriter or put up shelves at work. Perhaps you have helped orchestrate your firm's move to new quarters. (For one young attorney this was the highlight of an entire year and a troubling comment on her job.) List below three tasks you have performed recently at work and outside of work which fall into the Realistic category.

WORK	NON-WORK
1. ____________	1. ____________
2. ____________	2. ____________
3. ____________	3. ____________

Circle the number that best answers each of the following questions from 1. ("Very little") to 5. ("A great deal"):

How much of your time at work is spent on such activities?

Very little 1 2 3 4 5 A great deal

How much of your time outside of work is spent on such activities?

Very little 1 2 3 4 5 A great deal

How much have you enjoyed these activities at work?

Very little 1 2 3 4 5 A great deal

How much have you enjoyed these activities outside of work?

Very little 1 2 3 4 5 A great deal

The Investigative Type

Do you enjoy research for the sheer sake of finding out? Would you rather work through a complex problem on your own than with a committee? Ever have an assigning attorney complain that your memo told him more about the subject than he cared to know? List below tasks you have performed recently which best fall into the Investigative category.

WORK	NON-WORK
1. ____________	1. ____________
2. ____________	2. ____________
3. ____________	3. ____________

Circle the number that best answers each of the following questions from 1. ("Very little") to 5. ("A great deal"):

How much of your time at work is spent on such activities?

Very little 1 2 3 4 5 A great deal

How much of your time outside of work is spent such activities?

Very little 1 2 3 4 5 A great deal

How much have you enjoyed these activities at work?

Very little 1 2 3 4 5 A great deal

How much have you enjoyed these activities outside of work?

Very little 1 2 3 4 5 A great deal

The Artistic Type

The arts may not much intrude on your practice unless you happen to be an entertainment lawyer, but self-expression is not denied the lawyer. Good writing and communication skills can be a source of artistic satisfaction. And, increasingly, desktop publishing with personal computers will become an important part of a lawyer's persuasion skills. Then again, perhaps hanging a picture in your cubicle was the last act of artistic significance you committed at work. For what it's worth, list three tasks performed recently at work and outside of work that might fall into the Artistic category.

WORK	NON-WORK
1. ____________	1. ____________
2. ____________	2. ____________
3. ____________	3. ____________

Circle the number that best answers each of the following questions from 1. ("Very little") to 5. ("A great deal"):

How much of your time at work is spent on such activities?

Very little 1 2 3 4 5 A great deal

How much of your time outside of work is spent such activities?

Very little 1 2 3 4 5 A great deal

How much have you enjoyed these activities at work?

Very little 1 2 3 4 5 A great deal

How much have you enjoyed these activities outside of work?

Very little 1 2 3 4 5 A great deal

The Social Type

Do you enjoy client contact? Amongst colleagues do you pour oil on troubled waters? Enjoy training and mentoring? Promote collegiality and loyalty at work? The characteristics of Social types are important to the executive and managerial functions increasingly required by the business aspects of law practice. List tasks you have performed recently which fall into the Social category.

WORK	**NON-WORK**
1. ____________	1. ____________
2. ____________	2. ____________
3. ____________	3. ____________

Circle the number that best answers each of the following questions from 1. ("Very little") to 5. ("A great deal"):

How much of your time at work is spent on such activities?

Very little 1 2 3 4 5 A great deal

How much of your time outside of work is spent such activities?

Very little 1 2 3 4 5 A great deal

How much have you enjoyed these activities at work?

Very little 1 2 3 4 5 A great deal

How much have you enjoyed these activities outside of work?

Very little 1 2 3 4 5 A great deal

The Enterprising Type

You will not be astonished that lawyers are assigned to this category although you may have seen much of yourself in the other types. Nevertheless, perhaps you are most drawn to advocacy, to pushing through a deal or transaction, to reversing a ruling or a wrong. List tasks performed recently in which you were truly the Enterprising type, "leading, dominating, persuading."

WORK	**NON-WORK**
1. ____________	1. ____________
2. ____________	2. ____________
3. ____________	3. ____________

Circle the number that best answers each of the following questions from 1. ("Very little") to 5. ("A great deal"):

How much of your time at work is spent on such activities?

Very little 1 2 3 4 5 A great deal

How much of your time outside of work is spent such activities?

Very little 1 2 3 4 5 A great deal

How much have you enjoyed these activities at work?

Very little 1 2 3 4 5 A great deal

How much have you enjoyed these activities outside of work?

Very little 1 2 3 4 5 A great deal

Work Style Preferences

Now, to summarize your type-analysis, enter below the number ratings for each Type for at work and outside of work:

	AT WORK			OUTSIDE WORK	
	Time Spent	*Enjoyed*		*Time Spent*	*Enjoyed*
REALISTIC	______	______	**REALISTIC**	______	______
INVESTIGATIVE	______	______	**INVESTIGATIVE**	______	______
ARTISTIC	______	______	**ARTISTIC**	______	______
SOCIAL	______	______	**SOCIAL**	______	______
ENTERPRISING	______	______	**ENTERPRISING**	______	______

Now list the three top-rated character types from each column above:

TOP RATED CHARACTER TYPES

AT WORK		OUTSIDE WORK	
Type *Time Spent*	**Type** *Enjoyed*	**Type** *Time Spent*	**Type** *Enjoyed*
1. ______	1. ______	1. ______	1. ______
2. ______	2. ______	2. ______	2. ______
3. ______	3. ______	3. ______	3. ______

The top three enjoyment ratings in the work column define your vocational type according to your work style preferences, the top rating being your primary type. Enter these Types in the space provided in Exercise 15 on page 89. By way of contrast, you have your top three enjoyment ratings in the outside work column as an expression of your character in the rest of your life.

You may discover unsuspected implications in this Exercise. For instance, to the extent that you recognize yourself as a Social Type who prefers to solve things by discussion, you will understand why you might be more drawn to negotiation than to more adversarial kinds of problem solving. Or perhaps as an Enterprising Type you realize that your facility with words does not extend to the patience for writing them down—the need for feedback makes the conference table and the telephone the more satisfying mode of communication.

Turning to the Time columns, if you spend

most of your time in vocational activity types that vary greatly from your Enjoyment ratings, you have a clear indication of a clash between your preferred work style and your present job.

What if your outside activities and interests are more in harmony with your character than those at work? Many lawyers may feel that there is no adequate reward, now or in the future, for work which they do not find deeply self-fulfilling. On the other hand, some professionals seem to find exhilaration in a strong contrast between professional and spare time activities.

Looking, for example, at research on the vocational interests of lawyers who say they feel alienated in their profession, we have found that some of these people truly fail to share many interests with their peers. Another group fares differently, however. They share most of the basic interests of lawyers but they simply have a great many other interests as well.

You should not neglect the importance of outside interests in your self-assessment. If you have many interests, centering your life on a career may be very unsatisfying, no matter how seriously you take your work. As you analyze your needs and your situation, remember:

It is the ratio between expectation and reality that determines job satisfaction.

Work need not be the major source of self realization—even in the exalted realm of the professions.

Perhaps, also, in the above Exercise you were uncertain whether to describe an activity as enjoyable when you were not particularly good at it. In a culture that is driven by achievement, the distinction between what we like to do and what we can do well can become very cloudy. Many people cannot conceive of enjoying anything at which they cannot excel.

For instance, in the great surge in technical education in the post-sputnik era many children with mathematical talent received significant attention and reinforcement to go into scientific fields. The message was some form of "you're so good at this, you'd make a great engineer." These students may have become engineers only to discover that they had allowed themselves to be bribed into excelling at what others valued more than they did. Even so, they were luckier than those who no longer knew what they enjoyed. Many lawyers may remember being told "you're so good at debate (or so argumentative!) you should be a lawyer." Although we can't avoid such feedback, which is an indispensable part of career choice, it may prematurely pre-empt a more independent discovery of our real preferences.

Over-response to praise for achievement leads to excessive fear of failure. The fear of failure, especially in areas in which we might be truly interested, forecloses all possibility of professional development in the sense propounded here. A point some unfulfilled lawyers may need propounded into their heads.

To summarize, in assessing your present position it will be helpful to remember three points:

- **You may be choosing to excel at what others value more than you do, either at the lawyer/other occupation level or the specialization level.**
- **You may be expecting too much or too little self-fulfillment from your job.**
- **You may be overlooking sources of gratification at work that are particularly suitable to your own mix of character types.**

EXERCISE 4: Role Models

Evaluation of others can be almost as enlightening as evaluation of yourself. Especially evaluation of those you admire.

Exercise 4 asks you, after extended reflection, to list real, living individuals who have developed personally and professionally in a manner that you admire. You should list each such individual's personal attributes and the skills and characteristics that seem to have contributed to his or her career accomplishments and satisfactions. Often the best way to do this is to first describe the person in prose and then analyze the traits that are inherent in the description.

Here is a sample role model description from which a young lawyer gained substantial insight regarding his own path into, and within, the law:

Sample Role Model Description

Mark O. Polo, a family friend, had returned to his college town to practice law in a small firm after graduation from law school. A general business practice that included negotiating unusual contracts for small entrepreneurial companies prepared him for the interesting problem of representing a recently graduated athlete of his alma mater who had prospects for a professional career. A few other athlete clients followed over the years, but such work was never the bulk of his practice.

Mark began to realize that the work in athletics, whatever the service provided or the role he played, was the most enjoyable part of his practice. Rather than a business counselor, some of whose clients were in the sports business, he wanted to be a sports lawyer performing whatever types of services and roles were required. But he did not relish the seedier side of client acquisition and competition with "agents" not restrained by any ethical canons.

He decided to expend some time learning more about the full spectrum of the sports business and did so by first securing a job as Assistant Commissioner of a collegiate athletic conference and later as an Athletic Director at a school in a different conference. After five years of these pursuits, he knew much about the sports business and had numerous contacts. He also had confirmed his views about not aggressively entering the player representation circus. Instead, he drew up a business plan for representing coaches, institutions, and conferences on a broad spectrum of sports-related legal matters. He convinced a medium-sized firm in a large city to hire him and to support his efforts to build such a practice. Today he is spending 100% of his time in sports law, without the show biz aspects of player representation, and is extremely happy with his life-style.

The lawyer who wrote this Role Model Description realized that he was particularly impressed by Polo's calculated pursuit of an ideal practice even though it fit no pre-existing specialty definition and by his use of non-legal experiences to prepare himself for his life's work. The writer decided to keep in mind these options in pondering his own career.

After you have written a few descriptions of Role Models (or simply "admired professionals", if "Role Model" seems too grandiose), list the traits, skills, style, etc. that most led you to such admiration:

Role Model Traits

Role Model 1	***Role Model 2***	***Role Model 3***
1. ________	1. ________	1. ________
2. ________	2. ________	2. ________
3. ________	3. ________	3. ________
4. ________	4. ________	4. ________
5. ________	5. ________	5. ________
6. ________	6. ________	6. ________

EXERCISE 5: The Party

Another handle on those who have influenced you has a broader sweep. We all admire or despise on a far wider range than just our friends and acquaintances. Exercise 5 addresses that broader sweep.

Break away from your narrow past. Imagine that you are hosting a party and may invite any ten guests. The guests may be friends, family, historical or public figures (of any century), entertainers, and, of course, the role models you have already mentioned. Now this covers a lot of territory. One key to the Exercise is to limit yourself to ten people and thus force some hard choices. Take some time to ponder the matter and be sure to work in pencil since tomorrow, or next week, you may decide to substitute Pee Wee Herman for Augustus Caesar.

Your guests:

1. ______________________
2. ______________________
3. ______________________
4. ______________________
5. ______________________
6. ______________________
7. ______________________
8. ______________________
9. ______________________
10. ______________________

Now, let's ponder your guest list. Were the guests more alike than representative of a spectrum? If alike, how? Did you purposely invite antithetical individuals to observe their interaction (e.g., Hitler and Buddha)? Can you spot positive traits, beyond those of the real life Role Models of Exercise 4, that you admire and would like to cultivate in yourself. If so, list them here.

Compare these with the traits you circled in Exercise 4, and transfer the most important traits from the two Exercises to Exercise 15 at page 89.

Party Guest Traits

1. ______________________
2. ______________________
3. ______________________
4. ______________________
5. ______________________

EXERCISE 6: Coping Strategies

How you cope with stress is important to any self-assessment and to considering the value of your present job or the specification of a new one. Even those who believe that pressure incites them to higher performance have limits on the stress-level that is needed. Excess stress is always coped with in some way.

Exercise 6 identifies coping strategies drawn from a recent survey given to third year law students and first year associates. Rank order the strategies, once for your law school period, and again for your current life. Then enter your best coping strategies at the specified place in Exercise 15 on page 89.

EXERCISE 6: COPING STRATEGIES

LAW SCHOOL	NOW	COPING STRATEGY
		BUY EXTRA TREATS (CONSUMER GOODS, HOUSING,. ETC.)
		ALCOHOL, MARIJUANA OR DRUG USE
		EXERCISE
		WORK HARDER, LONGER
		MAKE TIME FOR THINGS YOU LIKE TO DO
		CHANGE ATTITUDE OR PERSPECTIVE; SENSE OF HUMOR
		TALK ABOUT IT WITH A CURRENT IMPORTANT OTHER
		TALK ABOUT IT WITH PEERS OR ASSOCIATES
		TALK ABOUT IT WITH SUPERIORS OR AUTHORITY FIGURES
		TALK ABOUT IT WITH FAMILY MEMBERS
		TALK ABOUT IT WITH A COUNSELOR OR THERAPIST
		TAKE TRANQUILIZERS
		OTHER:
		OTHER:

EXERCISE 7: Career Choices and Reasons

Let us now see if you can learn a little more about your goals, desires, and motivations through a close examination of significant decision you have made.

In the chart below, list briefly your major decisions regarding your education and choice of jobs. The most important decisions for young lawyers usually are the choice of college, college major, law school, summer positions, and subsequent permanent jobs. For each such choice you should describe the other alternatives that were available to you, the rationale behind your ultimate decision, and your retrospective view of the quality of the decision. Feel free to add any important decisions in your life that do not fall within the items listed.

A sample Career Choices and Reasons Chart follows the blank Chart of Exercise 7.

In Exercise 15, you will be asked to study your Career Choices and Reasons for themes and patterns.

EXERCISE 7: CAREER CHOICES AND REASONS CHART

CHOICE	ALTERNATIVES	RATIONALE	IN RETROSPECT
College:			
College Major:			
Law School:			
First Summer:			
Second Summer:			
First Position:			
Second Position:			
Other:			

SAMPLE CAREER CHOICES AND REASONS CHART

CHOICE	ALTERNATIVES	RATIONALE	IN RETROSPECT
College: Dartmouth	Football scholarships at Memphis State, Colorado State and Lake Forest.	The timely intervention of a high school counselor who persuaded me to apply to Dartmouth.	Very naive. Paltry group of alternatives. Shudder to think what would have happened if turned down at Dartmouth.
College Major: English	History, economics, political science	Not math, science or pre-med. Social sciences seemed weak. English was a demanding major. Enjoyed reading and writing.	Good choice. But really no viable alternatives. Very demanding. Volumes of reading; many papers; Learned English & European history as a byproduct.
Post College: Peace Corps, Nigeria	Divinity schools. Grad program at Harvard in guidance and counseling.	"No" to grad school in English. "No" to empl. in business. Doubts re divinity career. Did not consider law or bus. school. Peace Corps new; appeal of adventure, travel, purpose	Wonderful experience. Frontier environment. Teaching stimulating, then boring. Got off conveyor belt. Opportunity to observe and reflect. Entrepreneurial.
Post College: Fuller Brush Salesman	Intern in big business.	Only honorable way to make big $ to finance law school.	Great learning experience. Six months seemed forever. Self reliance and discipline critical.
Law School: U. of Chicago	Harvard, Yale, Northwestern, Stanford.	Rejected at Yale. Wait list at Harvard. Accepted at N.U. and Stanford. Chicago my home, home of fiance. U. of C. seemed more stimulating and demanding from visits.	Good choice. Great school. Small size definite plus. Academic & policy orientation mirrored my own interests. Considerable success in law school. Great classmates. A nuturing competition.
First Summer: Santa Fe RR Law Dept.	Fuller Brush, manual labor.	Excellent and scarce opportunity. Many research and writing assignments. Good training in a quality corp. law dept.	Good practice. Confidence builder. Chance to experience corp. alternative. Large volumes of good work.
Second Summer: ½ Kirkland, Ellis ½ Holme, Roberts	Big firms in Chicago. Variety of big firms in med. size quality-of-life cities.	Good chance to sample two quite different approaches to law. Best of alternatives in each category. Very fortunate set of options.	Knew Chicago. Love the summer at Kirkland. Wife did not give Denver a real chance. Too much Italian family.
First Position: Kirkland, Ellis	Santa Fe; Home, Roberts; and a few other firms from fall of the second year.	Very good friends and work at Kirkland. Wife wouldn't consider other locations. Some question in my mind about permanent commitment to law. Good learning experience and credential.	Demanding studs. Learned to think in terms of industries, black books, and the self-contained "big" memo. Like working BCG or McKenzie in terms of the residual value of the experience.

How You Became a Lawyer

Now, continue the self-assessment with an interview with us, your friendly counselors. The questions we are about to ask are rather simple ones that any career counselor would ask in an opening interview. They are not rhetorical, however. Take pen (or keyboard) in hand and write down, at any length that seems necessary, your response to each question. Then read our commentary on that question. The commentaries, which follow the complete set of questions, reflect on the sorts of issues commonly raised by these questions, and are intended to prompt you into reflection on the implications of your own answers and into adding depth to your first draft answers. Obviously, there are no "correct" answers. There are only more and fewer insights to be gained from more and less thoughtful efforts on your part.

From the foregoing Exercises and discussion you should be aware by now of some of the many the forces and influences that usually underlie the stages and decisions of career development. As innocuous as they may seem, the questions below are leading questions . . . in the sense that they should lead you to some unsuspected views of yourself, your wants, and your needs. The previous Exercises were designed to get you thinking about matters that are about to become more overt.

Exercise 8 requires time (a minimum of an hour) and thoughtfulness. Reserve adequate time. Or, if you are not in the mood for this, make a mental or physical note to return to Exercise 8.

EXERCISE 8: The Self-Interview

1. **When did you first entertain the notion of being a lawyer?**
2. **Who were the people who supported or influenced you to become a lawyer? What were their personal attributes, skills, and characteristics that seem to have contributed to their accomplishment and satisfaction? Were there those who discouraged you?**
3. **How did you choose your college major?**
4. **At the time you applied, what were your reasons for applying to law school?**
5. **What was your experience your first year of law school?**
6. **What was your attitude towards attempting to make the Law Review?**
7. **What was the evolution of your study methods?**
8. **Did you like the second and third years better? Why or why not?**
9. **Did you take time off before or after law school? Why or why not?**
10. **Did you ever seriously consider dropping law school? What was the turning point that changed your mind?**
11. **What did you find most stressful about being in law school? What did you do to cope with the stress?**
12. **What impact did your summer jobs during law school have on your self-image and career plans?**

Commentaries on Self-Interview Questions.

1. When did you first entertain the notion of being a lawyer?

Some people seem to have known they were going to be lawyers shortly after they gave up the idea of being a firefighter or cowperson. They always knew, or it was known for them. Others took the notion seriously rather later, perhaps in the last year of college.

As the next question may illustrate, the age and stage at which an occupational image becomes imprinted on your mind has a lasting impact on your later relationship to that occupation.

The people who have the most influence on your thinking vary considerably at different periods in your life. Which leads to the next question.

2. Who were the people who supported or influenced you to become a lawyer? Were there those who discouraged you?

Role models can be as real as our parents and as imaginary as Perry Mason. Whatever their source, in identifying with them you often absorb not only their attributes but their outlook on life as well. Role models seem to have the key to whatever is important in life. Sometimes their choice of occupation seems to be that key, often because that is what the role model believes too. Other times it is the way in which role models pursue their occupations that has the greatest impact.

Of course, your notion of lawyering will be very different if you acquire it from an attorney/mother when you are 10, than if you acquire it from someone like role model Attorney Polo of Exercise 4 when you are of college age. For that matter, your most important role models may have had nothing to do with lawyering (perhaps by choice). If so, what mattered to them and why does that matter to you? Exercises 4 (Role Models) and 5 (The Party) should have stimulated some thoughts to launch you into a solid response to this question.

You should take note of when you first became acquainted with any real people on your Party list, of the age and stage at which they first made an impression on you. This is most critical when parents or other loved and respected authority figures have been role models, especially if they were lawyers. We need not be unduly Freudian to make this point.

Take, for example, this actual episode from the early life of a litigator.

> When she was thirteen, she went shopping with her mother in search of a pretty party dress. Never too confident about her appearance, she was thrilled to find a dress that truly flattered her. Although slightly damaged, the dress seemed easy enough to mend. However, the mother, who happened to be a lawyer with a keen sense of justice, refused to buy the dress when the store manager refused to lower its price. To pay the full price would be unreasonable, the mother explained, and would encourage bad practices which might cause other people to suffer. The daughter pled in vain. She was told by her mother that if she could come up with a convincing reason her mother would be glad to purchase the dress. For years the daughter fell to sleep trying to think of reasons. Repeated conflicts of this nature convinced the daughter that her mother was not to be approached on any issue without "a good reason," however beside the true point that reason might be be. Eventually, she forgot the point of being pretty or of any other feelings. For a long time she discounted her own needs, although she always remained sensitive to the needs of others who had been cheated in life. Not until many years later did she recognize her bitterness toward her mother. And only then did she realize her continuing attempts to make law do what it was never intended to do: To make someone say "I'm sorry."

Suppose, instead, that the mother had succeeded in using her lawyerly skills to help the daughter obtain the dress. Or we might take the case of the daughter in *To Kill a Mockingbird,* who discovers that her lawyer father's occupation is connected with his basic sense of fairness and objectivity in a society governed by strong passions.

The real point of the above anecdote is the complicated power our role models have, for good or for ill, or some mysterious mixture of the two. For most (perhaps all) of us, it is far too late to negate that power. Careful analysis and introspection can, however, help us to account for it in our planning.

3. How did you choose your college major?

Did you, in fact, give much attention to the choice, or did you have other developmental concerns on your mind, like dating or social issues? Were you already thinking law, and as an Enterprising personality chose one of the traditional majors considered a good preparation for law school? Or, as an Investigative Type, did you choose something that tickled your interest, regardless of your future goals. Looking back, do you have any regrets about the choice or feel you missed critical opportunities? As with all these decisions, how you made them is as important as the outcome. What were the criteria you used to make the decision, and are the same kinds of considerations important to you today?

4. At the time you applied, what were your reasons for applying to law school?

How did you feel writing the answer to this question? Were you writing about yourself or someone who seems rather different from the person you've become? We are not referring to the possible naivete of your reasons for going to law school. It is not uncommon, after all, for legions of people to choose law for a profession with only the vaguest notion of what lawyers actually do. Rather, we are asking if the basic values underlying your decision still seem sound and if you are still in sympathy with them today.

Look again at what you have written. If you mostly emphasized what you planned to do (e.g. practice commercial law or go into government), write a little more about what you hoped to achieve through those activities. Some of the considerations in the back of your mind could have been power, change in society, job flexibility, job security, wealth, prestige, or intellectual stimulation. Whatever they were, are they still on your private agenda?

Think carefully about some of the outside, or auxiliary, factors that may have contributed to your decision to apply to law school. Compensatory motivations should bear special scrutiny. Was applying to law school designed to offset a quixotic undergraduate career? Was it a reasonably practical capstone to a rigorous exploration of the liberal arts? Was it to help you recover from a loss or failure of some kind in your personal life? Was law school a solution to an economic crisis or some other cataclysm in your life? The importance of these questions lies in the fact that compensatory motivations seldom yield more than partial satisfaction and you must be able to sort out the elements in any unhappiness with your job which are not wholly work-related.

5. What was your experience your first year of law school?

A deliberately open-ended question.

That first year may not, in truth, be very representative of legal practice. But it does create an impression of the profession which, if not indelible, is difficult to erase. It is a question of successful bonding. What aspect of the experience did your answer emphasize? The competition? The daily pressure of being obliged to be prepared? Was it the workload? The intensive homogeneity of the course work? The novelty of "legal thinking"? The character of your classmates? Every one of these factors can have positive or negative aspects.

For some, the workload is experienced as a desirable challenge, the opportunity for intensive immersion; for others it is a shock, the first premonition of a way of life threatening to basic assumptions about the relationship between work and personal pursuits. The homogeneity of the work strikes some as stultifying compared to the breadth of undergraduate work. For others the specialization seems a proper complement to a liberal arts background, the time to choose depth. Similarly, the legal approach to problem solving is to some a straitjacket, to others an intriguing new tool. In your own case, what vestiges of these first experiences color your perception of law today?

Also, once again consider the impact of extraneous factors such as the adjustment to a new part of the country or separation from friends and lovers. Could your adjustment to law school have been different had these factors not applied?

6. What was your attitude towards attempting to make the Law Review?

Did you resolve merely to do your best and let things take their course? Or, did you deliberately reach for the brass ring? If you didn't make Law Review on grades, did you enter a writing competition or draw the line and call it quits? If you made Law Review, was it a positive experience despite the extra work and lost sleep? How much did you involve yourself in other "resume-building activities" in law school?

In counseling law students we have found that the Law Review issue can become almost a crisis of conscience, testing the outer limits of the strong achievement orientation common to most law students. More revealing than the failure to make Law Review, however, is a decision, expressed or not, to voluntarily abstain from the competition. As with many of these early decisions, one can often see the seeds of later and continuing concerns.

7. What was the evolution of your study methods?

Your answer to this question may reveal the origins of your current approach to structuring your time and workload. It may also begin to cast some light on your particular cognitive style and methods of learning. The intensive workload in law school forces some people into their first deliberate analysis of their learning style and work habits.

In this regard we would be interested to know if you preferred to study alone or in study groups; if you enjoyed talking to other students about your studies; if you found course outlines helpful; if you participated much in class; if you took elaborate notes in class or while preparing for exams; if you studied most during the day or night; if you attended class regularly. These questions have to do with whether you are a collegial learner, a compulsive communicator whose capabilities are enhanced by what science essayist Lewis Thomas calls "touching antennae," or whether you are more classically the Investigative Type who likes to take a challenge into a corner and chew it like a bone. Any uncontrived pattern that evolved in law school may reveal the work approach you would prefer today, unconstrained by firm culture or specialty necessities.

Coupled with these cognitive style issues, is the question of how much you felt part of the social/intellectual culture of law school. Did you master the challenge as a participant, or did you feel like a solitary salmon swimming upstream? Are you a collegial learner/worker or a competitive loner?

8. Did you like the second and third years better? Why or why not?

Leaving aside for the moment the probability of a better psychological and social adjustment in the last two years, what were they like as an intellectual/professional experience? Some find the law school experience front-loaded with the most theoretically interesting courses in the first year, the subsequent years being a more dreary, albeit essential, plunge into the nuts and bolts. Others are glad to be getting down to the fitting of practical nuts to practical bolts. We'll ask you in a moment about clinical opportunities and summer jobs, but you may have already addressed that topic here if those experiences outweighed all the coursework of the second and third years.

9. Did you take time off before, during, or after law school? Why or why not?

This question is grounded in your openness to recognizing the breadth of your developmental needs and whether you can set aside time to deal with them. In our experience, those who have actually taken the time off have seldom regretted it, finding that the experience had significantly enriched their ability to profit from their legal education, and had also enhanced their professional and personal development. The practice of law, after all, is the imposition of processes on the affairs of humankind. Real world experience is seldom a negative in the training of a lawyer.

On the other hand, those who yearned to take time off and never did (for reasons other than financial constraint) usually continue to regret the decision. From a career-diagnostic point of view, it seems that these people were almost afraid of what they would discover about themselves and their commitment to law. They felt compelled to stay in law school lest they lose momentum. In fairness to the bulk of people who never considered taking time off, that does not make them workaholics. But for those who did take time off, their decision says much about the strength of promptings from their personal lives and about their ability to heed those promptings.

As we have said, Freud defined a mentally healthy person as one capable of love and work. The personal side of this Exercise is there to remind you how the two aspects of life are constantly interacting. Failure in one area can offset success in the other, and vice versa. Deep investment of energy in one area can make the other seem unreal. Thus time spent in an intense relationship can make even an academically successful year pass without much meaning, a time when many actions and decisions took place on automatic pilot. The interplay between these two factors constantly colors our evaluation of every stage of life and makes it difficult to say just what we mean when we refer to "good times". This pairing of personal and academic accomplishments should help you to figure out the balance during your law school years and its relationship to your career planning at that time.

10. Did you ever seriously consider dropping law school? What was the turning point that changed your mind?

Every year at law school has more than one winter of discontent. What experiences plunged you into doubt, and what did you do to work your way out? What happened to shore up your self-esteem? Clearly, your resolution to such a crisis may set a valuable precedent for any comparable feelings you have about your work subsequently. Here it is important for you to recognize whether any present career dissatisfactions are replays of earlier doubts and conflicts. This leads to the question about stress and coping strategies.

11. What did you find most stressful about being in law school? What did you do to cope with the stress?

You may have touched upon this topic in your previous answers, but we hope you became more expansive here and more specific about your methods for coping with tension.

In helping you to reflect upon the nature of your own witches' brew of stress, we could arm you with an endless array of psychological terms . . . enough to fill a dozen self-help books. However, the most helpful, and critical, distinction is whether you were in conflict mostly with yourself or mostly with your environment.

If your description of stress focused on the difficulty of external challenges, with the implication that you were willing, if not entirely able, to meet them, then it is likely that you were reasonably well in harmony with self and setting. If the description focused on ambivalence about the challenges and opportunities of law school, then the underlying conflict in values need examination to see how and if they were resolved.

Here you must ask yourself if your usual methods of coping with stress are well adapted to your present situation. A person whose strategy is to redouble his or her efforts is not necessarily well-adapted to long term survival in a high pressure practice. You must figure out your optimal level of stress for sustained performance and mental health, and then decide whether your coping strategies are ultimately reinforcing or self-destructive. Whether you cope by changing circumstances or your attitude will affect the energy with which you will seek new employment.

A look at the success of your coping strategies in law school may establish a frame of reference for your present situation and, in particular, tell you if you are still inclined to make the same trade-offs. One sobering way to think on this is to remember the words of one old law professor who admonished his student, "the way you deal with your problems in law school is probably how you will cope for the rest of your life."

12. What impact did your summer jobs during law school have on your self-image and career plans?

Were there any significant shocks to your expectations or changes in your stereotypes? Did those jobs cause you to revise your plans or did they reinforce your sense of direction? Looking back on the experience, were your initial impressions of practice fairly accurate, or did you fail to perceive something important in that limited exposure?

So ends our interview. Reviewing your replies, what have you learned? We hope that you can see a little more clearly how much you are a product of the encounters, influences, and decisions you have just recounted. At this point you have reminded yourself of why becoming a lawyer was important, of whether law was a natural outgrowth of your early interests, of the history of your intellectual development in the law, of your social adjustment during the professionalization process, of the origins of your characteristic means of dealing with stress, and of the inevitable interaction between your professional and personal growth. For one integrated example of the rich information the self-interview can evoke, take the case of Max, a fourth year associate on his second big firm job after a move to another city. Answering the self-interview questions yielded the following information.

MAX: AN ILLUSTRATIVE SELF-INTERVIEW

Max first got the notion of being a lawyer from his father, the owner of a lumber yard in a small town in New England. The father had mixed feelings about his dealings with local lawyers, whom he alternately experienced as a help and a hindrance, but whom he always viewed as powerful persons.

Max, who saw his father in the same light, listened to his father's suggestion that he consider law, but he was more preoccupied with the desire to see more of the world and, incidentally, escape his father's closed domain of the lumber yard. The lumber yard was a well organized, tight ship where Max spent a lot of time working for his father. As soon as Max could get off to college, on the West Coast, he proceeded to major in East Asian studies and anthropology, which he picked because of their emphasis on wider world views. His major was also influenced by the politicization he underwent in those last days of the Vietnam era.

In reviewing why he picked his college major, Max recognized the pleasure he took in the systematic schemas of anthropological analysis, not unlike the elaborate classification of lumber. Also appealing to him was the focus of "primitive" peoples on the simple economics of survival and, he had to admit, a small town background gave him a special empathy for the dynamics of tribalism in closed communities. He also enjoyed the exoticism and complexity of Far Eastern languages.

Upon graduation, he got a masters in anthropology and a fellowship to study the breakdown of traditional cultures in refugee camps in Asia. In the course of his researches, because of his political interests, he also become interested in local economic development aimed at reestablishing the refugees' independence. Returning to graduate school, he found himself a little impatient with the ivory tower aspects of his program, which was beginning to seem a little claustrophobic. Nevertheless, he prepared to pursue his doctorate.

Instead, he applied to law school. Fate

intervened in two ways: his father died, unexpectedly, and he got married, more or less unexpectedly. His reasons for applying at that time were complex. He felt an overwhelming sense of economic responsibility, as a new husband and the only son of a mother barely familiar with the family business. At the same time, he was deeply ambivalent about returning home to replace his father at the helm. Going to law school seemed to serve several purposes. It would insure economic security, and it would give him a kind of practical training arguably useful to his mother in absentia. (He would try to help her with her business problems while in school). In any case, the decision seemed consistent with recent changes in his own outlook on life, especially the cooling of his political passions and the growth of his interest in more pragmatic economic issues. The notion of law school had crossed his mind more frequently lately and now, after his father's death, he acknowledged a strangely felt desire to please the old man and stand vindicated in his eyes.

His experience of law school, in yet another city, was intense but not unsatisfying. As an older, married student, he lived off campus and, although friendly, was somewhat detached from other students. He studied mostly alone. In truth, he was a participant observer, a role for which he was prepared by nature and by anthropological training. The stance helped him to maintain objectivity and was congenial to examining different doctrines and points of view.

His organizing, systematizing skills were also adaptive to his new profession. He became preoccupied with doing well, although he eschewed law review because of family responsibilities, which were increased by the arrival of his first son. The same responsibilities directed his attention to the high incomes earned in big firm practice. He had something to offer these employers because he graduated in the top ten percent of his class, doing well in courses such as property and commercial law and receiving a prize in estate planning.

There were seemingly inexplicable lapses in his grades, which he understood perfectly to reflect his disinterest in the intellectual or moral underpinnings of the courses in question. These flashes of alienation he took as normal, and he never considered time off. He felt he had done his share of that.

As for stress, he relied pretty much on talking to his wife and a few old friends. Never afraid of hard work, it gave him satisfaction to throw himself into and master a new field. Always a very active person, he did chaff under the sedentary routine of a student and tried to keep up some exercise. He was adamant about keeping up reading in his old field, if only on a symbolic level.

Both of Max's summer jobs were in large firms, in the same city. He enjoyed being in yet another setting, amongst older people and with a chance to prove himself in his new field. His employers found him a little quiet and reserved, although not unwilling to participate in the firms' social life. He was an excellent writer, with good research skills. He got offers from both firms.

On the down side, on reflection Max found the intellectual life of the firm less stimulating than law school, and although he enjoyed the challenge of the work, he found himself largely unempathetic with the clients, who were mostly commercial real estate developers. He began to question, somewhat, the wisdom of accepting his offers, but momentum and financial pressure caused him to stay on course.

This much about Max emerged from the twelve questions. At the time he began the exercise he was most definitely unhappy with his work. He was beginning to dream at night of getting a doctorate in anthropology. Recognizing the dire nature of his affliction, he immediately sought a career counselor who led him through the foregoing history.

While Max had many influences absent from the backgrounds of large numbers of lawyers, all have been subjected to far more, and subtler, influences than they perceive without intense, and directed, effort.

We have provided this summary of an actual Max to illustrate the richness that the self-interview questions can evoke. See if, on the strength of this information alone, you can raise some hypotheses about what new directions Max's career might take.

The analysis of your background, traits, and style in this Chapter begins to have greater immediacy in Chapter 7 where we turn to your experience, skills, and competence.

Chapter

7

Self-Assessment II: Taking It A Step Further

"... seeing the root of the matter is found in me."
Job 19:28

ANALYZING YOUR EXPERIENCE, SKILLS, AND COMPETENCE

If you have faithfully completed the work in Chapter 6, undoubtedly you now know more than you care to know about how you landed in your present position and certainly more than prospective employers will care to know. These practical people are more given to wondering if you are any good, just how good you are, and what you are good for. Such a focus is apt to inspire some doubts in yourself. To deal with these questions you need a general framework for understanding the development of competence as a lawyer over the full span of a career. And you need means of analyzing your skills and experience in a manner helpful to yourself and to future employers.

As we suggested earlier, building legal competence usually takes about nine years. Graduation from law school at the three year mark is a milestone, not a finish line, as is plain from that tripartite definition of legal competence as espoused by an ABA task force: (1) *knowledge* of the law, (2) *skills* to turn knowledge into solutions of client problems, and (3) *productivity* to do so efficiently.

Remember, these three components are, in large measure, learned in successive three-year training segments. First, three years of formal law school focusing principally upon knowledge of the law. Second an "internship" of roughly three years during which basic legal skills are polished. Third, a "residency" period during which an attorney acquires greater depth of experience and expertise so as to provide services to clients more cost-effectively and to achieve a richer involvement within a specialty.

Thus, you are mostly in transit in those first six years after law school. Plainly, you should apply a somewhat different analysis to those first years than you would apply to the later years. An early focus on achieving the highest level of competence in the areas you like most will permit the most economically and personally satisfying remainder of the rest of your career. Said another way: The best ways to use your first six years may be quite different from the best long term position for you.

How do you assess your competence at your present stage? By now you probably agree that success in practice requires a decathlon of skills and abilities. Success in law school may be tied to the single event of examination grades but a host of characteristics and skills bear upon success in law practice. The successful lawyer draws upon knowledge of the law, fact finding, law finding, negotiating, evaluating options, personality, productivity, creativity, appearance, and social, management and leadership abilities.

EXERCISE 9: Achievement Stories

Whether you feel successful as a lawyer, or even feel the potential for success, depends upon your mastery of these sorts of skills. Often the groundwork for a sense of mastery has been laid well before your formal professional training. Therefore, the following Exercise asks you to develop brief writeups of several Achievement Stories from your entire life. Things that you have done successfully and well at any stage of life are apt to be windows on your talents and interests. They are also useful ammunition in interviews.

Write briefly about up to ten significant or memorable achievements in your life. You should strive to identify the skills that contributed to your success in each of these activities. You should also be attentive to the details of the satisfaction they afforded. For example, being a captain of a sports team in high school or college could have been the result of athletic skills, leadership abilities, physical endurance, or the ability to make social connections.

Look for common threads in your Achievement Stories. If you have a broad spectrum of talents and interests, a theme may be hard to find. Upon reflection, many people find, however, that things they did well and enjoyed have similarities even if done at ages 10 and 30.

Here are some sample Achievement Stories of a hypothetical young attorney to show you the spectrum of possibilities.

SAMPLE ACHIEVEMENT STORIES OF OLIVER WENDELL BRANDEIS, JR.

Achievement 1: Swimming Merit Badge

As a scout, I wanted to achieve certain levels of accomplishment. The Swimming Merit Badge was required, but I was a non-swimmer and terrified of the water. I overcame my fear, took lessons, and got my Swimming Merit Badge, thereby opening the gate to further achievement via Merit Badges more easily obtainable for me.

Achievement 2: Election Campaign

In High School senior year I became the campaign manager for my best friend in his effort to be elected class president. My friend and others later told me that my clever campaign posters and other gimmicks lent interest to a dull campaign and probably had a major influence on my friend's election as class president.

Achievement 3: PR Coup

As an officer of the Young Whigs in college, I noted that a lack of publicity was a serious problem of our club. To overcome this, I conceived of and implemented a plan whereby each club member would wear an outrageous wig to some function at the school. For example, a band member wore a French Provincial wig rather than his hat during a half-time show at the homecoming football game.

Achievement 4: Thinking on my Feet

During Moot Court competition I was a district attorney pitted against a public defender appointed to represent a juvenile who had vandalized a police car. After my opponent had made little of the seriousness of the crime, I rose and noted that "the Public Defender seems to place little value on de fender of de public".

Achievement 5: Major Merger

At my firm of Filla & Buster, I managed the closing of a merger between two major HMO's. I had solved many problems en route and had drafted many of the documents needed. By the time of the closing I was the only one with sufficient familiarity with all of the problems to oversee the closing and did so despite much high-priced legal talent in the room.

EXERCISE 10: Problem-Solving Approach

Now that you have developed a set of Achievement Stories, you can go on to pinpoint just why and how you succeeded in each instance.

List the titles (or other identifying words) for each of your Achievements on the slanted lines at the bottom of the Exercise 10 chart. List them twice, actually, once for each of the right and left halves of the chart. Then, in the boxes of the chart check off each time each particular Achievement involved the use of each mental or personality factor listed in the left-hand column of each half of the chart. Tally the number of check marks for each factor and write the totals in the right-hand column of each chart half. Circle the factors with the highest scores in the Totals columns. Finally, list the five key (i.e., highest scoring) factors in the space provided in Exercise 15 on page 89.

	1	2	3	4	5	6	7	8	9	10	TOTAL
Analysis											
Artistic											
Budgets											
Controls											
Coordination											
Creative											
Design-art											
Decision-making											
Energy											
Economical											
Figures											
Follow-through											
Foresight											
Human Relations											
Ideas											
Imagination											
Individualist											
Initiative											
Inventive											
Leader											
Liaison											
Manager											
Mechanical											
Memory											
Negotiations											
Observation											

	1	2	3	4	5	6	7	8	9	10	TOTAL
Organizer											
Outdoors/Travel											
Ownership											
People											
Perspective											
Perservering											
Personnel											
Persuasive											
Planner											
Policy-making											
Practical											
Problem-solving											
Production											
Programs											
Promotion											
Research											
Sales											
Service											
Showmanship											
Speaking											
Systems											
Things											
Training											
Trouble-shooting											
Words											
Writing											

Very likely, the result of the Exercise 10 analysis was a little general. You may not be quite sure what such a list means in the context of legal practice. The next step is to make an Inventory of Legal Skills that takes account of your professional stage and the clients, services, and transactions typical of your experience to date.

EXERCISE 11: Inventory of Legal Skills

In all practice, but especially in large private law firms, there seems to be a relatively predictable hierarchy of stages of increasing competence and responsibility assumed by lawyers. The typical progression begins with legal research. Young lawyers—even law students—can perform legal research and craft their findings into memos for partners, judges, or clients, or into written arguments to be furnished to arbiters and adversaries.

The next stage involves the discovery, organization and communication of facts: "discovery" in the context of litigation, but also the accumulation and proving of facts in various types of transactional settings. These two stages typically are encountered in what we have called the "internship" phase of professional development.

The next stage may be called the "second chair" or "assistant operating officer" position. This involves the integration of all aspects of a case—law, facts, strategy—in the context of an adversarial setting, albeit in a support position. This stage might correspond to that of a first year resident in medicine.

Subsequently, in the "first chair" stage the lawyer is operationally responsible for efficiently moving a matter forward toward the result desired by the client.

There follows a "designer" stage during which one is responsible for disaggregating a problem into its legal, factual, emotional, political, and irrational components, and then reorganizing them to form a coherent strategy and game plan . . . basically, diagnosis of a problem, design of a solution, and quality control. In law practice, senior associates and young partners often fill the roles of these latter two stages.

Finally, there is the "rainmaking" stage based, mostly, on reputation. Clients come to "rainmakers" because of their expertise, fame, prior experience, or because they have developed an image in the marketplace as a cost-effective provider of particular types of solutions.

In Exercise 11 we have grouped various legal skills with the career stages at which they are most important or first introduced. The objective is, for each skill, to rate yourself as to *Ability* (a combination of knowledge, aptitude, and skill level), *Satisfaction, Frequency* (with which you employ these skills in your practice), and the current importance, or *Priority,* of improving the skill. We have used the standard grades of A, B, C, D, E (prior to grade inflation) for *Ability* and *Satisfaction* ratings and numbers for *Frequency* and *Priority* Ratings. You should circle the appropriate letter or number in each of the four columns to the right of each specified skill. If our "standard" list of skills doesn't fit your job or specialty, feel free to add, subtract or change skills and stages as seems appropriate.

SKILL	ABILITY	SATISFACTION	FREQUENCY	PRIORITY
The Law Stage				
Analysis skills	A B C D E	A B C D E	1 2 3 4 5	1 2 3 4 5
Research	A B C D E	A B C D E	1 2 3 4 5	1 2 3 4 5
Objective writing	A B C D E	A B C D E	1 2 3 4 5	1 2 3 4 5
Argument writing	A B C D E	A B C D E	1 2 3 4 5	1 2 3 4 5
Oral communication	A B C D E	A B C D E	1 2 3 4 5	1 2 3 4 5
The Fact Stage				
Interviewing	A B C D E	A B C D E	1 2 3 4 5	1 2 3 4 5
Discovery	A B C D E	A B C D E	1 2 3 4 5	1 2 3 4 5
Synthesis	A B C D E	A B C D E	1 2 3 4 5	1 2 3 4 5
Interpretation	A B C D E	A B C D E	1 2 3 4 5	1 2 3 4 5
Client communication	A B C D E	A B C D E	1 2 3 4 5	1 2 3 4 5
Second Chair				
Integrate Law/Fact	A B C D E	A B C D E	1 2 3 4 5	1 2 3 4 5
Management Law/Fact	A B C D E	A B C D E	1 2 3 4 5	1 2 3 4 5
Client relations	A B C D E	A B C D E	1 2 3 4 5	1 2 3 4 5
Productivity	A B C D E	A B C D E	1 2 3 4 5	1 2 3 4 5
Legal substance	A B C D E	A B C D E	1 2 3 4 5	1 2 3 4 5
Team Play	A B C D E	A B C D E	1 2 3 4 5	1 2 3 4 5
Interpersonal skills	A B C D E	A B C D E	1 2 3 4 5	1 2 3 4 5
First Chair				
Project management	A B C D E	A B C D E	1 2 3 4 5	1 2 3 4 5
People management	A B C D E	A B C D E	1 2 3 4 5	1 2 3 4 5
Operating tactics	A B C D E	A B C D E	1 2 3 4 5	1 2 3 4 5
Negotiation skill	A B C D E	A B C D E	1 2 3 4 5	1 2 3 4 5
Happy settlements	A B C D E	A B C D E	1 2 3 4 5	1 2 3 4 5
Adversarial skills	A B C D E	A B C D E	1 2 3 4 5	1 2 3 4 5
Project leadership	A B C D E	A B C D E	1 2 3 4 5	1 2 3 4 5
Project efficiency	A B C D E	A B C D E	1 2 3 4 5	1 2 3 4 5
Legal operations	A B C D E	A B C D E	1 2 3 4 5	1 2 3 4 5

SKILL	ABILITY	SATISFACTION	FREQUENCY	PRIORITY
Designer				
Client counseling skills	A B C D E	A B C D E	1 2 3 4 5	1 2 3 4 5
Creativity	A B C D E	A B C D E	1 2 3 4 5	1 2 3 4 5
Deal structuring	A B C D E	A B C D E	1 2 3 4 5	1 2 3 4 5
Strategy formulation	A B C D E	A B C D E	1 2 3 4 5	1 2 3 4 5
Quality control	A B C D E	A B C D E	1 2 3 4 5	1 2 3 4 5
Staff relations	A B C D E	A B C D E	1 2 3 4 5	1 2 3 4 5
Rainmaker				
Business development	A B C D E	A B C D E	1 2 3 4 5	1 2 3 4 5
Firm leadership	A B C D E	A B C D E	1 2 3 4 5	1 2 3 4 5
Financial analysis	A B C D E	A B C D E	1 2 3 4 5	1 2 3 4 5
Marketing	A B C D E	A B C D E	1 2 3 4 5	1 2 3 4 5
Public relations	A B C D E	A B C D E	1 2 3 4 5	1 2 3 4 5
Planning	A B C D E	A B C D E	1 2 3 4 5	1 2 3 4 5
General management	A B C D E	A B C D E	1 2 3 4 5	1 2 3 4 5
Networking	A B C D E	A B C D E	1 2 3 4 5	1 2 3 4 5

We recognize a circularity problem in rating *Priority* before having carefully defined the ultimate job you are seeking. Most young attorneys, however, do have a general sense of the type of work they enjoy and of the type of abilities that work would require. They also have a sense of what they don't do so well. Priority, then, becomes a blend of likely need in the future and likely deficiency at present.

There are some obvious questions to ask yourself in the wake of Exercise 11. For instance, how much time do you spend employing the skills you enjoy versus those more valued by your employer? Levels of expectation will affect your response to this question because we are all raised with varying notions about how "real and earnest" work is supposed to be. There are those who will remind us that enjoyable work is not guaranteed in the Bill of Rights. Nonetheless, if there is little overlap between your greatest Abilities and greatest Satisfactions you may have been sidetracked in the course of your "internship" training. For now, however, your subconscious probably helped you identify "Priorities". Circle the five highest rated Priorities and then transfer them to the space provided in Exercise 15 at page 90.

Many lawyers, at all stages of experience, get stuck with specialties simply because their proficiency is fortuitously discovered and then exploited to the hilt. For example:

> Tyrone, senior associate in a major law firm, once had been in journalism. He developed, against his will, a reputation for interpreting banking regulations merely because he had once written a very clear memo on the subject. Repeated assignments in banking only increased his knowledge and writing skills in that field. Writing, a skill in which he excelled but which he hoped to de-

emphasize in his new career as a lawyer, helped to make him a reluctant expert in a subject that really bored him. The partners in his firm could hardly be blamed for appreciating and exploiting his ability, which certainly enhanced his position with them, but he was nonetheless trapped.

You can become typecast at any stage in your career, potentially a problem even when it is to your financial advantage.

Now, let us consider your strengths and deficiencies. How many of your skills are recently developed versus old standbys from your past? The Career Paths Study, mentioned in Chapter 3, revealed that, except for analytical ability and legal research, most lawyers feel that their skills were acquired during internship and residency rather than in law school. However, you may feel that such things as negotiation skills or business acumen are natural abilities that have been in your arsenal even prior to law school. In that case, the question is whether your work has contributed to professional growth recently or whether you are coasting on polished, but aging, skills.

Of course, despite your best intentions, your job might not provide much of an environment for correcting deficiencies or testing new skills. You may feel forced into a purely defensive position, constantly playing to your strengths and hiding your weaknesses. Dan Hassenfeld, a Boston attorney, once instituted a tremendously popular seminar in his law firm on the subject of "making mistakes". In it he stressed the impoverishment of professional development in a climate of nervous failure avoidance. In such a climate you can feel more stupid by the day and the whole process of growth is thrown into reverse.

EXERCISE 12: Career Geometry

Looking at your skills in isolation is of limited utility. The setting of clients, services, and transactions typical of your current or desired practice is the relevant environment. However, most lawyers carry an analysis of their practice little beyond a simple description of their general area of specialization and the legal subject matter of client problems they have worked on. There is little attention to client or industry types, settings, or the roles which characterize the stages of professional development. We have devised a simple organizational device—the Career Matrix—which permits a more organized and insightful analysis.

We have found that almost any legal experience can be described in terms of three parameters: Types of clients served, types of services performed, and types of roles assumed. The intersection of clients, services, and roles will define a graphic rendering of the nature of an existing practice or experience level. The simple matrix provided below thus can map the contours of your current practice. The gaps in the matrix will point out areas where further experience may be necessary or where there is the potential for practice expansion. And, with respect to your skills, you can map them in conjunction with various kinds of clients and services.

Do this Exercise, therefore, with the understanding that it will be the basis for more self-assessment and for planning the subject matter content of your next training investment (read, job) in your legal career.

In the left-hand column of the matrix below list your clients either individually or by types of industries and companies. For each column list a type of service you have performed in terms of transactional types, legal subject matter, or legal skills involved (whichever service description makes most sense in your practice area). Then, in each cell of the body of the Matrix describe the particular roles you played in rendering such services. In many areas of the law we have found that lawyers typically progress through the roles we described in the Inventory of Legal Skills (Exercise 11). However, whatever description of roles seems best for your practice is the one that you should use. A sample Career Matrix follows the blank and additional illustrative Career Matrices are found in Appendix D.

The sample Career Matrix shows the expected concentration in law, fact and second chair roles for Oliver Wendell Brandeis, Jr., a young attorney who chose law after a losing battle with organic chemistry in college canceled his plans to follow in the footsteps of his doctor father. His greatest concentration of services has been for various elements of the health industry. He would obviously like to expand his roles into higher levels and there are evident gaps in his services supplied to various client types that could be filled in to increase his value and to develop his practice.

From your own Matrix, identify the key gaps in your experience and transfer those to the appropriate space in Exercise 15 at page 90.

As a specific variant of the Careers Matrix Exercise, you might now plug in the results from your Problem Solving Approach and Inventory of Legal Skills exercises. Instead of listing roles in the cells of the Matrix, you may substitute ten problem solving approaches or five greatest skills, showing wherein lies the greatest concentration of strength in your experience. Of course, you can as easily substitute the skills Priority list from Exercise 11, thus graphically delineating the greatest concentration of deficiencies in your experience. Obviously, the potentially instructive variations are limited only by stamina and attention span.

It might become apparent for instance, that most of your opportunities for indulging in business planning occurred while working with small, individual proprietors. Or that certain litigation skills were necessary for almost any client or transaction in your experience. The versatile or narrow application of your skills becomes apparent. You can easily map out expanded lists of clients or services that utilize your strengths.

The skills and experiences that you can currently bring to any job are only part of the picture at any career or job decision point. What you want to do and how you want to do it must be addressed.

EXERCISE 12: CAREER MATRIX

Services					
CLIENTS					
	1. 2. 3.	1. 2. 3.	1. 2. 3.	1. 2. 3.	1. 2. 3.
	1. 2. 3.	1. 2. 3.	1. 2. 3.	1. 2. 3.	1. 2. 3.
	1. 2. 3.	1. 2. 3.	1. 2. 3.	1. 2. 3.	1. 2. 3.
	1. 2. 3.	1. 2. 3.	1. 2. 3.	1. 2. 3.	1. 2. 3.
	1. 2. 3.	1. 2. 3.	1. 2. 3.	1. 2. 3.	1. 2. 3.
	1. 2. 3.	1. 2. 3.	1. 2. 3.	1. 2. 3.	1. 2. 3.
	1. 2. 3.	1. 2. 3.	1. 2. 3.	1. 2. 3.	1. 2. 3.

EXERCISE 12: SAMPLE CAREER MATRIX

Services	Gen. Corp.	Deals	Mergers	Tort Litig.	Financing
CLIENTS					
HOSPITALS	1. Law 2. Facts 3. 2nd chair	1. Law 2. 3.	1. Law 2. Facts 3. 2nd chair	1. Law 2. Facts 3.	1. Law 2. Facts 3.
HMO's	1. Law 2. 2nd chair 3.	1. 2. 3.	1. Law 2. Facts 3. 2nd chair	1. 2. 3.	1. Law 2. Facts 3. 2nd chair
GROUPS	1. 2. 3.	1. Law 2. Facts 3. 1st Chair	1. 2. 3.	1. Law 2. Facts 3. 1st Chair	1. Law 2. Facts 3. Design
MED/TECH	1. Law 2. Facts 3. 2nd chair	1. Law 2. Facts 3.	1. 2. 3.	1. Law 2. Facts 3.	1. Law 2. Facts 3. 2nd chair
OTHER TECH	1. Law 2. Facts 3. 2nd chair	1. Law 2. 3.	1. 2. 3.	1. Law 2. Facts 3.	1. Law 2. Facts 3. 2nd chair

EXERCISE 13: Work Satisfactions

This exercise will assist you in determining your career/work factors crucial to your professional satisfaction. Consider each item separately and rate it accordingly: A = Very Important, B = Important, C = Not Very Important.

_____ Achievement
_____ Advancement
_____ Affiliation
_____ Authority & Power
_____ Autonomy
_____ Being Needed
_____ Boss You Respect
_____ Collegiality
_____ Commitment to Goals
_____ Competition
_____ Control
_____ Creativity
_____ Direct Impact
_____ Discovering New Things
_____ Ethics
_____ Excellence
_____ Excitement & Adventure
_____ Financial Reward
_____ High Risk/High Reward
_____ Identification with client goals
_____ Independence
_____ Influencing People
_____ Intellectual Challenge
_____ Interesting Work
_____ Interpersonal Challenge
_____ Job Security
_____ Leadership of Others
_____ Mentoring
_____ Personal Time
_____ Pleasant Surroundings
_____ Pleasure & Fun
_____ Pressure & Fast Pace
_____ Prestige
_____ Public/Client Contact
_____ Public Service
_____ Recognition
_____ Respect
_____ Responsibility
_____ Results of Work Seen
_____ Security
_____ Stability
_____ Self-Development
_____ Self-Expression
_____ Service
_____ Specialization
_____ Status
_____ Structured Environment
_____ Supervision
_____ Teamwork
_____ Training
_____ Travel
_____ Variety
_____ Other:
_____ Other:

Now, review the work satisfactions you ranked "A" and then rank-order these from 1 to 10 in order of importance to you.

1. ______________________________
2. ______________________________
3. ______________________________
4. ______________________________
5. ______________________________
6. ______________________________
7. ______________________________
8. ______________________________
9. ______________________________
10. ______________________________

ANALYZING YOUR VALUES AND MOTIVATIONS

Almost every Exercise you have done so far has forced you to confront your basic values and motivations beginning with Work Style Preferences (Exercise 3) in Chapter 6. You may find it helpful, however, to summarize your impressions in the following two Exercises. These deal primarily with your values as they bear on your work. If, as we hope, you are seeking a wider basis for introspection, you will find more food for thought in Chapter 8, where we address issues of personal development.

Having just sorted out your ten most important work satisfactions, you might wish to look at how adequately they have been realized in your past or current experience.

EXERCISE 14: The Job Satisfaction Matrix

Now, take your top ten Work Satisfactions from Exercise 13 and insert them in the left-hand column of Exercise 14. Across the top label the other columns with your clients or transaction types (which ever seems most appropriate for your practice).

In each box in the body of the Chart, score each client or transaction with a +1, 0 or -1 for each Work Satisfaction. The column totals then tell you just how positive or negative a motivation was associated with that satisfaction for that one client or transaction. Row totals tell you how often that satisfaction occurred across all clients in your practice.

The motivational complexity of work would be plainly demonstrated, we believe, if you were to ask colleagues to fill out the above exercises naming the clients or transactions you have shared in common. We suspect that you would discover that the same task can be very satisfying (or dissatisfying) to two individuals for very different reasons.

In any case, transfer your top five job satisfactions to the space provided in Exercise 15.

EXERCISE 14: JOB SATISFACTION MATRIX

Clients or Transactions } / **SATISFACTIONS**								**ROW TOTALS**
1.								
2.								
3.								
4.								
5.								
6.								
7.								
8.								
9.								
10.								
COLUMN TOTALS								

EXERCISE 15: Summary of Self-Assessment Efforts

EX.#	EXERCISE DATA	ANALYSIS AND COMMENT
EX. 3	From page 62 enter "Top Rated Character Types": 1. 2. 3	What jobs or specialties might feature these Types?
EX. 4,5	From pages 64 and 65 enter key traits of Role Models and Party Guests. 1. 2. 3. 4. 5.	Which of these do you wish or need yet have not yet developed? 1. 2. 3. 4. 5.
EX. 6	From page 66 enter your primary Coping Strategies 1. 2. 3.	Comment on the adequacy of these for your anticipated career stresses:
EX. 7	Page 67, Career Choices and Reasons.	Comment on any themes or patterns that you can discern.
EX. 10	From page 79 enter your key problem-solving approaches: 1. 2. 3. 4. 5.	What jobs or specialties might be best suited to these approaches? What problem-solving approaches might be needed for jobs or specialties of interest to you?

EXERCISE 15: (con't.)

EX.#	EXERCISE DATA	ANALYSIS AND COMMENT
EX. 11	From page 81 enter the highest Priority skills you need to acquire: 1. 2. 3. 4. 5.	Comment on types of "next" jobs that would give you these skills.
EX. 12	From pages 85 enter gaps in your experiences that must be filled: 1. 2. 3. 4. 5.	Comment on types of "next" jobs that would give you these experiences.
EX. 14	From page 88 enter your leading Work Satisfactions: 1. 2. 3. 4. 5.	Comment on types of positions that would be consistent with these Work Satisfactions.

YOUR IDEAL NEXT JOB

You should now be ready to make a stab at describing your ideal next job, if indeed you haven't mentally tried to do so at the conclusion of each Exercise.

If you were to try to envision an ideal, but realistic, next job, what would be its substantive content? What types of clients? What types of industries? What skills and experiences would you hope to obtain from the position? Would this be a permanent position or a learning experience on the way to obtaining a long term goal? What should be the appropriate setting or work atmosphere? What basic values should be served?

All of the Exercises above should yield information and insights that will help the diligent to answer these questions.

Summary answers to these questions are best organized in a Chart that can accept data and insights from prior Exercises in this Chapter. We have provided Exercise 15 as a convenient repository of self-assessment insights.

Commenting on the leftish tone of a Supreme Court opinion written by Felix Frankfurter, a journalist asked the Justice, "If you believe thusly, why aren't you a Communist." Justice Frankfurter replied, "Because I can't capture life in a phrase."

Nor can your professional and personal and material and psychic needs be captured in a single Chart. The Chart of Exercise 15 is but a tool to help you keep key points in mind. A thoughtful review of what you have learned about yourself (and perhaps additional summaries to supplement the Chart of Exercise 15) is what is needed. The mechanics are secondary. The goal is to define the realistic professional position that will maximize your own satisfaction and growth.

The purpose of Exercise 15 is to gather your insights to help you to complete a Position Statement that defines with some particularity what next job is best for you and what you expect to get out of it. That Position Statement, such as the the format of Exercise 16, is really the end product of all of your assessment efforts.

A very important threshold question is whether your next job is plainly a training experience or potentially a permanent position. This, of course, depends upon where you are in your career and what your ultimate goals are. Having made that determination, however, you are ready to attempt to distill the collected information and self-knowledge into the final product, your Position Statement:

EXERCISE 16: Position Statement

I am seeking a position as a lawyer at the ________________ level and in the practice area of ______________________________________ working on the behalf of ______________________________________. This position would utilize my special traits, skills, and knowledges such as ____________, ____________, and ____________ and would provide resume-building experiences such as, ________, ________, and ________. The position should be with an employer suitable to my Work Satisfactions such as ________, ________, and ________. My goals in taking such a position are ____ ____.

For Oliver, our young ex-pre-med lawyer, this transposition yields:

> I am seeking a position as a lawyer at the senior associate/first chair level and in the practice area of general business counsel working on behalf of clients who are HMO's, group practices, or med/tech companies. This position would utilize my special traits, skills and knowledges such as Social Type work with medical professionals and would provide resume-building experiences such as expansion into intellectual property work, first chair responsibilities and direct client contact. The position would be with an employer suitable to my Work Satisfactions such as Self-Development and Public/Client Contact. My goals in taking such a position are to prepare myself for the ultimate position of house counsel to an HMO or med/tech company or of department head in a major firm having medical industry clients.

Having done these Exercises you may have a better idea of what you are doing and what you would like to be doing and for whom and at what level of authority. You may also see better which activities you wish to augment or de-emphasize. At the least, you should be able to expound upon your experiences in a more organized and positive fashion in an interview situation.

Now that you know what you want, all you have to do is go out and get it, right? If you feel this way, proceed directly to Chapter 9 and begin the plunge into your Planning and Job Search. However, if you still feel that something critical has been omitted from your self-assessment, you may need to search your soul a bit longer or deeper before you take the field. If so, Chapter 8 may be just the soul-searching tool you need.

Chapter

8

Self-Assessment III: Taking A Deeper Look

" . . . the price of wisdom is above rubies."
Job 28:18

Re-read your Position Statement, the end product of Chapter 7. Does it really capture what you want from a job or career? Compare the sample Position Statement with the following quote from the physician and epidemiologist Hans Zinsser describing the clarification of his career goals as a physician during military service in World War One:

> "I remember one dark, rainy day when we buried a Russian doctor. A ragged band of Serbian reservists stood in the mud and played the Russian and Serbian anthems out of tune. The horses on the truck slipped as it was being loaded, and the coffin fell off. When the chanting procession finally disappeared over the hill, I was glad the rain on my face obscured the tears that I could not hold back. I felt in my heart, then, that I could or would never be an observer, and that, whatever Fate had in store for me, I would always wish to be in the ranks, however humbly or obscurely; and it came to me suddenly that I was profoundly happy in my profession, in which I would never aspire to administrative power or prominence so long as I could remain close, heart and hands, to the problems of disease."

Granted, this may not be quite fair to young Ollie Brandeis or to your own Position Statement. Neither of you were instructed to reach down quite this deep. Now is a good time to do that, however. To ask yourself if that Position Statement is truly consonant with your goals as a lawyer — and as a person. We admit we were tempted to put this Chapter into a thoughtful Appendix, but couldn't bring ourselves to do it. It would have been tantamount to saying "turn to Appendix M to figure out the meaning of life."

So, without pretending to quite so grandiose a plan, let us pursue the implications of your Position Statement a bit further. It really breaks down into two main components: (1) special knowledge and skills applied to (2) special settings and constituencies.

The Kind of Person You Are

A very important question frequently omitted or forgotten in a profession that so often assumes a pose of neutrality, is the exact nature of your relationship to those settings and constituencies. At heart, that relationship will define the kind of lawyer and person you are or wish to become. If there seems to be more to understand about yourself as a lawyer, the answers probably lie in a mix of sociological, personal, and organizational tensions centered on the question, "what kind of lawyer are you?"

After all, there are many kinds of lawyers (only partly defined in terms of skills and specialties) whose feelings about their role in life are exceedingly varied. The reason for this, if you stop to consider, is that law has no independent reality apart from the richness of life it regulates. Although once we become absorbed in the study and practice of law, it seems to take on a life of its own. To some lawyers that life has an absolute reality and the exercise of professional skill has a beauty and fascination comparable to the performance of music. Yet, even for such a person, the hall and audience, the setting and the clients, must define the impact he or she has in life as a lawyer.

Since the practice of law is also an exercise in power, it affords a certain concrete, nonspecific pleasure comparable to flexing one's muscles. The pure pleasure of being where power is, of being part of the power structure, is not necessarily the corrupting and ignoble motive some would have it be. There are those who have felt so powerless at times that the dignity and excitement of power are a healing balm. Those young lawyers in the big firms who gravitate toward investment banking do so for many reasons, but the desire simply to be "where the action is" ranks high among them. As one lawyer puts it in a *New York Times Magazine* article, ("The Faster Track", August 10, 1986):

> "I think most lawyers are highly paid drones who have no real control of their lives. I'm interested in management consulting, because instead of being a technician working on deals, I'll get to the guts of the deal."

One is tempted to ask, "What is the big deal?" A question that contains the seed of an answer. For although several motives are implicit in this lawyer's statement, it is clear that a deal's bigness figures as prominently as its content.

Ultimately, law is powerful because it regulates important human activities that should ultimately matter more to us than than the rules that govern them. Perhaps, from the self-interview questions on your choice of career, you suspect how many are drawn to law simply because it promises to allow them control of some important part of their lives. That importance can be measured practically, emotionally, or philosophically, but it has strong links with life prior to and outside of the law.

The power of law to influence so many domains is, then, one of its major appeals. But which domain is most important to you? What is your constituency? What is the "on the behalf of" part of your Position Statement?

For instance, service to society seems to mean different things to different people. Legal services lawyers seem bent on ameliorating the problems of individuals whose lives other lawyers wish to influence from a distance via manipulation of social policy. The latter kind of lawyer is actually more concerned with modifying attitudes in the minds of legislators, administrators, and all those in the policy establishment. These two kinds of lawyers may have similar social values and objectives, but they are drawn to using the power of law in different ways. Arguably, if either kind of lawyer could see a better way to change policy or help clients they would choose it. Law to them is primarily a means to an end, however freighted with its own pleasures.

Consider the case of young prosecutor who had majored in philosophy and psychology in college. After an internship in private practice in which his early interests were for a time submerged, he became a prosecutor "in order to deal with the question of how people should act, in the most practical way I could, as a lawyer and central character in a real life morality play."

This attraction to law as a means of practical participation in a vital part of life might be most overt in those who espouse social causes, but it is pervasive throughout the profession. It can be just as strong an attraction in business law. And, as we have suggested, if you find yourself more interested in your client's work than in the work you are doing for the client, then you may have been attracted to law as a closet business person. For that matter, as a legal services attorney you may be discovering yourself a closet social worker. (Ironically, not a few social workers doing battle for their clients discover in themselves a latent lawyer.)

The question to be decided here is whether your relationship to your clients, your constituency, makes you feel "like a central character" in a real life play. Since law is a superb introduction to a wide variety of pursuits, it is constantly capable of creating a vocational crisis in those who are open to the opportunities for real life participation to which they are exposed. Whether you respond with a real career shift will depend on the intensity of attraction for you to that participation and on whether you are an armchair traveler or a determined explorer.

The fact is, however, that as an armchair traveler you can go many more places if you are willing to accept a certain detachment and vicarious participation. For many lawyers this is the supreme pleasure of law. Like journalism, it is a license to learn everybody's business through important, but limited, involvement.

This matter of detachment brings us to another form of power conferred by a career in the law. The power of autonomy.

As we have discussed, changes in the profession have challenged the old image of the lawyer's independence and insulation from his clients and the world around him. But there are still many ways in which law appeals to a sense of autonomy. One of the strongest is its appeal to intellectual independence. As we have seen, this is an area in which the profession is sometimes failing to live up to its appeal.

Even so, law offers a chance to bring problem solving skills to bear on practical problems and yet remain a participant/observer with an independent, thoughtful frame of reference. According to Holland's typology, lawyers are supposed to be Investigative Types. If they are also Intuitives they are apt to have a strong theoretical bent.

The prosecutor, mentioned above, who loved having a practical role in a morality play, also said this about his work:

> "Of all the principals, — the police, the criminals, and so forth — I felt that as a lawyer I had the best chance to reflect on what was going on. I was always interested in the 'whys' as much as the 'whats' and 'hows'. I would enjoy being a judge, but I'm not sure if I wouldn't prefer being a professional juror!"

Another form of autonomy traditionally appealing to those going into law is the notion of controlling the choice, content, and flow of one's work. Indeed, this notion lies deep at the heart of the mythology of the professions, as self-regulating and accountable only to the canons of their discipline. Despite modern assaults on this traditional aspiration of lawyers, opportunities to be the controller of one's work still abound. They take many forms, from the municipal bonds specialist in a large firm who is proud of being "our bonds man" to the beginning solo practitioner who would rather "reign in hell than serve in heaven."

The image of the solo practitioner, the sole proprietor, brings us to yet another form of autonomy, the drive to be an entrepreneur. (Increasingly, even partners in large firms are obliged to become entrepreneurial.) An important personal issue is, do you prefer to practice law apart from the marketing function or do you want to be an owner-manager? Do you want to assume the roles and risks of management and business development? Do you want to deal with the marketplace, the competition, and the bottom line? These are critical questions when the profession is undergoing major economic transitions. Those in a firm that is foundering can only preserve control of their work by assuming control of the firm.

This issue of entrepreneurialism is by no means confined to private practice. Institutions and the public sector need entrepreneurial managers too, especially in an era of uncertain funding. Thus, any lawyer should address the entrepreneurial/managerial issue in his or her self-assessment. Appendix G, Building Your Practice, presents some views on the role and scope of entrepreneurial thinking in the face of the current realities of the legal marketplace.

In truth, the entrepreneurial motive combines several forms of the need for autonomy. Surely it includes the desire for financial independence, which touches every aspirant to the professions.

Yet, money alone is not independence. Many professionals lapse into wealthy wage-slaves. It is more the desire to conceive, build, and control one's own work that makes the entrepreneur. The word autonomy shares the same root with "author." To author something, to create a product, is a drive in all of us. The entrepreneur feels this especially strongly at work; sometimes to the detriment of those other products of our lives: Spouse and children.

To summarize, we are suggesting that the principal work-related motivators of lawyers are: Intellectual challenge, association with power, practical and effective participation in important life arenas, and autonomy: intellectual, creative, organizational, and financial. Many others, including the love of conflict, come to mind, and you will probably add to our list of motives to fashion your own. Those motives that we have emphasized, however, seem reasonably universal, present to some degree in all lawyers.

The Kind of Person You Are Becoming

An arduous business this self-assessment. And you have just arrived at the hardest part.

In most cases of career indecision, personal development issues provide the extra dimension that gives the indecision its intensity. When we come to the next Chapter on making choices and taking action, you will see that the toughest trade-offs will involve the balancing of your professional and personal development.

All of the above discussion of skills, values, and personal development is rather theoretical, even while we have been insisting that reality is richer and messier. The Exercises, we hope, have helped to elicit and organize your personal needs, traits, and development to date. Professional counselors typically find all of the material from these Exercises spilling forth in their work with lawyers. It is just more interwoven and gut-driven in a counseling session than in a series of discrete Exercises.

Listen to the following monologue by Tony, a thirty-five year old tax partner in a west coast firm. He has only recently joined this firm, as a partner, after moving to a new city in order to facilitate a job change by his wife and also to live closer to his aging parents. The new firm thinks that by adding two new attorneys it is expanding its tax practice, but Tony is doubtful whether they are really committed to innovative approaches. In his darkest moments Tony is wondering whether he even wants to be a tax specialist:

> "I just don't know. It seems I'm losing control on a day-to-day basis. I haven't been home for dinner more than two nights in a row. I caught myself making a phone appointment with my son the other night.
>
> "And as for tax, it seems more draining and stressful these days. We're a small department, which I like in some ways, but we're understaffed. The pressure is always on because it's always a sensitive issue which must be resolved before others can move on with any transaction. It's like being a neurosurgeon, every move has to be right. I take the work home every night, worrying about it.
>
> "You're a specialist, and by definition never called upon to answer the easy questions, it's always the grey areas. And you know, the way tax is practiced here, you're never called upon to work through the whole deal, never able to have an ongoing relationship with a client or follow the whole outcome of their projects. The corporate guy is like the internist who gets to treat the whole person; you're called in only at certain points. It doesn't have to be that way, not the way I practiced it before. Your tax specialist can be a kind of general business advisor. I guess I do like tax if I can practice it my way. I like the camaraderie of client contact, but I sometimes feel that tax attracts very bright people who don't like clients particularly.
>
> "Actually, I got into tax because I liked business law and I thought that you should be good in tax to have a real foundation in that area. My first firm didn't have a separate

tax department, and I really enjoyed using the specialty within the general corporate practice. But then I began to feel I was losing my edge in tax because I wasn't doing enough of it, so I got a graduate degree in tax and then rejoined the firm. I got involved right away in some very interesting, complicated transactions where I could immediately show off my new knowledge. I did very well. They were impressed. I was impressed! I made partner in three years. So for a while it was just exciting and I was so pleased just with the acceleration in knowledge and status in the firm.

"But you know, I cracked up. No, not mentally . . . well, not exactly. I had a motorcycle accident, and you might say it was work-connected. My wife had been after me to get rid of the thing, especially after our first kid was born, but I was loathe to give it up. And I got home through traffic a lot faster than in a car. But on this occasion it was dark and wet, and I was tired out. I spun out and woke up in the hospital. Over the next two months recuperating at home, I had the chance to do some hard thinking and spend some more time talking to my wife — about her work as well as mine. Well, when I got back to the firm I tried to put my foot down, limit things.

"No, I know it sounds contradictory, but I balk at the idea of a 'smaller pond'. I've thought about it, talked to some of our clients who'd be happy to have me, and it is tempting. But I'm not happy being a service person; I do like a challenge to drive me. I'd take less of my work home if I were less frustrated here. It is not just a case of how many hours, but how much control I have over them. I tell you, if I could have the green light to develop some business, revamp things a little, I'd feel a lot better.

"And you know, I'm not sure how to get my case over here, it's a rather sedate and gentlemanly crowd in comparison to my old firm — or the kind of home I grew up in, for that matter. I keep looking for a polite way to remind them of their commitment to innovation, but I guess I'm just going to have to be more assertive and start bugging them. But I'm not hopeful. Maybe I should be considering a smaller firm that would be willing to give me a free rein, but I'm not keen on the financial cut at this point. I've got my parents' care over the coming years to consider, and the kid. And I don't like having to explain so many recent job changes."

This is a typical outpouring from an initial interview with a career counselor. As a virtual stream of consciousness meditation, it is a good example of how all the work-related and personal issues are interwoven in our first efforts at self-assessment. So many themes are packed into these first statements, beginning with Tony's general feeling that he has lost control of his life.

We see that he is going through something like a second Age Thirty Crisis. The first occurred when he went back to graduate school to get his tax degree, feeling that he needed to rededicate himself to the intellectual rigor of his specialty. There followed a BOOM phase in which he exploded into productivity, rapidly establishing himself as a more-than-junior member of his profession. Then, the motorcycle which seemed to embody all his youthful energy and to symbolize his ability to cut through traffic, collapsed beneath him. Old questions emerged again, as they often do, to be solved in a new form.

We see how Tony's initial impulse to specialize in tax arose more from a general interest in business than an interest in tax per se. Yet, at this point he feels the tension between being the master of a rigorous specialty and his resistance to being locked into a socially isolated corner of practice. We see, also, how he tries to resolve this tension by being able to redefine the nature of tax practice, which requires more autonomy than he has in his present firm. Yet other tensions make it difficult for him to go out on his own, among them the status and importance he feels being associated with a large firm. Then again, he feels that he has fallen in with a bunch of pleasant enough characters who don't really fit his style or his social background. He is enough of an owner/manager to want to satisfy his business leanings by client development, but his new firm doesn't seem to be the hospitable environment in which to do this.

That he finds himself a politically weak, "new boy partner" comes from following his wife's own career change, which is in turn a consequence of the reassessment they gave their relationship at the time of his accident. Like many of this generation, he is also sandwiched between aging parents and young children; to meet some of their needs he must work harder, and to meet others he must work less. He is like the character of Dylan Thomas in the biographical play Dylan, who provides a poignant interpretation of the lines:

Ba Ba black sheep, have you any wool?
Yessir, yessir, three bags full.
One for my master, one for my dame,
And one for the little boy who lives down the lane.

The master, he explains, is his work. The dame is his wife, and the little boy who lives down the lane is himself. What, he asks, is left for that little boy who persists in all of us? Or, in Tony's case, the little boy who loved motorcycles. How to serve all these masters, and so order his priorities in life, is the great challenge of Tony; and the rest of us.

Your self-assessment should bring you to a similar picture of your position in life. What begins with typologies and checklists ends with a living portrait. The picture may be clearer, but it will include contradictions requiring you to set some painful priorities before you can act. Creating that portrait, contradictions and all, is the most crucial phase of taking control of your life and of skillfully managing the transitions that ultimately define a career. You have some sense of where you are and how you got there. You have a general feel for where you would like to get to and what way-stations there may be along the route. Optimizing that route and evaluating possible way-stations is the next task, and, not so coincidentally, the subject of our next Chapter.

Chapter

9

Planning and Investigating A Career: Taking Control

"Multitudes, multitudes in the valley of decision."
Joel 3:14

Your self-assessment ended with a Position Statement, a definition of an ideal next job. That definition now must be matched with a reasonable job-locating plan having a reasonable chance of achieving your goals.

ORGANIZING YOUR THOUGHTS

Your efforts to date should have provided you with time and incentive to reflect on key personal and professional questions to be resolved before investigation and planning can proceed:

1. **How do you want to be living in five years?**

   Personal. Married? Children? House? Location? Time spent on work? Significant non-work interests and activities? Household income required to finance such a lifestyle? Your contribution to household income?

   Work Competence. Industries and client types? Primary practice area specialty and role? Knowledge, skills, information, techniques, experiences, transactions, and matters in which you need competence to perform the intended role in the intended specialty? Necessary administrative, managerial, and personal-productivity skills? Secondary practice area specialties, roles, and required legal and non-legal competence?

   Work Setting. Law or non-law? Firm or corporation? Big or little? Entrepreneurial or institutional? Secure or risk taking? Fast paced and pressured (investment bank, high stakes litigation) or steady and orderly (banks, 1960's type law firms)? Ideal characteristics of co-workers? Work atmosphere? Work ethic? Image and prestige? The cultural values of the organization?

   Role. Star or team player? Owner (management responsibility, bottom line risk, practice development responsibilities) or professional? Risk taker or risk assessor? Principal or advisor?

2. **What alternative career paths can you see for yourself after five years?**

   It would be naive to believe that all lawyers in the early years of practice can define a single ideal mainstream career position. Most can, however, define various alternatives and look for similar competence needs and prerequisites in them.

3. **Which are the competence deficiencies you have to fill in order to be**

suited for the position you want five years in the future?

What area of legal skills, experience, or competence are you missing? What industry knowledge? What business, organizational, or non-legal experience or skills? What about project or task design and leadership? Extending the breadth of your primary legal specialty? In this analysis your Career Matrix will help to show you gaps in your experiences and skills that need to be filled in before you can realistically expect to fit into your ideal position. Those gaps (be they in client types to be served, work content, roles, or settings) will help to define the next job that you need to propel you on your way to your ideal.

The investigation and planning efforts, then, should lead to answers to the remaining key questions:

4. **What are job specifications and categories of employers who can provide you with your missing work experiences?**

Can your needs be satisfied with the experiences from one employer? Can you achieve your objectives with your present employer? Can pro bono activities provide you with experiences you need?

5. **What arguments can be made to the gatekeeper at a new employer that it would be in their interest to provide you with your desired work experience?**

What skills and experiences do you already have which are relevant to their needs? What are your potential contributions to the new employer? What is the likelihood the new employer will capture your potential contributions? What are your strengths and weaknesses for the new position? How do you rate with others seeking the same position?

Having a pretty good idea of your desired long-term career goals and your life-style and location preferences, you can plot a course to reach those goals. Lawyers have some fine advantages when it comes to planning careers and conducting job searches. For one, they are well versed in research and analysis, skills which can be trained on the employment market as easily as on a legal topic. For another, lawyers are investigators, interrogators, and advocates—they can be effective in obtaining information and planning campaigns of persuasion. Moreover, they are compulsive communicators, documenting all of their activities for the edification of other lawyers and participating in various professional networks that are replete with information and opportunities.

We suggest that you model your career plan and job search on two activities very familiar to lawyers: investigation and litigation. Although overlapping, these activities require different attitudes or frames of mind. In the first, starting with a few good leads, you put your intuition on a leash and let it sniff around. In the second, having caught the scent, you go straight for the quarry through hell and high water.

Psychologists call this the difference between divergent and convergent thinking. Divergent thinking elaborates possibilities: although you may have a pretty good idea of what you are seeking, you don't want to ignore potential leads. Convergent thinking is what the words imply: converging upon a solution after eliminating distractions, false leads, and less desirable alternatives.

Ideally, one process ought to shade over into the other. In law, the investigation turns into litigation as the facts begin to point toward a course of action. In career planning, information gathering crystallizes into a job search.

Unfortunately, many people feel they need a fully formulated plan before they take any steps to investigate a way out of their situation. It offends their sense of efficiency to engage in tentative exploration. Asked, what are their plans, they are apt to reply: "Oh, I don't know. I don't know what's out there yet."

They are at an impasse. On the one hand, they are reluctant to look because they don't know precisely enough what they want. On the other hand, they don't know what they want because they haven't looked around enough. Not realizing that planning is a marriage of self-assessment and investigation, they remain stuck in writing and re-writing their ideal job specifications. Forced by circumstances to a job search, they find they are as ignorant of their opportunities as a frog at the bottom of a well. A rushed or limited investigation ensues, followed by an overly directed job search that prematurely narrows knowledge of possibilities both within oneself and within the job market.

Reluctance to investigate is but one pitfall. It is also possible, at all stages of planning or searching, to become insatiably addicted to information, never reaching enough closure to mount an effective campaign. There are at least two reasons for this information addiction, both dealing with the tension between one's plans and reality.

By now you will probably have realized that several alternative career paths may emerge from even the most rigorous self-assessment, despite the intention of finding a unique solution. In the early stages of planning and investigation these alternatives may appear as an embarrassment of riches, equally attractive for different reasons. It is reasonable to suppose that more information may enable a selection between them. But, when the alternatives reflect competing values rather than choices all consistent with a single value, additional information may only intensify the attractions of each alternative. In such cases the purpose of investigation should be to heighten, rather than reduce, conflict until a choice must be made. This is very hard for most people to do. Those initially reluctant to investigate alternatives simultaneously, for fear of conflict, may go on endlessly hoping to find that key piece of information to tip the scale. They may fail to realize that the decision must be made on the basis of priority of the underlying, competing values.

Besides conflicts between alternative career paths, there are the conflicts between career and personal goals. Chances are, your efforts to harmonize these in the foregoing Exercises have been only partially successful, and you will have to proceed in the company of some conflict and uncertainty. It will help to remember that conflict can create an even deeper craving for perfect information. Much of the most fruitless information searching is a hopeless effort to circumvent some hard emotional dilemma. It is like a scrupulously mounted scientific expedition to find a hybrid creature like the centaur, when there is no such beast.

We are reminded of Red.

> Red was married to another lawyer who was much more ambitious than he. In his perception, his wife thought the less of him because he was in a low pressure job as a contracts administrator in a small college, while she was in a hard driving, large law firm. However, she also seemed to appreciate his greater flexibility and availability for child care and household management. Rather than confront her with the emotional dilemma that she was creating for him, Red insisted that there must be information somewhere that would allow him the best of both worlds. He pored endlessly over law firm directories looking for indicia of a non-existent job.

A career plan that is broadly based and takes the long term view will protect you from some of the pitfalls we have just described. Since your investigations relate to long term goals, the job search and its outcome may be only a partial step toward their fulfillment, but a step nonetheless. If you keep that in mind, you can plan and act without falling into paralysis or compulsive activity. A young lawyer with a plan is unlikely to be completely dissatisfied with a current or prospective job, however imperfect, which progresses toward ultimate goals. A career plan is less an exact blueprint and more an anchor against the unpredictable storms in professional life.

Your personal plans should also take the long view, and you should expect to realize them partially, or in sequence. You should accept the inevitability of trade-offs, and not be afraid to create conflicts or contradictions in exploring opportunities. The necessity to simplify will become apparent as you go on, or when you actually have to choose between real possibilities.

Therefore, do not expect your first efforts to immediately clarify or resolve your issues. It takes longer than most people think to accomplish a job change, sometimes as much as a year, and only toward the middle of that period does a highly focused search become possible. You should proceed in a spirit of perpetual experimentation. Since you cannot foresee all solutions to your needs, the best you can do is be alert to reconsideration when knowledge and opportunity beckon in unforeseen ways.

On the other hand, without your career plan and an ideal job description, you have no way to structure even the most flexible job search. Even a partial element of your career plan can form the basis for an initial exploration — a geographical limitation, a credential requirement, money, a practice opportunity. As the saying goes, to put up a tent in a storm you must get one corner securely pegged down. Or, from another point of view, you might remember that the most satisfying form of travel always has a destination . . . whether you get there or not.

RESEARCH: FROM FROG TO SPIDER

We have suggested that you should approach your job search as if you were engaged in appellate litigation. Perhaps Certiorari is an even more apt analogy. You will be your own advocate before a bench of employers who must be persuaded merely to hear your case, and then to pass favorably on it.

To be successful, you will have to: (1) conduct effective research, (2) prepare good documentation, (3) submit written briefs, and (4) make strong oral arguments. In other words, you will: (1) target your employers, (2) develop the best case for your value to the new employer, (3) prepare a Lawyer Portfolio which will get their attention, and (4) interview effectively to sustain their interest and obtain a job. In these efforts, as in litigation, there will be obligations of truthfulness and strategies to emphasize facts and concepts to get a favorable ruling. Research, writing, and oral presentations will need to be complementary and reinforcing. The following are our suggestions on how to utilize each step in the process.

You will need at least four types of information regarding: a) the profession, b) specialties, c) practice and job descriptions, and d) employers. However, before addressing these types of information, we would like you to consider your sources.

If you begin as that frog at the bottom of a well, the object is to turn yourself into a spider in the middle of a web. As a job searcher, you may resemble the spider in having limited mobility in pursuing your prey, be it information or employers. You are probably working, and probably not yet prepared to share your intentions with your employer. Stuck where you are, you cannot work full time on your investigations. What is the most effective way to extend your range of information? The illustration below shows you—the researcher/spider—in the middle of a web of expanding information sources.

As you can see, this web begins with sources directly accessible to observation or interrogation. From your job, including bosses, associates, and clients, it expands to include friends, family, classmates, and other lawyers in your vicinity. Beyond these direct sources are entities that organize and transmit information to you: Associations, conferences, courses, and placement and search services. The outer perimeter of the information web includes libraries, books, journals, newspapers, and the new, computer-based information systems. Let us look at the use of each of these.

Your Job

By now you should know by heart our dictum on using work as a source of career information. It is simply regrettable that some lawyers can pride themselves on their ability to serve their clients without curiosity about their clients' affairs. However, job dissatisfaction can shake this attitude by forcing a disengagement from the

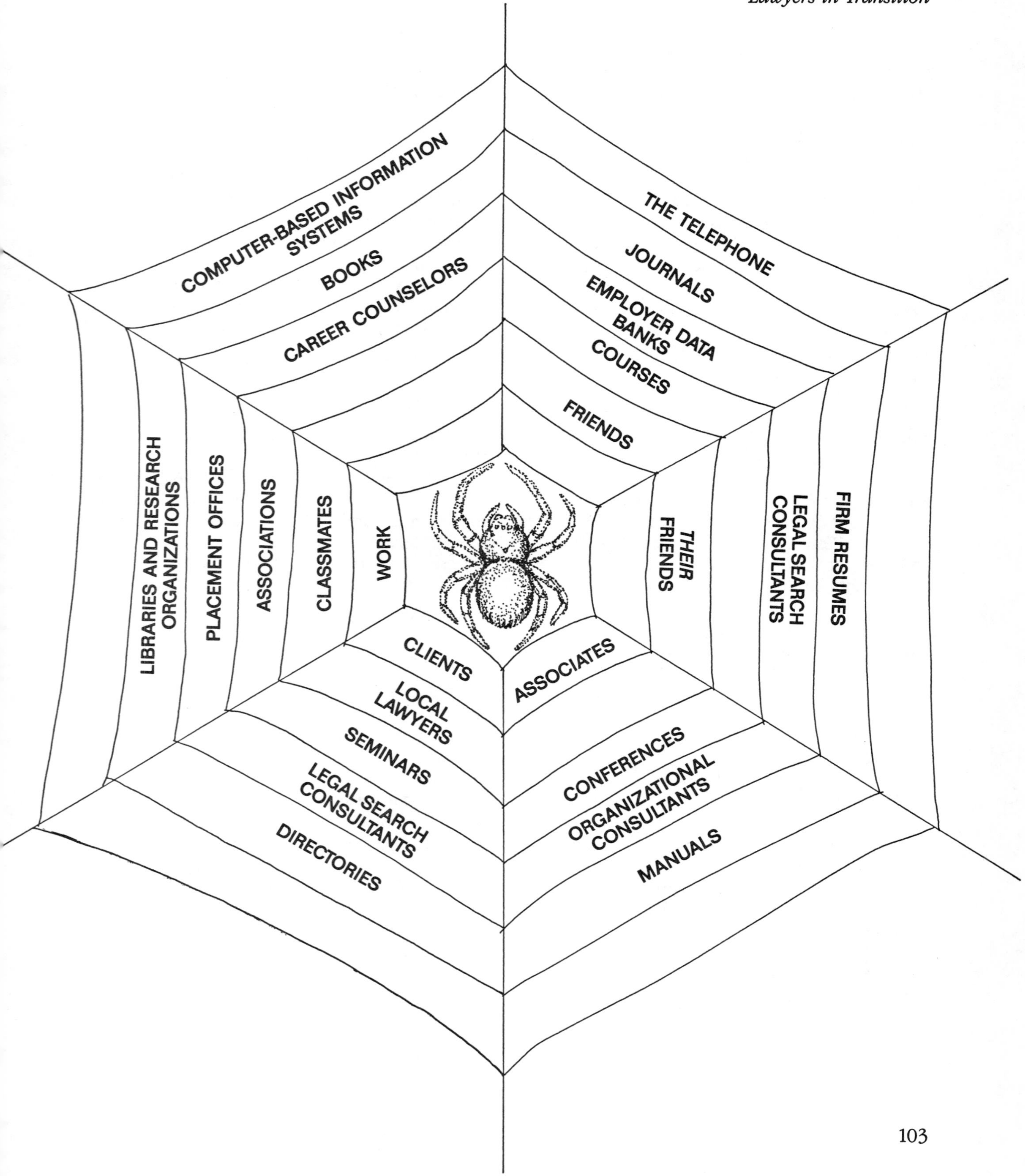
COMPUTER-BASED INFORMATION SYSTEMS
BOOKS
CAREER COUNSELORS
THE TELEPHONE
JOURNALS
EMPLOYER DATA BANKS
COURSES
FRIENDS
LIBRARIES AND RESEARCH ORGANIZATIONS
PLACEMENT OFFICES
ASSOCIATIONS
CLASSMATES
WORK
THEIR FRIENDS
LEGAL SEARCH CONSULTANTS
FIRM RESUMES
CLIENTS
LOCAL LAWYERS
SEMINARS
LEGAL SEARCH CONSULTANTS
DIRECTORIES
ASSOCIATES
CONFERENCES
ORGANIZATIONAL CONSULTANTS
MANUALS

values of one's employer. If you have reached this state, you have an opportunity to substitute something positive for alienation. As others have done, you may find that the decision to leave a job makes it possible to stay a while as a participant/observer, enjoying and learning what you can. In this liberated mood you can redirect your energies and do your work a little differently, as research for your own benefit.

For instance, one young associate who had begun to realize his boredom with his job and his possible disinterest in law, began to approach his most "boring" work in a new spirit. When put to work incorporating someone who was setting up a printing business, and afterwards helping the client with some commercial leasing problems, the associate decided to pay some housecalls. The results were interesting. On the one hand, the legal problems were somewhat more interesting on site. On the other, conversations with the client opened up unexpected vistas on business. The printing trade was not exactly his cup of tea, but he did enjoy time spent with the client. Did this mean he might consider in-house counsel? If so, what could he learn about other clients? Life definitely became more interesting.

Approaching your work with a hidden agenda may go undetected by your employer, but, in time, your intentions are apt to betray themselves by a change in the style or quality of your work. Then, you will face the issue of whether, and how, to involve your present employer in your investigations.

Certainly, if your employer believes your performance is deteriorating you may have to speak up. Failure to voice your feelings leads others to suppose that poor performance reflects inability rather than unhappiness. Your employers' respect and willingness to provide you with information or opportunities will wane if they begin to suspect you of incompetence or disloyalty. Your ideal next job could well be with your current employer. Rather than face such a consequence of silence, this is rather the time to find out if other opportunities are available within your organization or whether your present role can be redefined. Surprisingly few lawyers attempt this. Even in the worst case where a parting of ways is inevitable, employers can be very forthcoming with advice, contacts, and time. They may even help by underwriting outplacement services or counseling.

Then again, they may also just decide "off with her head". This is an area of such delicate judgement that we dare not issue much advice, except to remind you that in any job one is apt to have many masters, some of whom are more benevolent than others. Those for whom you have done your best work and with whom you feel somewhat identified are often in the position to act as confidential advisors, without your having to go wholly public with your intentions.

Letting the cat out of the bag may have yet another benefit. Going public before God and your employer usually means facing a deadline by which you must obtain the next job. Though the idea may send chills up your spine, this is not always such a misfortune. For you, the deadline, if imposed under supportive conditions, may be a galvanizing factor that will drive you into a targeted job search without further procrastination. This is equally true if a departure is unplanned and involuntary.

Friends, Classmates, Local Lawyers

Sometime, long before this stage, some of your peers at work will have been drawn into your confidence or have discovered your intentions on their own. Their involvement can be unwelcome and a source of some anxiety when you are trying to maintain some privacy and to protect your present status. Moreover, you may be in direct competition with some of them in edging toward the exit. On the other hand, with friends there also comes a time when secrecy and lack of candor can be counter-productive. The close-lipped are lonely, and nobody helps them. Brainstorming with peers does more than shore up your morale. It can provide some good leads. It often happens that a sidekick in discontent is someone who shares many of your problems but whose knowledge, contacts, and plans will be somewhat different from yours.

These differing perspectives will often be mutually reinforcing and enlightening rather than competing.

Outside of work, old classmates and friends at other jobs can be almost embarrassingly active in providing information and soliciting opportunities on your behalf, not to mention offering jobs. (We are not referring just to friends in the legal community. All friends can be surprisingly helpful.) Informal contacts remain the classic means of accessing employers. According to one associate,

> "I called several friends who practiced in [the desired city] . . . and simply discussed the general legal community [there]. I defined for them what I thought I was looking for, which was a smaller firm—I did not want to jump from one large firm to another large firm, but I wanted a smaller firm, preferably in the ten-to-thirty lawyer range—preferably a youngish firm, but one having a sophisticated business-oriented practice, as close as possible to the kind of practice that I had enjoyed at [Firm #1]. And I was told that that probably limited my choices to about three firms in that city at the time, all of which had been spin-offs from larger firms."

Useful, specific information is not an unusual product of a few casual contacts.

Associations

We are a gregarious nation. There are more associations in this country than in any other. Witness the Encyclopedia of Associations, a basic resource with which you should be familiar. (All references cited in our text are discussed in full in Chapter 13, Resources.)

Law-related associations may be organized around geography, as in your local bar association or the Council of New York Law Associates; around some specialty, as in the American Corporate Counsel Association; around some combination of specialty and activity, as in plaintiff-litigation support groups; around ideology, as in the National Lawyers' Guild; or around business aspects of law, as in the National Association for Law Placement. Many of these associations are multi-purpose. The American Bar Association, mother of us all, does everything, of course. All associations, to greater or lesser degree, offer career-related programs, conferences and publications, and sometimes even placement services. Unfortunately, most lawyers remain relatively uninformed about these services.

Conferences, Courses and Seminars

Even when these activities are not directly career-related, they are used in furtherance of many a career. The techniques involved are similar to those of client development.

As you may have discovered from experience, it is not always clear in using these techniques if you are marketing yourself or your business. Principal techniques are "circulating" and what we call "voyeuristic conversation", just shy of "informational interviewing". Circulating covers a host of activities, some informal—such as local bar association get togethers, others formal—such as speech making. One of the best is continuing professional education. Utilizing educational opportunities outside your place of employment has obvious advantages.

More experienced attorneys may derive all of the afore-mentioned benefits by giving, rather than taking, courses. The faculty are good sources of information to each other and provide good employment contacts. In the case of law firm seminars for clients, one's pupils become resources on many levels. This is also true for speech making to a wide, public audience.

A case in point is the opportunity created for attorneys involved in the creation of the Tax Reform Bill of 1986. As a 1986 article in the *Legal Times* pointed out, merely "having worked in this particular tax bill (did not) necessarily make lawyers on Capitol Hill and in the treasury better catches for tax practices in . . . firms" once the law was down for every one to see. It is not strict grasp of the substantive law, but the willingness to come alive to all the ramifications of their work, that gave these attorneys real opportunities. Constantly interacting with the corporate and other special interest groups that come before them, government lawyers do more than meet possible future clients. It is true that maintaining visibility allows them, as one lawyer put it, "to cut the best deal you can while people know who you are." However, the tax lawyers who speak at trade association meetings or professional conventions have the chance to follow the impact of their work out into the world. They not only find jobs that are an obvious outgrowth of their current work, they may learn of jobs just beyond the periphery of the obvious.

There also are the middlemen, the merchants of all other sources of information concerning careers and jobs. Your humble servants most certainly included. As non-profits, they may be sponsored by associations or schools. As businesses, they may take many forms. Each has a specific mandate or purpose, but they share many features. To differing degrees, they can help with much of your work: Self-assessment, planning, research, and the location of employers. This is an obvious advantage to people who are pressed for time and in need of confidentiality. Now, a word about each.

Placement Offices

Never neglect your law school placement office in your investigations. Even recent graduates should be aware that many law schools have greatly expanded their services for alumni as well as for students, and that these services are constantly evolving. Indeed, some have begun to give serious consideration to entering the legal search business themselves, since they have unparalleled contacts and resources among employers.

Your law school placement office may have a graduate placement program offering a good deal more than informal advice. Some have well-organized computer-matching programs and regular job bulletins listing opportunities in a wide variety of fields. The staff specialist handling these services is a crossroads of information about alumni and employers, and is often in touch with his or her counterpart at other schools which maintain reciprocity. (For example, if you are an east coast graduate looking for jobs in the west, your school may be able to arrange for you to use the facilities at a western school's placement office.) If your school has a reputation for producing graduates who concentrate in some area such as state government, its graduate placement program may be richer in that specialty than is the roster of any headhunter.

Even the most informal contacts with your law school placement office can be helpful. Placement directors and counselors are constant recipients of gossip about the hiring needs, at all levels, of their client employers. Over the years they accumulate personal databases of esoteric information about unusual employers or graduates who are especially helpful contacts. Through placement offices you may reach student groups that maintain their own information such as lists of alumni willing to advise on employment matters. (For instance, the Harvard Black Law Students' Association has published a *Directory of Black Alumni/ae* indexed by geography and specialty.) For that matter, your school's alumni association can not only provide you with directories but may also put you in touch with alumni willing to do some informal placement. Faculty can also fill this function. Indeed, some seem to run their own informal placement service.

Your undergraduate placement office can also be a rewarding source of information. This is certainly so if you are facing a radical career change. But, even if you are pursuing law-related jobs, an undergraduate placement office will have a broader base of information on non-legal employers. Graduate schools of business and public administration are similar in providing services and information not available in law schools.

Employer Data Banks

Through your placement office, or ads in journals, you may discover a variety of employer data banks which, for a fee, will give you access to job listings or more general information about employers. This is a growing field with a growing spectrum of players. Some resume-mailing services are also able to search their mailing lists by employer category. Private placement agencies and legal search consultants sometimes have expanded the capacities of their information systems to provide general as well as specific job information. The American Trial Lawyers' Association has put together a job bank based on its membership information. Obviously, all of these systems are only as good as the information that they contain. If careful scrutiny satisfies you that the information base is relevant to your search, then such a system can be tremendously helpful.

Legal Search Consultants

Naturally, legal search and placement consultants have a major interest in placing you quickly and, from their standpoint, efficiently. At the worst, with very little input or overhead, they function merely as resume brokers. At their professional best, they are a source of counsel and information transcending their particular function. Many of them can augment your search with an excellent grasp of economic and professional developments within their own geographic area. Furthermore, they are veritable wailing walls of lawyer dissatisfaction, collecting much information about conditions at many local firms. This information may be limited to the natural selection that brings clients to their door, but it is information hard to come by through other channels.

Of course, their employer universe comprises clients that are large or affluent enough to pay to retain them. But, within this range they will have a very good idea of how you compare with others seeking similar jobs.

Their perception of your marketability is affected by their understandable preference for easy searches and instantly placeable lawyers. One of them recently described his greatest challenges as (1) partners with competence but no clients, (2) overly-ripe associates, (3) senior partners looking for a cap to their careers, and (4) those without credentials looking for an internship to upgrade their resumes. This is discouraging if you fall into any of these categories. On the other hand, you can count on getting a frank assessment of the odds against you in the current market, which has at least the value of keeping you from false starts down foreclosed paths.

How can you judge the quality of a legal search consultant, and further, ascertain if they are able to help you? *The American Lawyer's* national directory of headhunters is useful up to a point, particularly in describing the specialties of different consultants and in reporting their placement records when those have been made available. *Lawyers Weekly Publications* publishes *The Attorney's Guide to Executive Search* which lists the members of the National Association of Legal Search Consultants, an organization which takes seriously the necessity for professional standards and a code of ethics.

Beyond consulting these publications, you can rely on certain other guidelines. For one, you can be more assured when a consultant attempts to ascertain your needs and interests, and is candid and soberly realistic about your chances. If they also specialize in outplacement, human resources, and law firm management, the diversification in services may mean they are less dependent upon placing you at any cost and that they have a broader base of expertise. Some might also argue that if the headhunter is mostly a search consultant, operating on retainer, with an exclusivity agreement with employers, then their services will be somewhat more thorough and they will be less susceptible to the seductions of the quick-but-jerry-built placement. (You are warned that one of the authors has pioneered the legal retainer search industry. As with all advice and comment in this or any book, your own evaluation is important.)

In the last analysis, your best guarantee is your judgement of character, and your ability to detect professionalism in any service. If you have that kind of confidence in a search consultant, you should also take their suggestions seriously and at least follow the leads they recommend rather than rejecting them out of hand.

Organizational and Management Consultants

A growing number of management consultants, accountants, publishers, and personnel consultants are taking an interest in the legal profession. Their utility to the job searcher is probably limited to their publications, unless one has personal contacts among them. They are often a good source of information on recruitment and hiring, evaluation, salaries, and business policies among legal employees. With respect to non-legal employers they may be even more valuable. For instance, if you were interested in learning more about well-managed municipal governments in your state, a consultant in municipal government might be worth calling.

Career Counselors

We would like to think full use of this book precludes resort to career counseling. But we know better. Indeed, reading this book may have the opposite effect. It may make you want to sit down with someone to discuss its implications. Generally, the stock-in-trade of career counselors is personality and aptitude assessment, occupational information, and strategic planning. But their expertise is seldom equally distributed across these categories. Some excel in helping their clients to identify skills and clarify priorities; others are specialists on particular job markets.

In order to choose a career counselor effectively you must decide whether you need more information about yourself or about your alternatives. Career counselors with sophistication about the legal profession are hard to find, but do exist, especially in those centers where lawyers abound. Sometimes they can be located through law school placement offices or local bar associations. As we have said, some legal search consultants do career counseling.

A career counselor who is frank about his or her limitations can still be useful if you supply the missing expertise from other sources. Career counselors can also serve the important function of support and encouragement in what can, after all, be a pretty solitary and discouraging process, especially if they have organized support groups of other lawyers or professionals who are slogging through the job search odyssey. Job search support groups can also greatly extend your research web.

Libraries and their Contents, Including Librarians

Lawyers spend a large portion of their lives in libraries of one kind or another, yet seldom use this resource to their own advantage. And there are so many libraries available.

If large enough, your firm may well have a library worth a little extra attention. Law school libraries are an obvious place to begin a library search. Law school placement offices maintain career resource centers. Trade associations, corporations, and advocacy groups maintain their own collections. Professional associations have their libraries, as do law centers and think tanks. Nor should you underestimate public libraries. Large systems often have separate business reference collections which are especially rich in information on regional employers.

You would be foolish not to enlist the aid of librarians (i.e., information specialists) in your investigations. One of the authors was recently trying to track down information about the National Association of Black Broadcasters, about whom he had read in *Opportunities in Communications Law,* published by the National Association of Broadcasters. Not having handy a copy of the directory, he called the NAB and was referred to their reference librarian whose existence had gone unsuspected. This godsend provided the requested information and a dozen unsolicited leads as well, including the fact that the association shares a building with a venture capital company specializing in seed money for black-owned television enterprises.

Librarians, archivists, and researchers are often this pro-active and generous. Many libraries have reference specialists who are knowledgeable in certain fields or in conducting specialty searches. When you are in doubt as to how to structure your research, their help can be invaluable.

A perusal of our Resources Chapter should remind you of the multitude of books, directories, manuals, journals, newspapers, newsletters, and catalogues to be found in any library. This material ranges from the raw to the predigested. You must avoid, however, becoming mesmerized by the "directory mentality," flipping endlessly through the pages of *Martindale-Hubbell.* (For the true aficionado there is the *Directory of Directories,* published by Gale Research Company, which is organized by a vast number of fields.)

Using reference publications will be especially fruitful if you are a bit creative and follow what we call a constituency, or client-centered approach. For instance, you might work backward from transactional records or client lists in search of the lawyers who service them. Two very obvious examples of references designed for this approach are *The Corporate Connection,* which lists major U.S. corporations and their outside counsel, and *Washington Representative,* which lists the law firms and lobbyists of many industries, interest groups and countries. Other sources may lead you through less direct connections to even more useful lists. U.S. government publications such as the *Commerce Business Daily* or *Consultants and Contractors: A survey of the Governments' Purchase of Outside Services,* not only tell you where government business is going, they also classify the recipients of that business by region and type of contract.

Thus, if you were interested in a corporate counsel position in the electronics industry in the Boston area, you might go to a regional industry list in the *Directory of Corporate Counsel.* But that strategy would not be helpful if you also wished to avoid working for an employer that relied heavily on defense contracts. By consulting the *Commerce Business Daily* initially, you could identify the most frequent recipients of non-defense contracts, after which you could look up their corporate counsel. With increasing ingenuity, this kind of research becomes detective work.

Computer Based Information Systems

Tools for creative research often at hand, but seldom used in this fashion, are the computer-based legal research systems such as *Westlaw, Lexis,* and its business counterpart, *Nexis.* These systems can be used, for example, to search out firms, clients, and attorneys involved in litigation in almost any substantive area. Thus, one might obtain the names and firms of toxic torts litigators obtaining verdicts in any jurisdiction of interest. Use of a system like *Nexis,* which comprises a huge collection of legal, general, and business periodicals, would then provide considerable contextual information on those cases. It may not always be necessary to use a sledge hammer computer to swat a single fly of information, but the obvious advantage of a computer search is its comprehensiveness and speed.

The Ultimate Research Tool

While extolling the virtues of high technology we should include the telephone, the most flexible, magical instrument ever invented for the gratification of human curiosity. Generally, lawyers wield a powerful telephone. So, here again is a professional skill that can be used on your own behalf. If we seem to be laboring the point, consider the following true life example. It not only shows the telephone at its best, but portrays good use of other research tools as well.

Suppose that you were working in a large firm on the east coast but interested in moving to the west coast. Moreover, within the corporate department you have gravitated toward the high tech part of their practice. Now, you are more interested in a smaller, boutique firm specializing in high tech and concentrating on start ups and venture capital funded enterprises. Where are they on the west coast?

Browsing in your firm library, or flipping through the pages of a book catalogue, you come upon Richard D. Harroch's *Start-up Companies: Planning, Financing, and Operating the Successful Business.* Reading this book will turn up many nuggets useful to a job search, but the catalogue listing is already helpful. For in it you learn that Mr. Harroch is with the San Francisco firm of Orrick, Herrington and Sutcliffe. You decide to give Mr. Harroch a call. That gentleman, not having been too badgered with requests for information in the past week, is able to spend a few minutes chatting with you during which he quite reasonably suggests you read his book.

However, Mr. Harroch concedes that listings of law firms involved with venture capitalists in the high tech field are a little harder to come up with. He shares with you those firms he knows from personal knowledge, and that's it.

But wait, it strikes him that he has seen in the directory of the American Electronics Association a list of associate members who are mostly law firms of this description. Thanking him, you hang up and head for the *Encyclopedia of Associations,* which informs you that the American Electronics Association is a substantial organization representing a big segment of the electronic components industry. Not only does it publish a directory and other useful documents, it has a standing lawyers' committee.

Picking up the phone again, you are soon chatting with a very helpful attorney at the AEA who directs you to any number of employers exactly fitting your criteria. Since their directory costs a hundred and twenty five dollars, you put back your checkbook and go to the nearest engineering library to duplicate the relevant pages.

All of the above actually happened through the miraculous agency of the telephone. More than any computer search, doing your own hunt by phone enables you to capitalize on fortuitous discoveries. The interaction of two minds at each end of the line can strike sparks—and deals.

The Information Most Difficult to Obtain

So much for sources. The telephone takes you to the edge of the known world. As we have said, you will be looking for certain types of information dictated by your ideal job description. There are numerous publications concerning the profession, considerable technical and general material concerning specialties, and a growing collection of employer descriptions. Unfortunately, the type of information most critical to many is much less well-documented and tantalizingly illusive.

We are referring to meaningful practice descriptions, living pictures of how different practitioners pursue their goals, the competencies they develop, and the satisfactions they experience. Something like this emerges from some specialty descriptions, but they tend not to be dynamic.

Legal digests and firm resumes sometimes help. Often informal job descriptions—more in the form of personal portraits—are found in association journals or newsletters. Excellent examples from diverse areas are the journal of the American Corporate Counsel Association and the newsletter of Trial Lawyers for Public Interest. Both are in the habit of sketching practice areas or the work and careers of interesting individuals in their membership. The sometimes maligned legal newspapers do portray the economic and human dimensions of various practices. Sometimes reliably. They also cover evanescent developments that may be critical to the timing of your job search.

In the end, there is probably no substitute for informational interviewing which at this level requires conversations with trained lawyers performing at the design and management levels of practice. You will have contrived to do some of this through the kinds of networking described above, but, unfortunately, access to many gurus is sometimes available only through job interviews. Your research will thus continue "on the battlefield," so you should plan a portion of your job interviews to be primarily informational.

To supplement your own research, we offer the following listing of potential employers which was developed by NALP:

Employers of Lawyers

Accounting Firms
Advertising Agencies
Banks

Community Organizations
Consulting Firms
Corporations
Educational Institutions
Entertainment Industry
Federal Government
Hospitals
Insurance Industry
International Trade
Investment Banks
Labor Unions
Law Firms
Libraries
Lobbying Organizations
Local Governments
Military
Nonprofit Organizations
Political Organizations
Prepaid Legal Plans
Private Foundations
Public Interest Agencies
Publishing Houses
Real Estate Developers
State Bar Associations
State Government
Trade Associations
Transit Companies
Trust Companies
Various Small Businesses

BATTLE PLANS

Once you have determined employers who will provide the experiences and training you need to move toward your career goals, you need to list them and then convince one or more of them to offer you a position. Many lawyers seeking new opportunities view this as an unpleasant obstacle. It need not be. Remember that the process is virtually identical to selling an appellate panel on your client's position, involving both written and oral arguments. Your ability in advancing you own case is good evidence of your ability to advance a client's case.

Having collated the fruits of your researches in a divisional notebook or a series of files, you should prepare the working documentation necessary to a good job search.

This will mean compiling a job prospect or employer list and assembling what we call your Lawyer Portfolio and what we address in the next Chapter.

Prospective Employer Lists

List perhaps twenty employers you have targeted for different purposes. Your target list should be fleshed out to include all data you will need to avoid later scrambling or embarrassment: names, addresses, phone numbers, contact individuals, key hiring-influence people, etc.

Rate the potential employers as best you can, before direct contact, on the basis of two criteria: desirability in light of your goals and the likelihood (to the extent you can estimate it) that you would be hired. Then divide your list into three categories, say A, B, and C. All on the A list should be contacted before any B's or C's are approached. From such contacts, however, you may well generate new leads or may gain information that causes you to re-evaluate the initial ratings you gave to one or more employers.

Once you have armed yourself with your Lawyer Portfolio, you will be ready to exchange information with those on your priority list and let each of you evaluate the other. It is often best to give yourself a schedule. For example:

1/15—1/18 Send Portfolio to A group.

1/22—1/25 Follow up with a phone call.

1/26—1/31 Schedule interviews. Reassess priority list. Decide whether to send Portfolio to B group.

You must take pains that your cover letter introducing yourself and transmitting your Portfolio is appropriate for all recipients. If it is not, create individual letters for all addressees that need them. The cover letter should contain a few arresting statements to secure attention, but should not be your autobiography. Your Portfolio carries the burden of your argument—as the next Chapter illustrates.

Chapter

10

Your Lawyer Portfolio: Taking Pen in Hand

"Write the vision, and make it plain upon tables . . . "
Habakkuk 2:2

The creation of a well organized and concise, yet thorough, professional Portfolio will get you off on the right foot with any potential employer. Keep in mind that a Portfolio (even if only a resume) does much more than merely convey skeletal data about yourself. It also conveys a very fleshy statement about your abilities at information accumulation, organization, and presentation, and about your talents at persuasion. How you present yourself can be more important than the facts you present.

A well-constructed Portfolio will parallel an employer's decision criteria and will also address your own agenda. In form, it will permit each individual who receives it (e.g., multiple lawyers at a single employer) to find quickly the information that he or she considers key. While there are always exceptional cases, we have found that a four part Portfolio, when skillfully constructed, lets you meet all of these goals. Specifically, we advise supplying the following items to any potential employer (although different versions may be desirable for different potential employers):

1. **Overview Resume**
2. **Statement of Specific Experiences and Skills**
3. **Work Evaluations**
4. **Work Product**

For experienced lawyers wanting to demonstrate their future value to a firm and for lawyers asking an employer to venture into something new, a fifth item is desirable:

5. **Business Plan**

(Business planning is discussed in Appendix G.)

Working together, these items can let you address the employer's agenda:

- What have you done for someone else?
- What can you do for me?

as well as your own:

- Here is what I like and know how to do.
- Here is how my experience is relevant to you.
- Here is how you will benefit as I acquire new skills.

The Overview Resume. We recommend that the Overview Resume start with a maximum of two-thirds of a page of credentials including (a) academic chronology and highlights and (b) employers and positions.

For experienced lawyers, the most important part of the Overview Resume will be the description of prior legal work experience. Convert you Career Matrix analysis (Exercise 12 of Chapter 7)

SAMPLE RESUME

Oliver Wendell Brandeis, Jr.
1234 S. First Street
Megalopolis, Illinois 11111

Home Phone:	312-999-1111
Work Phone:	312-263-0033

Academic Experience

1984	Goode Law School, J.D. Upper 20% of class LSAT 675 Note Editor, Journal of Health Law
1981	ESU, A.B. 3.3/4.0 Political Science Major Active in campus politics Catcher, Javelin Team

Vocational Experience

1985-87	Filla & Buster Associate, corporate law
1984-85	Clerk Judge Rudolph Hardass
1983	Filla & Buster Summer clerk
1976-82	Various jobs to finance education

Work Content

During the three years at Filla & Buster, in 60% of my work I have represented companies and associations in manifold corporate matters including acquisition evaluation and government regulation compliance. In this work, my role was ____

____

Of that 60%, about half of the time was spent for clients that were hospitals, HMO's, or group practices.

The remaining 40% of my time was spent on assessing potential tort litigation against corporate and association clients. My role was ____

____

My year of clerkship involved legal research and draft opinion writing in a wide variety of legal matters, about 80% civil and 20% criminal. Contractual matters were the most common cases before my judge.

Objective

My objective is to broaden and deepen the services I can render to Health Care Industry clients. I have further developed a pre-existing natural rapport with physicians and health care administrators and find working with them stimulating and mutually rewarding. I would like to expand my experience to include intellectual property counseling and exploitation.

into concise language that will be meaningful to another experienced lawyer. Describe lengths of time, percentages of work, practice areas, client and industry types, settings, roles, and responsibilities.

There remains substantial debate among career counselors as to the inclusion of an Objective section in a resume. There are two arguments against including them. First, it is hard to develop solid, meaningful content. Bromides, platitudes, and "motherhood" are too often the result. Second, any statement of specificity can be the basis for exclusion from consideration. On the other hand, a statement of desired experiences can suggest maturity and purpose and can focus both parties on the substance of the position under consideration. On balance, we think that the advantages of including objectives outweigh the disadvantages, particularly when the resume results from the type of career assessment and planning procedures that this book, we trust, will have forced upon you.

Statement of Specific Experiences and Skills. This document will expand upon the experiences described in your Overview Resume by describing actual cases, deals, and transactions, your roles in those matters, the types of clients involved, the services performed, and the setting. Your goal is to describe to an informed professional reader the specifics of your experience and competence. Where possible, tie these illustrations back to the Overview Resume. In addition to the sample below, additional samples are found in Appendix E.

Oliver Wendell Brandeis, Jr.
Statement of Specific
Experiences and Skills

HMO Merger

I served in a second chair capacity in advising a major HMO client on all phases of a merger with another large HMO. The work included the analysis of employee benefits of both firms, antitrust considerations, extensive discussions with administrators at both firms regarding organizational and legal goals and alternative ways of achieving them, drafting of various documents to effect the merger, and managing the closing.

Entrepreneur Seed Funding

With the permission of our hospital client, we represented a physician affiliated with the hospital in obtaining seed capital from a private source to finance research and development efforts on an improved intravenous fluid supply system. My role was largely confined to research on use of intellectual property as security for debt and as adequate contribution to capital by the physician.

* * *

Work Evaluations. All potential employers would like to hear what previous employers have to say about a candidate. For experienced lawyers interested in changing positions, there is the delicate matter of whether or not to inform your current employer of your plans and at what point in the process to do so. Many people in this position are reluctant to authorize contact with their current employer until rather far down the road to an offer-in-hand.

The potential employer's needs can be partially met, however, by offering written statements of evaluations that you have received. Somewhat like a warranty in a contract, you are telling the potential employer, "I know that you will want to speak with past employers at some point, in the meantime, here is what you will hear when you do so."

In almost all jobs there are official annual reviews, sometimes official semi-annual reviews, official two or three year review points with respect to partnership, and a host of unofficial feedback or commentary from superiors, colleagues, clients, and others on the quality of one's work. These reviews and evaluations are the equivalent of law school grades, except that they are more pertinent. More pertinent because they are more recent and because they grade your performance as a lawyer rather than as a law student. Additional samples are provided in Appendix F.

Oliver Wendell Brandeis, Jr.
Work Evaluations

1. I received a superior grade in my formal annual review for each of the three years I have been with Filla & Buster. Manfred Dorkkinger, Chairman of the Associates Committee, has told me that I am "very bright, hard working, excellent at organizing and writing about complex legal and factual issues, and that I have the ability to see a situation from a variety of perspectives, most importantly, the one most practical in the eyes of the client." Referring to the Chairman's renown as a lawyer (I assume), I have overheard others in the firm referring to me as "a little Dorkkinger".

2. While a clerk for Superior Court Judge Rudolph Hardass, he told me that I am an "independent and creative thinker and have a deep sense of concern for others, including my coworkers and support staff." (I assume that Judge Hardass intended this as complimentary.)

* * *

Representative Work Products. As compared to a law student, a lawyer seeking a new position is fortunate in being able to demonstrate the quality of his work through written work products. This is not just a "writing sample". Rather, it is a representative sample of prior legal work. Work such as objective writing, argumentative writing, analysis, strategy, communications to clients, etc.

All samples should either be purely your own analysis, organization, and language, or should include careful explanations of the contributions of others to the finished product.

Naturally, it is also important to protect the confidentiality of the work product. In most cases, the writing will have resulted from addressing the real problems of real clients. Unless in a public document (e.g., a brief filed in court), obliteration of names and other material may be required and should be done with care. Not only do you owe that to the client, but your potential employer may tag you as sloppy if you slip up.

Keep in mind that non-client materials may be of value in demonstrating your talent. "Work-Product" should be broadly interpreted to include thoughtful writing on management, organization, and business development issues, as well as on non-legal subjects (e.g., the annual report of a charity or club).

The Complete Package. For the best impression, as well as to be sure that all reviewers see all of your Portfolio, the materials should be tab-indexed in a thin, easily handled binder.

With your research-produced list of potential employers and your written argument (Lawyer Portfolio) in hand, you are ready to proceed to oral argument . . . the Interview, and the subject of Chapter 11.

Chapter

11

Interviewing: Taking Action

"A soft answer turneth away wrath . . . "
Proverbs 15:1

You may have been through a lot since law school, but we doubt you've done much interviewing since that third year frenzy. You probably haven't had to change a flat tire recently either, although you've done it before. Interviewing is like that, one of life's experiences for which we are always a little unprepared.

Moreover, even if still a young, relatively inexperienced attorney, you face something different from an entry-level interview. As with the resume, you must pay much more attention to presenting your legal work experience and yourself in a way which parallels employers' hiring criteria. Your position at the employment "bargaining table" is improved to the extent that you have a broader background of knowledge and experience. On the other hand, the longer your track record, the more likely it is that it contains liabilities as well as assets. To that extent, you have a heavier burden of explanation and interpretation. As years go by it gets harder, alas, to rely on the glow of your potential.

Employer Concerns

In general, four factors will always be important to employers, though each may weigh them differently. Each will be asking:

1. *What can you do for us?* To any employer this is the most important issue. In some cases the requirements will be virtually codified, in others the employer will be almost challenging you to write your own job description.

2. *Can we afford you?* This question is the mirror image to your own, "Can I afford to work for this employer?" If you have realistic expectations for yourself and an informed understanding of the employer's constraints, you will not be wasting anyone's time and will be able to bargain for an attainable arrangement.

3. *Are you a long-term resource?* You will need to fit in with their scheme of organizational and professional development, unless you are being considered for a short term role (which is not always easy to determine).

4. *Will we and our clients enjoy working with you?* The answer to this question may hang on anything from sports preferences to political ideology, but it accounts for an intangible social tension that pervades every interview, no matter what emphasis on credentials is articulated.

Employer Characteristics

The employers you have chosen and their immediate requirements determine just how these concerns get played out in interviewing. Obviously, your interviews will be wasted if you haven't learned as much as you can about the employer. Here, we just remind you of some basic characteristics of law firm, business, and government employers which cause them to approach interviews differently. Some of these points we have raised previously, some you will be aware of through your own investigations.

Law Firms. Whether a large firm can afford you and successfully insert you into their hierarchy depends upon your degree of seniority and its impact on their compensation and promotion policies. Which is, of course, one reason why third year associates are traditionally considered a "best buy." The mid-1980's explosion in new associates' salaries in some of the large firms created additional pressure on laterals and mid-level associates, not to mention partners, especially if there hasn't been sufficient business growth. Partners, who are loathe to give up the rate of compensation to which they have become accustomed, are inclined to put a cap on salaries down the scale.

Smaller firms in the process of becoming larger ones often control their overhead through salaries, since there is not much they can do about the rent on the plush new offices in the high-rise. On the other hand, stable small firms whose clients are by no means as affluent as those of some of the more "prestigious" practices may have so little overhead as to be surprisingly lucrative and to be able to provide surprisingly attractive compensation prospects. When you consider that some firms provide enough flexibility to permit participation in other paid pursuits, and that the cost of living varies in different cities, you may be able to afford them more than you think.

If a law firm is facing steady expansion, their interest in your long term potential will be obvious. If they are deliberately hiring to handle a temporary surge in workload, with no future guarantees, you can decide if it is worth the chance. Sometimes, however, a firm will advertise for "temporary help" as if it were looking for long term additions, either duplicitously or because they have deluded themselves into believing there will be more work down the road.

For instance, if a firm is looking for experienced attorneys to staff a weak or new department, or a branch office, it is important to determine whether they have the business to survive. You may be in danger of being hired to sail down a minor tributary that will dry up. Despite their optimistic assurances, they may need more of a rainmaker than you are capable of being. In interviewing, therefore, you should talk to troops in the trenches (other associates) to see if they have any confidence in reaching where the generals believe they are going. Of course, like many weary foot soldiers, they may have no idea. Then you will have to pay more attention to how partners from other departments regard the department you are considering.

A firm's interest in your long term potential is also affected by its size—the smaller the firm the more its members hang together or hang separately. A hire in this setting may mean that your immediate competence is vital. The more specialized the work or narrow the client base, the more they need to trust your competence and the more you need to trust their business prospects. If the firm is a small one looking for an experienced person to fill a niche in a tribe that is all chiefs and no braves, the partnership decision is almost synonymous with the hire. All of which makes their decision doubly critical.

A law firm's prevailing culture obviously affects whether they will find you likeable, much less promotable. True, the only dominant value at some big firms is sheer technical skill underscored by law school attended and grades achieved, criteria they will apply to even highly experienced attorneys. Some large firms seem to consider their associates to be like jewels in a Swiss watch, remarkable for their quality, uniformity, and durability.

Big firms, however, can display very distinct cultures. An excellent example would be Latham and Watkins, featured in a 1986 article in *The American Lawyer,* in which the firm is described as not just a firm but "a place of worship." One of their associates is quoted as saying Latham "offers a very different package for a young associate . . . I have a proprietary feeling about the firm. I feel like it is my firm. It took me six months to say 'we' at Cravath and it took me about six hours here."

The homogeneity and self-image of smaller firms can be equally intense, since some of them restrict their growth in order to remain "just a small circle of friends." Traits they may seek over others are flexibility and the ability to cooperate, since their functioning requires everyone to be a pinch hitter and utility fielder. Then again, some small firms may be virtually office-sharing arrangements for highly individual entrepreneurs, looking for someone willing to function independently.

Corporations. As you may have gathered from Chapter 4, compared to law firms corporate employers interview with rather different concerns. Business knowledge, managerial and interpersonal skills, the ability to get along with colleagues over the long term, and the ability to identify with corporate goals may be as important as legal expertise. This is especially so with respect to non-legal jobs in business. Some businesses, such as consulting and investment banking, will also put a premium on the parts of your legal experience which have fostered vigorous analytical skills. Your long term prospects in a corporate legal department are affected not only by the department's relationship to its client (corporate management), but by the corporation's economic health in general.

Government. The concerns of government in hiring are so varied and complex as to defy generalization. This variety is often expressed in such detailed job and qualifications specifications that interviewing seems irrelevant. That said, many other, highly non-objective criteria come to play in the more obviously political jobs such as legislative positions. Your fit with the employer culture in this case is going to be more of an ideological litmus test. Other desired traits are similar to those in private corporations: administrative, teamwork, and interpersonal skills, all of which bear on your ability to make the system work for you. Your long term prospects will often be hinged to funding, the equivalent of private sector business success.

The Interviewers

To be frank, our appellate model of interviewing has its limitations. Although your aim is to be persuasive, the means will be far more varied than those encompassed by courtroom technique. The style and expectations of interviewers are less consistent than those of judges. Moreover, interviewing is a two way street: you are trying to learn as well as teach. At times you will be interviewing them as much as they are interviewing you. At times they will seem like clients or colleagues requesting a consultation. Like judges, however, they may come on either like Mr. Rodgers or the Spanish Inquisition or, worse, both.

Interviewers are also unlike judges in that they probably exhibit a wider range of competence, although we won't argue this point too aggressively. On the one hand, you may fall into the hands of clumsy, bored, or indifferent interviewers who will need to be helped toward a useful understanding of your virtues. On the other, you may encounter highly skillful interviewers who combine the cunning of cross examiners with the sophistication of personnel consultants.

Jeanne Svikhart, an experienced interviewer who counsels firms on technique, offers this synopsis of good interviewers' methods:

- They will often focus on your *choices*, thus learning more about your values and priorities.
- They will ask about *transitions* between phases of your life, thus learning how you managed your choices.
- They will be most interested in your *recent experiences* and will closely scrutinize your motivation for moving on.
- They will want to know about the *expectations* you had at different stages of your career and whether you consider them met.
- They will want to hear you describe *problems you have solved* and why you are proud of your achievements.

- They will be as interested in your *self-appraisal* as much as third party evaluations of your performance.

In Appendix H you'll find a list of specific questions you may face in interviewing. In Appendix I we have reproduced the categories in which one firm rates its younger lawyers. Appendix I, should help prepare you for the dimensions in which an interviewer is likely to be sizing you up.

You may detect in these methods an approach reminiscent of the exercises you completed in Chapters 6 and 7. In fact, the good interviewer's purpose is the same as yours in self-assessment—to thoroughly understand what makes you tick. As an interviewee your object is to make sure that what they understand meets their criteria. The practical importance of your self-assessment becomes increasingly apparent —it parallels the methods of good interviewers and it increases the likelihood of a match between your background and the employer's requirements. If you have done all of your homework in assessing yourself and in finding an employer that is a good fit to your talents and needs, an honest self-presentation should be your best strategy. Honest, but not naive. The approach we shall recommend might be called "managed candor," coupled with some common sense techniques for putting your best foot forward.

The Interview

"Sit up straight — don't fidget — a firm handshake — don't forget to say 'thank you'. " Beginning with our mothers, we are bombarded with advice on how to "win friends and influence people". No doubt your mother may still have some tips for you, but we hope you will supplement such sound general advice with the following specifics.

Projecting a Coherent, Attractive Image

We might have said "confident" rather than "coherent". But we meant something broader, which encompasses an impression of confidence. The interview is no place to appear fragmented or ambivalent about yourself or your career, whether you feel that way or not. As mentioned in our discussion on planning, you will probably reach the interviewing stage still having unresolved questions, some of which can even be voiced in the interview. However, you must take care that you don't sound vague and confused. If you do express uncertainty, it should sound purposeful. In other words, you have to ask directions without sounding lost. This is done by raising questions thoughtfully, indicating you have some idea of the possible answers, and suggesting you have some preference between them.

"I always wear my lucky hat for job interviews."

Whether you convey an image of hot pursuit or of thoughtful quandary, you will also need to project energy. You needn't wave your arms or grind your teeth, but you have to look lively. Maybe "lively" isn't part of your self-image. If so, we are not suggesting that you do anything so fatal as putting on a party hat and pretending to be what you are not. We are referring to the necessity for "projection" in the sense of that term when applied to dramatics. Projecting a normal, conversational tone to the back row of the theater, an actor has to put a certain energy into speaking without shouting. And, to be seen, gestures have to be slightly exaggerated.

Similarly, in the interview you must give a slightly concentrated performance of yourself without seeming forced. Your excitement about the employer, if it exists, should be expressed in like fashion.

Physical appearance and dress do matter; less than we fear, but more than they should. It is best, therefore, especially if you have any doubt about the impression you make, to dress your best. Your soul may be more beautiful than your exterior, but even a very perceptive interviewer would need undivided attention to perceive this at the first meeting. There is no reason to allow dress and appearance to create a distraction from the other, more important factors you wish to present.

Styles of Communication

Interviewing lawyers have a tendency to lapse into an interrogatory/deposition mode of exchange, which is the death of spontaneity or any semblance of agreeable conversation. You will need to master the art of elaborating your answers, particularly to nudge talk in directions you wish it to go. Good interviewers will help you by asking "broad brush" questions which invite elaboration without much guidance from them. Your assessment of the diverse connections among your skills, interests, and values will enable you to broad brush right back, comfortably and convincingly.

Many people worry about assertiveness in the interview, wondering just what form it can take without overstepping often vague boundaries. At least three forms of assertiveness are at issue here.

The first has to do with evaluating your own work. Our unequivocal advice here is that the more genuinely proud you are of your work, and the more confident you are of its relevance to the employer's needs, the more serenely you should state your competence. You can do this because you needn't boast out of context; your abilities can be discussed, naturally, in connection with the employer's interests and activities.

The second deals with the problem of interviewers who provoke arguments, question your intentions or credentials, or simply prevent you from saying your piece. If they are obviously engaging in a stress interview, the rules of the game are clear, and you know you are supposed to fight back. Thus, if you truly question the propriety or relevance of a line of questioning, try turning it back on the interviewer by asking, "Why are you asking me this?"

When the interviewer's intent is less evident, the temptation is to be reticent or defensive when so much is at stake. At that point you must remember that there is no better defense than honesty, but your candor must adapt to circumstances and the temperament of the interviewer. If you feel compelled to disagree with an interviewer, perhaps because they have challenged a strong belief, then you should do so with rational restraint. The muting comes with the rationality and the care you take not to become too heated. You can say with quiet conviction that something is important to you. You should avoid pounding the desk or grabbing an interviewer by his tie.

The third form of assertiveness takes the form of your probing questions. Such questions can be asked in a non-accusatory manner implying that the employer is innocent until proven guilty. If you have first listened receptively to the interviewer's presentation and have indicated true interest, you can go on to suggest "there's much I like about you, but . . . " The tone is that you would like to make your way into the bosom of this wonderful organization, but there are a few obstacles to be resolved first. This approach is also effective when you have potentially debatable proposals or conditions; such as, "Could I work from noon to midnight?" (You chuckle? This is an actual proposal that was actually accepted.)

A Method for Getting Real Information

Your resume may not be the only document open to questions of superficiality. Consider the average firm resume. Specimens of this literary genre are to be taken with salt in multiple-grain quantities. They are often full of enthusiastic generalities that are difficult to decode and that require probing questions exceeding those discussed above.

For example, one Firm Resume says, "We are a dynamic firm serving a diverse client base, with the talents of young, aggressive associates and partners and the wisdom and experience of older partners . . . We are able to provide the necessary expertise for virtually all of our clients' needs." Such statements may be true, but how do you turn them into meaningful information about this firm as opposed to the spectrum of firms indulging in similar prose?

As you will have learned through networking, which is one of the best warm-ups for interviewing, asking questions about the interviewer's personal experience in his/her work is an effective way of penetrating the party line. It is as if you were an anthropologist dealing with what they call a "personal informant," someone who reveals the mysteries of the tribe through personal anecdotes.

Thus, if you are worried about putting in ungodly hours, you can get only so far asking what are the average billable hours of associates, or some such inquiry. Rather, while talking to your interviewer about his/her own work, you can ask when the last time was that he/she worked on a Sunday and what the occasion was. Answers to these questions will always be more vivid, and often more revealing.

Do not assume, by the way, that age peers are more truthful or more helpful. And an extra glass of wine at lunch can be as much your undoing as theirs.

However, as long as you are careful not to put the interviewer on the spot, these questions will at least establish rapport since you are expressing an interest in the interviewer personally. In taking this approach you will only be imitating your more skillful interviewers. And the more skillful your interviewer, the more likely the interviewer will be to recognize and appreciate the skill and perceptiveness you thus display.

Mixed Blessings (Like, Being Fired)

When answering questions about your liabilities, you must be candid. But you needn't go into the interview crying, "rotten meat for sale." Without sounding evasive, you must be brief and succinct, and then try to turn the conversation to something positive. In advance, you should have prepared explanations at different levels of specificity. If the interviewer wishes to pursue an issue you will have explanations at various levels to fall back on. You should smoothly acknowledge gaps in your skills or experience, but immediately put them in the context of those things that you do well while expressing your enthusiasm for learning new tricks.

If the liability relates to problems with your previous employer, including being fired, do not assume that the facts of the case will all be viewed negatively by the interviewer. Consider, for instance, Ruth, a third year associate "let go" after receiving a vehement negative vote from a senior partner with whom she had had chronic personality conflicts. She was not alone in the firm in having this problem, but she was the only associate who did, with predictable consequences.

In interviewing another firm, attractive to her for its real estate practice, Ruth found herself facing two interviewers, one male, one female. She liked both well enough, until the man said, with apparent relish and sincerity, "how about Smith [the obnoxious partner at the other firm], he's a wonderful guy, isn't he?" A long pause followed while Ruth struggled with a rising tide of dismay and uncertainty.

Having decided that unless she was candid she could well make a quick frying pan/fire transition, she was about to say what she thought of Smith, when the other partner interjected: "Really? I never thought that of him!" And she gave the interviewee an encouraging grin.

Ruth knew then that the truth could be in her favor. Since the friendly partner was the one from the real estate department, the prospects looked even better. Though some risk lingered, she went on to give an objective account of her problems at the other firm.

Before you can thus allow other people to give you the benefit of the doubt you must first have extended the same courtesy to yourself. If you have been fired, bluntly or insidiously, your self-esteem will have taken a beating no matter what your prior accomplishments or your inner core of confidence. Before interviewing you must work through the hurt and self doubt until they are expressed as normal regret and a sense of responsibility. You must also have rebuilt your self-esteem through conversations with supporters and deeds that remind you of your basic competency. Only then can you give a good account of yourself without flinching when faced with those inevitable questions. And remember, many a smug interviewer has been through a few unceremonious departures.

Bargaining

To modify the interviewer's verdict, a little bargaining usually helps. Remember, compared to your law school interviews you have both more assets and liabilities to bargain over. Whatever your rough edges, you would not apply for the job if you did not feel entitled to some consideration of your merits. Yet, the more radical the job shift, however logical it seems in the light of your self-assessment, the more you will have to bargain for the right to try your hand at something new.

The essence of bargaining, of course, is the quid pro quo. To get what you want you might first have to do what they want. In practice this means that you should have worked out before the interview the trade-offs you are able and willing to make. To gain experience in a new area of law, for instance, you may have to be willing to work with clients that are not your main interest. This might happen if you were trying to switch from litigation to corporate work and the new employer was willing to consider you because of your experience with certain clients gained through litigation. Or, you might be willing to relocate, hopefully not to the Baffin Island Office, for the opportunity. Whatever your concessions, you are looking for explicit assurance that in exchange you will eventually get the new experience you are seeking.

Besides new experience, another bargaining issue arises when the prospective employer is ambivalent about adding the function or specialty you represent especially if it seems to clash with their firm ethos. Since we have just been urging you to seek a good fit, you might be asking why you should now invite incongruity. The answer is that opportunities often exist where one can break new ground, and this may require some proselytizing.

Naturally, nothing overcomes resistance so much as bringing new clients, but this is not always so if your clients are perceived as Attila and other assorted Huns, or if the employer is otherwise uncertain about incorporating your type of practice. One strategy is to offer yourself as an independent profit center working out of the firm. If you can demonstrate that you are indeed profitable and your clients acceptable, they may well wish to consider incorporating you on a more regular basis. Variations on this theme are agreeing to a trial period or an "of counsel" arrangement. (The latter works best if you are a somewhat senior person whom the employer finds attractive but cannot comfortably "place" in the senior hierarchy).

These novel arrangements sometimes require novel forms of compensation. Thus you can work out an interim pay scale to fit your probationary or "of counsel" status, or you can devise various "payments in kind" involving office sharing or exchange of services. Flexible compensation schemes and provisional status are also bargaining chips when it comes to negotiating part-time employment. Since, in considering this issue, some employers are particularly nervous about the advancement issue, you can alleviate their fears by giving them a chance to know you better without too much pressure.

Postmortem

It is all over. On the elevator, afterward, you recall with a sinking sensation, not related to your descent, that you spoke disparagingly of the local sports teams to a partner with an autographed baseball prominently displayed on his desk. God knows what other gaffs you committed. You will think of them tonight while trying to fall asleep.

Experience will teach you that there is no point in becoming overly depressed, or overly elated, after an interview because it is very difficult to second guess the impression you have made. Interviews that are very affable and conclude on a pleasant note may come to nothing. Interviews that leave you limp with despair may result in an offer. Becoming fixated on your success in every interchange makes no sense, especially when you spent an afternoon interviewing everyone from the octogenarian partner to the office boy. These people may all compare notes of course, sometimes in a systematic way, so you must certainly be consistent. But you cannot, and should not, worry about each individual response to you. You do not know how input from each interviewer is weighted, and many may not even display their true reactions during the interview.

Keeping Your Perspective

Finally, this overview on interviewing: At times it will seem like a systematic exercise in rejection, something no sane person would willingly initiate. As important as it is, it cannot be survived without a sense of humor.

Consider the following anecdote from Arnold Kantor of when he was interviewing at law schools for Chicago's Sonnenschein, Carlin, Nath and Rosenthal:

> It was at the end of a long day at one of our nation's more prestigious schools. He had seen one radiant superstar after another, their accomplishments blending into one blaze of boredom. The next to last interviewee had been a towering individual who numbered among his many achievements having high jumped over seven feet in high school. Emerging from his interviewing office, Arnie spied the last applicant, one Jones, a small person in a three-piece suit and horned-rim glasses. In mock desperation, Arnie cried, "Jones, can you high jump seven feet? Because, if you can't I'm not even interested in talking to you!" Jones, without missing a beat, looked down at his loafers and said, "Not in these shoes, I can't." Of course, the story has a happy ending. Jones proceeded to Sonnenshein, where, reputedly, he leaped over all obstacles.

The moral, for interviewees and interviewers alike, is that the process cannot be allowed to become so grim that you lose all perspective and humanity.

Choosing Among Alternatives

Nonetheless, suppose that your wildest imaginings have materialized and through some combination of luck, native talent, and a thorough perusal of this book you have secured several job offers. What next? A useful tool in making your decision is to go back to your ideal and try to make meaningful comparisons among the options that you have, including the option (if it exists) of staying in your present situation. While intangibles will undoubtedly influence you, at least tabulate the pros and cons to assist with the decision making process. What better way to do this than returning to the Job Criteria Evaluation Scale (which we introduced as Exercise 1 in Chapter 3) and filling it out again for each of your options? For your convenience we provide it again here.

EXERCISE 1 (revisited)

Job Criteria Evaluation Scale

The twenty numbered phrases will be descriptive of your job to a greater or lesser extent. For each phrase circle the number that best corresponds to your feelings about the application of the phrase to your job. The number scale goes from zero ("Not at all") to 5 ("Very much").

Adding the scores for each of the 20 items will give a "score" for the job. The highest possible score (probably never reached by any real job) is 100.

1. Draws on my strengths.
   0 1 2 3 4 5 .... _____
2. Provides me with the training/experience I need.
   0 1 2 3 4 5 .... _____
3. Doesn't clash with the "real me".
   0 1 2 3 4 5 .... _____
4. Will not impede my long range development.
   0 1 2 3 4 5 .... _____
5. Provides my kind of intellectual stimulation.
   0 1 2 3 4 5 .... _____
6. Allows me to work in appealing areas of the law.
   0 1 2 3 4 5 .... _____
7. Meets my definition of social value.
   0 1 2 3 4 5 .... _____
8. Gives me the means to feel effective.
   0 1 2 3 4 5 .... _____
9. Will make me feel good when I tell others what I do.
   0 1 2 3 4 5 .... _____
10. Provides necessary and appropriate compensation.
    0 1 2 3 4 5 .... _____
11. Allows sufficient time and energy for a personal life.
    0 1 2 3 4 5 .... _____
12. Provides the company of people I enjoy.
    0 1 2 3 4 5 .... _____
13. Provides the right mix of formality and congeniality.
    0 1 2 3 4 5 .... _____
14. Meets my requirements for comfort and aesthetics.
    0 1 2 3 4 5 .... _____
15. Provides acceptable work facilities and staff support.
    0 1 2 3 4 5 .... _____
16. Provides reliable evaluation and review.
    0 1 2 3 4 5 .... _____
17. Is in the right geographical location.
    0 1 2 3 4 5 .... _____
18. Transportation to work is not a problem.
    0 1 2 3 4 5 .... _____
19. Provides a good mix of responsibility and supervision.
    0 1 2 3 4 5 .... _____
20. Provides participation in goal setting/management.
    0 1 2 3 4 5 .... _____

TOTAL SCORE _____

We suggest that you also take the time to discuss the options with all those who played a significant role in your first deliberations about a job change. Often, they can detect a departure from your original thinking or else agree that you are "only more confirmed in all that you knew."

Significant others will perhaps remind you of agendas in your personal life which you may be neglecting in your evaluation of options. Discuss the options with them and with non-lawyers for other points of view. Review your trade-offs, and recall our admonition while discussing planning, that most important objectives are accomplished partially and in sequence. All this done, bite your nails for a night, go for a long run or to a movie, then make your decision. Finally, give yourself permission to enjoy the fact that a decision has occurred. For better or worse.

Which brings your saga to an end . . . until the next time!

Communicating Your Decision

Once a decision has been made, it must be communicated to both your present employer and your future employer. Each communication deserves care and tact.

Be cautious in describing deficiencies in your present employer while explaining your decision to leave. Some firms and some individual supervisors honestly appreciate the constructive criticism uniquely available from departing employees. Others believe they do when they do not. Still others only see your departure as confirmation of their own exalted position in the scheme of things. It may be most tactful to emphasize the match between your special needs and the new employer's special features.

Your new employer will also appreciate your thoroughness in thinking through your decision. By being articulate in why you have decided to accept the offer, you will enhance your already positive image with your new employer. If it hasn't yet been arranged, it is appropriate to raise the question of a starting date and to suggest your own preferences, keeping in mind what is reasonable for the employer.

Looking Backwards and Forwards

Beginnings and endings are times of great delicacy and leverage. The good will and energy you show in assisting the transition of work-in-progress to others at your old employers' will not be quickly forgotten. Remember, that employer will always be a potential reference for any future career moves. Who knows, after you have achieved learning experiences elsewhere, you might even see your old employer as a new prospect. Law, like the rest of life, can be a circle game.

Chapter

12

Epilogue: Taking Leave

"Better is the end of a thing than the beginning thereof."
Ecclesiastes 7:8

If you have invested the effort that this book asks, you may approach your new job (or your old one if you decided to stay) with a new attitude. The self-awareness and directedness that you brought to a job search will retain an afterglow for some time, and perhaps forever. Ideally, assessment and planning are integral parts of existence and not quadraennial chores to be plowed through when your tolerance for a position wears thin.

Nothing is static; least of all a human psyche. Updating your self-awareness must be a high priority. But day-by-day updates would be enervating, confusing, and futile. Your birthday or New Year's Eve might be suitable trigger events to remind you to dust off your copy of *Lawyers In Transition,* to review the materials that you generated in doing the Exercises, and to ponder how far you have come and in what direction.

Oliver Cromwell once dissolved parliament with the immortal advice, "Gentlemen, we have sat here too long for the good that we have done, in God's name, let us go." Every book reaches a similar stage of diminishing returns—in both the writing and the reading.

This is, after all, a book in transition by authors in transition. In the course of our collaboration we have hatched new points of view, entertained endless—mostly valuable—suggestions, and wondered when to stop. In a fit of common sense, encouraged by the publisher, we decided to produce one book at a time, thus heeding our own advice that perfect solutions are reached in incremental steps. We rely on our readers in transition to use this book, and then to help us to transform it.

Write to us. (Care of the publisher, whose address appears in the copyright notice.) Tell us what else you might find helpful. Send anecdotes and advice—leave messages for those who come later. With luck, the next edition will be ready for your next transition.

Chapter

13

Resources: Taking A Look

"Hope deferred maketh the heart sick."
Proverbs 13:12

If you're at this point in the book, we hope that you are full of confidence and excitement over the prospect of taking some steps down a new (or at least a planned) career path. Don't stop now! A peek into this Resource Chapter may prompt you to set it aside for another day. That's all well and good but don't lose your momentum. Flip back and forth through the Chapter and get a feel for it. Review the Chapter Outline on page 130. While it may on first glance strike you as about as exciting to read as a Table of Authorities, a more careful look will reveal our purposes.

This Chapter is for those of you who are curious about some of the issues and trends, career paths, assessment tools and resources that we mentioned in the earlier Chapters. It is designed to give you the opportunity to take a deeper plunge into topics raised in the book. It's a guide to the many sources of information that are at your disposal as an individual about to take charge of planning your own career.

Don't be surprised if the clarity and confidence that you may feel as you approach this step wavers a bit as you begin to research new career options. That's only natural. It should be similar to the feeling you get when you move from having been given a research assignment to actually doing the research: Issues that once seemed clear now raise questions. Relax. Keep in mind that this is all part of the process. After immersing yourself in your research, paths and options will become clear again. And, we hope, you will once again feel the excitement of new possibilities unfolding before you.

The information that you will find here follows the basic outlines of the book as a whole. At the beginning of each new resource section you will find the Chapters in the book to which it pertains. This should facilitate moving from Chapters in the book to this Chapter and back again.

The Chapter is far more than a listing or compendium of resources. It's intended to be like a restaurant guide. While we haven't developed a rating system, whenever possible or practical we provide a summary evaluation of the resource and suggestions for its use. Information on how to obtain the source is also given. Many lists—of available positions, program requirements, firms that work in a certain practice area—are available for little or no expense. All that you need to do is drop a note (handwritten, if that's easiest) and a check in the mail, or pick up the phone and call.

For many resources you'll want to head to the placement office of your alma mater or to the careers section of your local public library. The Bar Association library and law school libraries are a source for much of this information, too.

You may find the Encyclopedia of Associations extremely useful but certainly not worth the expense to buy! You will find that often the placement office and the library both have a copy of these reference materials. As was stated in Chapter 9, placement offices have an enormous amount of good, general information for the job seeker. Your law school may have placement services particularly for alumni. In addition, law school placement offices usually have excellent information about local practice and career opportunities. Before setting off, you might find it useful to skim again pages 102 to 110 in Chapter 9.

If you are practicing law in a city far from your alma mater, often arrangements for access can easily be made with a local law school placement office. Call the placement office and speak to the director. Reciprocity between your school and a local one can often be arranged by a letter from your former school's placement office.

In keeping with the Preface of this book, USE this Chapter. You might want to go so far as to tear it out of the book and take it with you. And, while this certainly doesn't set forth everything that every reader would want or everything that exists, we've given you enough to get you well down the road to a new future. Bon voyage!

* * *

CHAPTER OUTLINE

* * *

THE STATE OF THE PROFESSION (Chapters 1 and 2)

General

Blodgett, Nancy. "Time and Money: A Look at Today's Lawyer." *ABA Journal,* 9/1/86, pp. 47-52.

Results of an ABA Journal study to determine the characteristics of the "typical" lawyer: male, 38 years old, earning close to $100,000 in business, personal injury or corporate law in an 8 person firm. Profiles five attorneys whose traits generally fit the pattern. Interesting, but don't be fooled into thinking that these are norms in the profession.

Curran, Barbara A. *The Lawyer Statistical Report: A Statistical Profile of the United States Legal Profession in the 1980s.* Chicago, IL: American Bar Foundation, 1985.

Statistics on the size, composition and geographic distribution of the legal profession in the early 1980s. Looks at changes in types of employment over time. Discusses differences in employment patterns between age groups, sexes and other characteristics. This might be useful to potential consultants to the legal profession or in terms of practice development planning.

Dembinski, Leslie A. & Frazier, Tracy R. *Legal Career Options 1988-89.* New Orleans, LA: Tulane Law School, 1988.

While a little basic in some areas, this provides nice profiles of different practice settings, opportunities from private practice to teaching and research, and descriptions of legal practice specialties. The cost of this version was not available at the time of printing. It should be no more than $5. Contact:

Tulane Law School
Office of Career Services
6325 Freret Street
New Orleans, LA 70118
(504) 865-5942

Flood, John A. *The Legal Profession in the United States.* 3rd Edition. Chicago, IL: American Bar Foundation, 1985.

An overview of what lawyers are doing professionally (i.e. practice areas), politically and socially. Analyzes the social organization of the profession. Also looks at legal education. Discusses changes in the profession. Has a good annotated bibliography. Again, might be useful for practice development. Could also help you in looking at what one can do with law.

Gibson, Dale & Baldwin, Janet K., Eds. *Law in a Cynical Society: Opinions and Law in the 1980's.* Calgary, Alta, Canada: Carswell Legal Publication, 1985.

A collection of studies on the perceptions of law and lawyers. Includes Barbara Curran's survey of what the public wants from the lawyer-client relationship. Good for raising issues that might be the basis for a partnership retreat or for better marketing strategies.

Hirsch, Ronald L. "Are You on Target?" *Barrister,* Winter, 1985, pp. 17-20.

Reports some of the results of the ABA Young Lawyers Division and the Board of Governors nation-wide survey of career satisfaction and dissatisfaction. Results indicate that 16% of all lawyers and 25% of junior associates and staff attorneys are dissatisfied. Again, the message from this is plan now for satisfaction over the course of your career.

Heinz, John P. & Laumann, Edward O. *Chicago Lawyers: The Social Structure of the Bar.* New York: Russell Sage Foundation, 1982.

A systematic analysis of the profession. Delineates the extent to which lawyers are channeled into areas of practice according to their social, economic, ethnic and religious origins and the standing of their law schools. Interesting but not immediately practical.

The Lawyer's Almanac. 8th Edition. New York: Prentice Hall Law & Business, 1988.

A goldmine of information and resources. Headings include: The Legal Profession (law firms, corporate counsel, compensation, etc.), The Judiciary, Government Departments and Agencies, Texts of Selected Statutes and Commonly Used Abbreviations. Includes trends in law school enrollments, law salaries, qualifications of judges, record locating information and the Declaration of Independence. Published biannually.

Lewin, Tamar. "Retaining Valued Attorneys." *The New York Times,* 5/29/84.

Discusses the trend to keep valuable, trained associates as senior attorneys or permanent associates.

Lhaman, Judith A. & Wrinn, David H. *Yale Law School Graduates at Work: A Selection of Legal Career Paths.* New Haven, CT: Yale Law School, 1987.

This is wonderful. It's a collection of the career path stories of Yale graduates. They each explain what they are doing, how they came to their current position and what about their work fascinates them. Extremely readable. Organized by contributors, professional settings and legal specialties. Available for $10 by contacting:

Office of Career Planning and Placement
Yale Law School
401A Yale Station
New Haven, CT 06520
(203) 432-1676

Matza, Michael. "The Paths Most Traveled By." *Student Lawyer*, May 1987, pp. 38-43.

An article summarizing the Career Paths Study (see below). Discusses rationale for looking at the classes of 1959 (Eisenhower), 1969 (Vietnam), 1974 (Watergate) and 1981 (Reagan). Profiles a lawyer from each class. Very interesting. Gives a sense of the breadth of paths and some of the determinative factors.

Munneke, Gary. *Opportunities in Law Careers.* Chicago, IL: National Textbook Co., 1986(1981).

This is a lively, well-written overview of what one can do with a law career. The areas covered include private practice, corporate counsel, teaching, government, public interest law and business careers. Also covers areas of law practice. This is geared to the person who is considering law (e.g. there are chapters on going to law school, etc.) but is a pleasant introduction to a variety of law careers.

National Association for Law Placement. *Employment Report and Salary Survey.* Washington, D.C.: NALP, 1987.

Data provided by responding law schools and graduates. Presented in table by region, sex and minority status. Often provides an overview with analysis and indications of trends. Starting salaries for graduating class is broken down by employer's location and type of practice. Very useful list of non-legal employment positions. Published annually. Available for $50 to non-members but most law school placement offices have a copy for reference. (202) 783-5171.

Singsen, Gerry. *Personal Legal Services: Problems and Possibilities in the Marketplace.* Harvard Law School Program on the Legal Profession, February, 1985.

A report on Services to the Poor and Middle Class. Discussion of the factors both within the profession and within the market that make servicing these populations difficult. Talks about pre-paid legal services, legal insurance and other trends.

Stewart, James B. *The Partners: Inside America's Most Powerful Law Firms.* New York: Simon & Schuster, 1983.

This is hot stuff. Stewart writes very well and is dealing with a fascinating subject. He seems to have really found his way to the inside of these powerful places and into the minds of these powerful people.

__________________ . *The Prosecutors: Inside the Offices of the Government's Most Powerful Lawyers.* New York: Simon & Shuster, 1987.

Another winner. Here we see the insides of the criminal justice system from the perspective of those charged with upholding it. He tells some wonderful stories: The investigation of Edwin Meese, the McDonnell-Douglas bribery case, insider trading investigations at Morgan Stanley. Great reading.

Vogt, Leona M. *From Law School to Career: Where Do Graduates Go and What Do They Do?* Harvard Law School Program on the Legal Profession, May 1986.

The Career Paths Study. A study of the career paths of graduates from seven Northeastern law schools. Develops a fascinating moving picture of the profession from how mobile law graduates are to what skills are most important to their work. Indicates that the first job out of law school may be the single most determining factor in terms of mobility. Average length of stay in first job: 2-5 years.

Wasserman, Steven & O'Brien, J.W., Eds. *Law and Legal Information Directory.* 4th Edition. Detroit, MI: Gale Research Co., 1986.

Wonderful compilation of information on law. Spans national and international organizations, bar association admission requirements, book publishers, CLE programs, awards, research centers, information systems, lawyer referral services and more. Good, basic information from a wide range of sources.

Zemans, Frances Kahn & Rosenblum, Victor G. *The Making of a Public Profession.* Chicago, IL: American Bar Foundation, 1981.

An in-depth study of the profession. Areas explored include entrance to the profession, specialization within the bar, career stability, professional status, skills and knowledge important to practice and the development of a sense of professional responsibility.

* * *

Minorities and Women in the Profession

Abramson, Jill. *"For Women Lawyers, An Uphill Struggle."* The New York Times Magazine. 3/6/88, p. 36.

Profiles of three women at Skadden, Arps who have struggled with the choices that a woman has to make between family and career. One is a young corporate partner who is planning to pursue a husband with as much aggression as she approached making partner. One is a litigation partner who has adopted two children without a husband. The third is a part-time associate who is no longer on partnership track because she wanted to have more time with her children. Also discusses women rainmakers. Fascinating.

Black Law Students Association-Harvard Law School. *Directory of Black Alumni/ae.* May, 1983.

A catalogue of the achievements of black alumni/ae of Harvard over the past twelve decades. For a copy, send $10 to:

Harvard Law School Alumni Center
Baker House
1587 Massachusetts Avenue
Cambridge, MA 02138.

Blodgett, Nancy. *"I Don't Think That Ladies Should Be Lawyers."* ABA Journal, 12/1/86, pp. 48-54.

Discusses issues of sexism in the courts, women's credibility and the ABA's positions on sex bias.

Chester, Ronald. *Unequal Access: Women Lawyers in a Changing America.* South Hadley, MA: Bergen & Garvey Publishers, 1985.

Profiles of women lawyers in the 1920's and 1930's in Washington, D.C., Boston and Chicago. Unprecedented numbers of women (albeit still very few) went to law school after World War I. Many ended up as legal secretaries. The message then, as now, seems to be that women need to be twice as good in order to get anywhere. This has a contemporary feel to it.

Couric, Emily, Ed. *Women Lawyers: Perspectives on Success.* New York: Law & Business, Inc. (Harcourt Brace Jovanovich), 1984.

A collection of case-histories of women lawyers in various stages of career and different areas of law. Sometimes hair-raising, often amazing and always inspiring stories of women who are going to make it.

Epstein, Cynthia Fuchs. *Women in Law.* New York: Basic Books, 1981.

A thoughtful study of women who moved into law in the 1960's and 1970's. Very interesting. Women in the beginning of the women's movement were often shunted into certain areas of law—often daddy's practice—or could only find law-related work. The Civil Rights Acts really made an impact on access for women. But, as we all know, the struggle ain't over yet.

Graham, Deborah. "It's Getting Better, Slowly." *ABA Journal,* 12/1/86, pp. 54-58.

Deals with the impact of women on leave policies, part-time employment and rain-making.

Lawyers for Alternative Work Schedules (LAWS) P.O. Box 956, Leesburg, Virginia 22075. (703) 777-7394.

This is an organization primarily of women all of whom are looking for viable ways to accommodate child raising and being a lawyer. Note that there is an Association of Part-Time Professionals in McLean, Virginia. Write to LAWS for their great bibliography listing articles and reports on child care, maternity leave and productivity in part-time employment.

Kanarek, Carol. "ABA Young Lawyers Survey: Maternity/Paternity Leave and Part-Time Work Policies." *Lawyer Hiring and Training Report,* Nov. 1984.

Report of a survey of 250 of the largest law firms regarding their policies. Might be helpful to determine to which firm one should go as a woman lawyer. Write or call Monica Patton for a copy. The issue will cost you $20 as a non-subscriber or $10 if you do subscribe.

LawLetters, Inc.
332 So. Michigan Avenue, Ste. 1460
Chicago, IL 60604
(312) 922-0722

New York State Task Force on Women in the Courts. Summary Report. New York: The Task Force, 1986.

The startling report on how the courts are biased against women as lawyers, witnesses, plaintiffs and defendants and jury members. This one was a real eye-opener for many. Similar studies have been done by NJ, RI, and AZ.

Rust, Mark E. "Why More Black Lawyers Aren't Recruited." *Student Lawyer,* April 1984, pp. 18-23.

An analysis of what's happening in recruiting blacks. Profiles of black partners and quotes from recruiting partners. Charts the numbers of minorities and women in the field.

Smith, Frederick F., Jr. "Are America's Law Firms Willing to Make Blacks Partners?" *Black Enterprise,* Nov. 1984, pp. 63-66.

Speculation about the effects of Hishon v. King & Spaulding in hiring and promoting blacks.

Sylvester, Kathleen. "Women Gaining, Blacks Fall Back." *The National Law Journal,* 5/21/84, p. 1.

An analysis of statistics from 92 of the 100 largest firms. Doesn't look great for either.

The Women's Bar Association of Massachusetts. *Report and Survey on Maternity/Paternity Leave, Part-Time Employment, and Related Subjects.* 1982.

Report on a study of law firms and public employers. Not much information was collected in this survey. This report is available from the Women's Bar of Mass. for $1.00. Unfortunately, they don't have an office. Information as to how to contact them can be obtained from the Massachusetts Bar Assn., (617) 542-3602. Check with your local Women's Bar Association for similar information.

Women's Law Association-Harvard Law School. *Employment Survey Directory.* June, 1985.

A survey of work and family policies in private and non-profit legal organizations in which some of Harvard's women students have worked. An analysis and summary of all respondents in addition to information presented on each organization. Somewhat limited in its scope. Check your local law school to see if they have a women's organization which has collected similar information.

* * *

ADULT DEVELOPMENT
(Chapter 5)

Baruch, Grace & Barnett, R. *Lifeprints: New Patterns of Love & Work for Today's Woman.* New York: New American Library, 1984.

A look at what all of the demands of our era have meant to the shape and substance of women's lives. Interesting reading. Really helps to look at how other women are dealing with the complex balancing act of their lives.

Cardozo, Arlene Rossen. *Sequencing: Having It All But Not All at Once.* New York: Atheneum, 1986.

This is one way to alleviate the pressure that career and child-bearing place women under. Yet, perhaps there is an underlying assumption here that all will work out when you have the time. Still useful for help with plotting future goals.

Erikson, Erik H. *Identity and the Life Cycle.* New York: Norton, 1980.

A classic. Erikson writes so well, too. This charts the major conflicts and struggles of the human being. Erikson is a little vague about women's development but it's truly worth reading by anyone interested in development.

Gilligan, Carol. *In a Different Voice: Psychological Theory and Women's Development.* Cambridge, MA: Harvard University Press, 1982.

A former dean at Fordham University School of Law gave this to women students who felt out of place in the system. A beautiful book. Since most developmental theory is based upon men, this is an important book for women. Also particularly good for lawyers because it deals with the concept of justice and what it means.

Grieff, Barrie S., M.D. & Munter, Preston, K., M.D. *Tradeoffs: Executive, Family and Organizational Life.* New York: New American Library, 1981 (1980).

A sensible, thoughtful guide to the complex tradeoffs professionals make. The case studies add personal interest and spice. The section on dual-career marriages is very good.

Levinson, Daniel J., et al. *The Seasons of a Man's Life.* New York: Ballantine Books, 1979.

Despite the title, this is not for men only. A thoughtful book about the movement of life.

Sheehy, Gail. *Passages.* New York: Bantam Books, 1977.

The popular classic. Combines Levinson's and Erikson's work in an engaging way. This really can give you a sense of the magnificence and possibility of the lifespan. Inspiring.

* * *

SELF-ASSESSMENT
(Chapters 6, 7, and 8)

On Your Own

Bolles, Richard N. *What Color is Your Parachute?* Updated edition. Berkeley, CA: Ten Speed Press, 1988.

The acknowledged best self-help book in the business. Goes far beyond the usual resume and interviewing tips to help you create your own niche in the workplace. Wonderful.

_________________ . *The Three Boxes of Life and How to Get Out of Them*. Berkeley, CA: Ten Speed Press, 1981.

Another fabulous book from Bolles. Here he aims to help those who know that they're in a rut but can't seem to break out of it.

Broadley, Margaret. *Your Natural Gifts: How to Recognize and Develop Them for Success and Self-Fulfillment*. Revised Edition. McLean, VA: EPM Publications, 1986.

An explanation of aptitude and aptitude testing. This may help you to decide whether professional aptitude testing is worth your while.

Drake Beam Morin, Inc. *The Career Navigator*. 100 Park Avenue, New York, NY 10017. (212) 692-7700.

Have PC? Then you can navigate. For $95 you can purchase this program for a personal computer which will run you through a series of career assessment exercises and analyze your responses. Great fun and useful, too.

Editors of the National and Federal Legal Employment Report. *The 30 Biggest Mistakes Legal Job-hunters Make (and How to Avoid Them)*. Washington, D.C.: Federal Reports, Inc., 1986.

Based on the questions that the Editors have received from lawyers looking for jobs, this is very informative, clear advice. They emphasize the fact that there are many jobs for lawyers that might not be found under the listing "attorney." To obtain this, send $3.95 to:

Federal Reports, Inc.
1010 Vermont Avenue, N.W., Ste. 408
Washington, D.C. 20005
(202) 393-3311

Gale, Barry & Gale, Linda. *Discover What You're Best At*. New York: Simon & Schuster, 1983.

A self-administered aptitude test with an informative guide to understanding the results.

Hall, Francine S. & Hall, Douglas T. *The Two Career Couple*. Reading, MA: Addison-Wesley Publishing Co., 1979.

Clear and engagingly written, this book gives a way of analyzing and coordinating the stages of career and family. The self-assessment exercises make this an extremely useful book.

Holland, John L. *Making Vocational Choices: A Theory of Careers*. Englewood Cliffs, NJ: Prentice-Hall, Inc., 1973.

A classic guide for careers counselors and career changers. While more academic than other sources, it also contains some very helpful self-assessment exercises.

Jett, Charles and Dory Hollander, "So You Want To Be A CFO? How To Ride The 'Doom Loop' To A Winning Career." *Cashflow* Magazine. December, 1986.

A new way of looking at job burn-out and skill development by analyzing the components of learning and anxiety. Helpful for individuals to assess when a change might be most productive and for persons involved in human resource development.

Kanarek, Carol, Ed. *Job Change Strategies for the Experienced Attorney* (working title). Chicago, IL: ABA Press, August, 1988.

At the moment of writing, this book had not been published. It is due to be out in August, 1988. Look for it, keeping in mind that it might appear under a different title.

Kennedy, Marilyn Moats, Ed. *Kennedy's Career Strategist*. Wilmette, IL 60091.

Kennedy, a specialist in career development and organizational politics, publishes this monthly newsletter on career planning and job satisfaction. Topics in an early issue included starting a side-line business, finding the 'hidden' job market and answering interview questions. This should be available in libraries or career counseling centers along with other such newsletters which you may find even more useful than this one.

Leape, Martha P. & Vacca, Susan. *The Harvard Guide to Careers.* Revised Edition. Cambridge, MA: Harvard Univ. Press (Office of Career Services & Off-Campus Learning), 1987.

Although this is primarily aimed at a young crowd, the extensive annotated bibliographies on different careers from accounting to broadcasting to health and human services to psychology to theology to veterinary medicine make this a wonderful resource.

Learning Style Inventory. McBer and Company, 137 Newbury Street, Boston, MA 02116. (617) 437-7080.

This is a self-administered and self-scored assessment of your preferred learning style. Quick, but can really help you to evaluate how it is you learn and, therefore, what environments might suit you best. They will send you a complimentary copy on request.

Magid, Renee Y. *When Mothers and Fathers Work: Creative Strategies for Balancing Career and Family.* New York: Amacom, 1987.

Good strategies for organizing your lives when stressed and blessed with the triple demands of career, family and marriage.

Provost, Maureen. *Charting Your Course: Identifying Your Success Pattern and Career Preferences.* New York: Fordham University School of Law, 1987.

This is a workbook of exercises for law students and attorneys developed by Provost, former Career Placement Director at Fordham. These are really inventive and terrific. Available by sending $10 to:

Maureen Provost
Assistant Dean
Fordham University School of Law
140 West 62nd Street
New York, NY 10023
(212) 841-5188

The Staff of Catalyst. *What To Do With the Rest of Your Life: The Catalyst Career Guide for Women in the '80s.* New York: Simon & Schuster, 1981.

Catalyst is an organization that does research and consulting into issues of women and work. This career guide begins with assessment exercises and continues with planning advice. While perhaps too basic for lawyers, this is valuable for its perspective on women as job seekers.

Trembly, Dean. *Learning to Use Your Aptitudes.* San Luis Obispo, CA: Erin Hills Publishers, 1974.

While a bit old-fashioned in its language, this little book explains how to understand the battery of aptitude tests administered by the Johnson O'Connor Research Foundation (see below). Different careers are listed along with an aptitude profile. Useful for determining whether or not to do the tests.

* * *

The Professionals

We clearly can't recommend career counselors in every city and state. Try your local law school placement office for referrals to career counselors in your vicinity who work with lawyers.

Catalyst National Network of Career Resource Centers. For a list of the Centers, specialists in career planning for women, write to:

Catalyst
250 Park Avenue South
New York, NY 10003
(212) 777-8900

Celia Paul Associates. Assists lawyers with career change, especially with change to non-legal careers. Runs very good support groups for lawyers who are contemplating change. Also does individual counseling.

Celia Paul Associates
Career Consultants
Suite 502
1270 Avenue of the Americas
New York, NY 10020
(212) 873-3588

Drake Beam Morin, Inc. 100 Park Avenue, New York, NY 10017. (212) 692-7700.

DBM is a nationwide career consulting organization specializing in outplacement. They have offices in 34 cities in the U.S. They also have a "Job Lead Bank" which is a database of thousands of job lads for management and executive positions. Call or write to the New York office for information on services nearest you.

Federation Employment and Guidance Service. For the unusually low fee of $250, they will do a complete assessment of your aptitudes and abilities, skills, motivational drives, awareness of style, personality and personal barriers. They then will work through this data to develop an action plan. While in the past they have not concentrated on professionals, they are beginning to develop programs in this area.

FEGS
114 Fifth Avenue
New York, NY 10011
(212) 741-7110

John C. Crystal Center. Crystal, a close collaborator and associate of Richard Bolles (see above), has this center to help individuals to create their own career paths.

John C. Crystal Center
111 East 31st Street
New York, NY 10016
(212) 889-8500

Johnson O'Connor Research Foundation. A fee of $450 covers three intensive aptitude testing and evaluation sessions. Aptitude testing is designed to tap your innate abilities. Knowing your aptitudes can help to determine what you might be most happy doing—since people usually like what they're good at. Centers are located as follows:

ATLANTA

Suite 911
3400 Peachtree Road, N.E.
Atlanta, GA 30326
(404) 261-8013

BOSTON

Human Engineering Laboratory
347 Beacon Street
Boston, MA 02116
(617) 536-0409

CHICAGO

161 East Erie Street
Chicago, IL 60611
(312) 787-9141

DALLAS/FORT WORTH

4950 N. O'Connor Road, Suite 250
Irving, TX 75062
(214) 258-0650
METRO: 256-1169

DENVER

Suite 690
One Cherry Center
501 S. Cherry Street
Denver, CO 80222
(303) 388-5600

HOUSTON

3200 Wilcrest, Suite 340
Houston, TX 77042
(713) 783-3411

LOS ANGELES

3345 Wilshire Blvd., Suite 210
Los Angeles, CA 90010
(213) 380-1947

NEW ORLEANS

1001 Howard Avenue, Suite 3800
New Orleans, LA 70113
(504) 524-6239

NEW YORK

11 East 62nd Street
New York, NY 10021
(212) 838-0550

PHILADELPHIA

230 So. Broad Street
Fifth Floor
Philadelphia, PA 19102
(215) 546-7050

SAN DIEGO

430 Nutmeg Street
San Diego, CA 92103
(619) 297-1823

SAN FRANCISCO

701 Sutter Street, 2nd Floor
San Francisco, CA 94109
(415) 885-3003

SEATTLE

1218 Third Avenue
Suite 900
Seattle, WA 98101
(206) 623-4070

TAMPA

5401 W. Kennedy Blvd.
Suite 651
Tampa, FL 33609
(813) 874-0542
PINELLAS: 442-1372

WASHINGTON, D.C.

201 Maryland Avenue, N.E.
Washington, D.C. 20002
(202) 547-3922

Lawgistics. Lawrence Richards, Esq., President. 419 S. Perth Street, Philadelphia, PA 19147. PA: (215) 923-3737. NY: (212) 874-6066.

Mr. Richards, an attorney and an organizational psychologist, provides individual coaching and consulting in the area of lawyer communications skills. "Career counseling for lawyers who are going through transitions—either those looking for a different law job, or those wishing to leave the profession entirely."

National Association for Legal Search Consultants. 1025 Thomas Jefferson Street, N.W., Ste. 400-East Lobby, Washington, D.C. 20007.

NALSC is the organization responsible for establishing guidelines and standards of ethics for the legal search business. More importantly, perhaps, for you, they also publish an annual list of legal search consultants who meet their criteria for ethical practice. Some of these specialize in outplacement work. Perhaps you might be able to get your firm to pay for their counseling services!

* * *

THE MAIN ALTERNATIVES (Chapters 4 and 9)

A word or two to the resource-seeker: Many of the sources listed here could easily fall into two or more categories. For example, the American Electronics Association publishes a list of law firms, investment houses, banks and other service suppliers to the industry. You'll find it under "Private Practice and Corporations" although it could be helpful in finding out about non-legal options in the business. Skim the entire list. That way you can be sure not to miss any important sources. In addition, the distinction between "Background" and "Investigation" can at times be less than cut-and-dried. "Background" sections are meant to give information about what it is like to work in the environment under discussion. "Investigation" provides resources for tracking down further information, openings and potential employers.

The national legal publications, *The American Lawyer, The Legal Times of Washington,* and *The National Law Journal* all publish an enormous variety of articles on practice areas, specialties, trends in law and business as well as information on publications in a variety of areas. The Current Law Index is a very useful tool in tracking down appropriate articles in these publications. These publications are especially helpful since they are available in most firms and offices which employ lawyers. While some articles are listed below, this list is not meant to be exhaustive. In fact, if you take a look into the Index you'll realize that the articles we include amounts to no more than a snowball on top of an iceberg.

Lexis, another law office feature, can be used to further your search also. Not only can you search for articles on industries, careers, companies and so forth through Nexis, but you can use Lexis to track down lawyers and firms whose specialty is your desired career.

* * *

Private Practice and Corporations—Background

American Bar Association Career Series. In recent years, the ABA has begun to publish a series of small books on particular specialty areas within law. Currently available or about to be published are the following:

Careers in Labor Law (1985)
Careers for Minorities (1988)
Careers in Natural Resources and Environmental Law (1988)
Computer Law
Corporate Law for Private Firms
Corporate Law: In-House
Entertainment Law
Family Law
Litigation
Sports Law
Tax Law

These books will introduce the reader to the particular practice area as well as profile individual career paths. They often have appendices of employers and resources. For more information, write or call:

ABA Order Fulfillment 511
750 N. Lake Shore Drive
Chicago, IL 60611
(312) 988-5555

Fishman, James J. & Kaufmann, Anthony S., Eds. *Practicing Law in New York City.* New York: The Council of New York Law Associates, 1975.

Practicing associates in New York City have written personal profiles on law specialties, types of legal environments, volunteer work, practicing as a minority, and the excitement of New York City life.

National Health Lawyers Association. *Careers in Health Care Law.* Washington, D.C.: NHLA, 1986.

Explores what health law is, what types of organizations use health lawyers, and tips on how to pursue a career in health law. NHLA also publishes a newsletter, Health Lawyers News Report. They also have job listings.

NHLA
522 21st Street, N.W.
Suite 120
Washington, D.C. 20006
(202) 833-1100

Orr, Lynn. "Lawyers for the Bottom Line." *Student Lawyer.* February, 1985, Vol. 13, No. 6, pp. 22-33.

Case studies of five young lawyers who decided to work in-house as corporate counsel.

* * *

Private Practice and Corporations—Investigation

American Bar Association. ABA section membership usually gives you access to a great deal of information about a practice area. The sections are as follows:

Administrative Law
Antitrust Law
Corporation, Banking and Business Law
Criminal Justice
Family Law
General Practice
Individual Rights and Responsibilities
International Law and Practice
Labor and Employment Law
Litigation
Natural Resources Law
Patent, Trademark and Copyright Law
Public Contract Law
Public Utility Law
Real Property, Probate and Trust Law
Science and Technology
Taxation
Tort and Insurance Practice
Urban, State and Local Government Law

There are Forum Committees on the following areas of law:

Air and Space Law
Communications Law
Construction Industry
Entertainment and Sports Industries
Franchising
Health Law

For membership information, call or write:

ABA Membership
750 No. Lake Shore Drive
Chicago, IL 60611
(312) 988-5522

American Corporate Counsel Association. 1225 Connecticut Avenue, N.W., Ste. 202, Washington, D.C. 20036. (202) 296-4523.

Publishes the *ACCA Docket,* a quarterly newsletter for corporate counsel which features articles and information of interest to corporate counsel. They will act as a clearinghouse for persons interested in in-house counsel positions.

American Electronics Association. P.O. Box 10045, 2670 Hanover Street, Palo Alto, CA 94303. (415) 857-9300.

Publishes a list of law firms, investment houses, banks and other associate members of AEA. This is great for determining who provides the booming electronics industry with advice. A list of potential employers.

AFL-CIO Lawyers Coordinating Committee Subscription List. 815 16th Street, N.W., Washington, D.C. 20006.

A state-by-state listing of counsel for the AFL-CIO. Good source for the aspiring labor lawyer.

The American Lawyer. 600 Third Avenue, New York, NY 10016 (212) 973-2800.

Check into the management reports (e.g., Life in the Trenches: Mid-level Associates Rank Their Firms; Annual Survey of Legal Recruiters). Available for $5. Also look for articles like Thirteen Great Small Firms and 147 Great Specialty Firms.

Art and the Law. Volunteer Lawyers for the Arts, 1560 Broadway, Ste. 711, New York, NY 10036. (212) 575-1150.

A quarterly journal on arts, entertainment and communications law published by VLA and Columbia University School of Law. Good for getting background on a growing area of practice.

The Association of Trial Lawyers of America. 1050 31st Street, N.W., Washington, D.C. 20007. (202) 965-3500.

Provides a free Attorney/Law Clerk Matching Service to pair ATLA student members who are seeking jobs with neighboring ATLA attorneys seeking law clerks. Publishes *Trial* magazine each month as well as *Law Reporter, Products Liability Law Reporter,* and *Advocate* (each published ten times a year). They also publish a directory each year which is useful for making contacts.

Ecology Law Quarterly. *Environmental Law Careers Directory, 1986-87.* Berkeley, CA: Ecology Law Quarterly, Boalt Hall School of Law, 1986.

Directory of non-profits, private firms and government offices providing opportunities for the environmental lawyer. Cross-indexed by state. Available for $1.00 from:

Ecology Law Quarterly
Boalt Hall School of Law
University of California at Berkeley
Berkeley, CA 94720
(415) 642-0457

Eis, Arlene, Ed. *Legal Newsletters in Print 1988.* Teaneck, NJ: Infosources Publishing, 1988.

A wonderful reference which most likely can be found at any law school library. The information is arranged by title, publisher and subject. While it does not evaluate the quality of the publications, it gives clear and concise information on the subjects and format of each newsletter as well as how to obtain them. See the entry under "Leader Publications" for an idea of what substantive newsletters are around.

Gerson, Ben, Ed. *The National Law Journal Directory of the Legal Profession.* New York: New York Law Publishing Co., 1984.

Firms of more than 50 lawyers responding to questionnaires sent out by the Journal. Gives firm specialties, locations, breakdown of partners and associates, management structure and client information. Too bad it's dated although it's still useful for general information.

Harris, Spencer Phelps, Ed. *The Legal Connection: Corporations & Law Firms.* 2nd Edition. Menlo Park, CA: Spencer Phelps Harris, 1982. (415) 321-4553.

A directory of 6500 publicly-held companies and the 4400 law firms that are linked to them as outside counsel, board members, special counsel or underwriting counsel. Gives three separate alphabetical lists: companies, law firms and law firms by city.

Law & Business Directory of Corporate Counsel, 1987-88. Clifton, NY: Prentice-Hall Law & Business, 1987.

This is the most complete directory available on corporate counsel. Gives biographic information on schools attended, professional affiliations and previous positions held, when possible. Gives phone, full title. Cross-indexed by geographic location. In alphabetical order by company. Great for personalizing letters and for determining credentials that companies might expect.

Leader Publications (The New York Law Publishing Co.) 111 Eighth Avenue, New York, NY 10011. 1-800-221-8195. (212) 741-8300.

Publisher of an extraordinary variety of newsletters and periodicals in legal specialties. Their introductory rates are often quite low. The newsletters that they offer are:

The Bankruptcy Strategist
Cable TV and New Media Law & Finance
Computer Law Strategist
Entertainment Law & Finance
Equipment Leasing Newsletter
Financial Services Law Report
Hazardous Waste & Toxic Torts Law & Strategy
Legal Tech Newsletter
The Matrimonial Strategist
Medical Malpractice Law & Strategy
Product Liability Newsletter
The Real Estate Syndicator Newsletter
Real Estate Tax Strategist

———————. The Corporate Counsellor. 111 Eighth Avenue, Ste. 900, New York, NY 10011. 1-800-221-8195. (212) 741-8300.

This is a relatively new publication focussing on issues for the corporation lawyer. It provides management advice and recent case information to aid the inside lawyer with the dual responsibility to the corporation as a member of management and as a lawyer. You may be able to get a month's trial subscription if you ask.

Leff, Laurel. "Firms of Endearment." *Savvy,* May, 1986.

The ten best firms for women based on a survey of 150 of the largest firms on the basis of numbers of women, upward mobility, parenting concerns, reasonable work schedule, pay parity, etc.

The Legal Times. 1730 M Street, N.W., Washington, D.C. 20036. (202) 457-0686.

Watch for articles and issues such as the "Legal Times 500", an annual survey of the nation's 500 largest law firms with salaries and profiles, or the "D.C. 50 Survey", a review of the largest firms in D.C., Maryland, Virginia and the metropolitan area firms.

Legal World Source, Inc. No. 15 D Street, S.E., Washington, D.C. 20003, (202) 544-6282 or 301 Vermont Street, San Francisco, CA 94103, (415) 431-6142.

This is a new, nationwide computerized job bank for lawyers. It is available to students and alumni of subscribing law schools. Legal employers pay to have their openings listed on the system which are then available to the school populations. A great idea but it will need time to catch on.

Martindale-Hubbell Law Directory in Eight Volumes. 119th Annual Edition. Summit, NJ: Martindale-Hubbell, Inc., 1987.

This behemoth has more services than you might think. While not every firm is in here, the list of lawyers by geographic location is as complete as you'll ever find. Also lists corporate counsel, government lawyers, ABA rules of conduct and special services for lawyers (e.g., couriers, corporation service companies).

National Association for Law Placement. *Directory of Legal Employers.* Washington, D.C.: NALP, 1988.

Check your law school placement office for this one. It's an in-depth listing of 1300 legal employers which includes information on the employer's specialties, salary and benefits, hiring projections and size of the organization. Also gives partner/associate ratios. Published annually.

The National Law Journal. New York Law Publishing Co. 111 Eighth Avenue, New York, NY 10011. 1-800-221-8195. (212) 741-8300.

The last issue of the year contains a list of publishers of law-related books and a list of current law and related books grouped according to area of interest (e.g., litigation, real estate, professional responsibility, law office management).

Smith, Larry, Ed. *Of Counsel Annual Survey.* Clifton, NJ: Prentice Hall Law & Business, 1988.

From the folks at Of Counsel magazine, their annual survey of the 500 largest law firms. They are looking for the basic information on size, partners, associates, laterals but are also asking about non-equity partners, staff attorneys, and so forth. Also has information on revenue and fastest growing practice areas. Available for $50. Call 1-800-223-0231.

Tarlow, Barry, Ed. *National Directory of Criminal Lawyers.* 2nd Edition. Los Angeles, CA: Darby Publishers, 1983.

Lists criminal lawyers in practice in all states but California. Tarlow screens candidates for competence. This may be slightly out of date but will provide useful leads.

United States Law News. *1987-1988 Employment Law Annual.* San Juan Capistrano, CA: United States Law News Company, 1987.

While targeted for law students, this compendium lists subscribing law firms by area of practice and the leading 1000 corporations with in-house counsel, and employments agencies/legal search firms. Plus there are articles on practice development, resume and letter writing, and computer software. This publication should be coming out every year.

* * *

Government (Legal and Non-Legal, including the Judiciary)

While applying for jobs in the government, at any level from your municipality to the Federal Government, may seem to be bewildering due to the volume of forms and red tape that you must wade through, there are fortunately a large number of guides to demystify the process. The United States Government Printing Office, for example, publishes a variety of aids to the government job seeker. See the listing below under U.S. Government Printing Office for further information. Job openings in Congressional offices are issued by the Personnel Office in Congress. These listings are available through your Congressperson. Lastly, information about state judiciaries which may be useful to a jobhunter is available through each state's court administrator's office. Perhaps before going any further you might want to read James Stewart's The Prosecutors, if you haven't done so. (See the listing under "The State of the Profession", above.) His book can give you a real feel for the excitement of government litigation. Government lawyers often mention how extraordinarily interesting their work is (being able to see inside the workings) as a chief reason for job satisfaction. Not a bad reason, either.

* * *

Government—Background

ABA Law Student Division & Economics of Law Practice Section. *Now Hiring: Federal Government Jobs for Lawyers.* Chicago, IL: ABA Press, 1987.

A basic resource on finding Federal jobs. Geared towards those who are just starting out. Describes opportunities for lawyers in the executive, legislative and judicial branches as well as in independent agencies. Annual.

Editors of the National and Federal Legal Employment Report. *Federal Law-Related Careers.* Washington, D.C.: Federal Reports, Inc., 1987.

Identifies over 80 government law-related careers for which a law degree is helpful but not absolutely necessary. Includes job description, number of positions, salary range, average annual salary and the leading Federal agency employers for each field. Available for $12.95 by contacting:

Federal Reports, Inc.
1010 Vermont Avenue, N.W., Ste. 408
Washington, D.C. 20005
(202) 393-3311

________________. *Landing a Legal Job.* Revised Edition. Washington, D.C.: Federal Reports, Inc., 1987.

A straightforward presentation of career advice which includes a list of government sources on careers. This has good information on identifying opportunities in the private sector. Explains how to tailor your SF-171, the Application for Federal Employment. Also of importance is a chapter on two paths to landing a federal job with sample federal employment applications. Available for $9.95 by contacting them as listed above.

Hermann, Richard & Sutherland, Linda. *Working for Big Brother: Government Still Wants You.* Student Lawyer, May 1986, Vol. 14, No. 9, pp. 26-28.

Discusses the distinctions between working in the public versus the private sector. Points out that public sector jobs have some significant advantages such as rapid promotion and benefits. Gives advice on getting through the application process.

Norton, Marilyn B., Ed. *National Association for Law Placement Employment Opportunity Survey of Government Agencies.* Washington, D.C.: NALP, 1987.

Lists contact persons and application deadlines for summer and permanent employment. Updated annually.

U.S. Department of Labor. *Career Paths in the Department of Labor.* Washington, D.C.: U.S. Dept. of Labor, rev. 1978.

Offers basic information about job functions, applications and positions. This is in the process of being revised. A new version should be ready in 1988-89. Free.

U.S. Government Printing Office. *How to Get a Job in the Federal Government.* Washington, D.C.: U.S. Govt. Printing Office, 1981.

Clear instructions on how to complete federal job application forms; explains working conditions, benefits, and holidays; also provides a list by state of Federal Job Information Centers. This title does not seem to be available any longer. Your library may have a copy. Keep in mind, too, that the Federal Government publishes an enormous variety of books that are useful to the government job seeker. For a catalogue, write:

Superintendent of Documents
U.S. Government Printing Office
Department 33
Washington, D.C. 20402

Zehring, John William. *Careers in State and Local Government.* Garrett, MD: Garrett Park Press, 1980.

A solid book for government job seekers. The job bank listings and periodicals in the appendices are especially helpful.

* * *

Government—Investigation

The American Lawyer.

Check for articles such as in the July-August 1983 issue: The Am-Law Complete Guide to Federal District Judges and, also, Federal District Judges: The Best and Worst.

Brownson, Charles B., Ed. *1988 Congressional Staff Directory.* Mt. Vernon, VA: Congressional Staff Directory, Ltd., 1988.

Gives biographical information and election results of the senators and representatives as well as providing lists of their staff members and committee staffs with biographical information on 3000+ staff persons. Not updated as frequently as Congressional Yellow Book.

Brownson, Charles B. & Brownson, Anna L. *1988 Judicial Staff Directory.* Mt. Vernon, VA: Congressional Staff Directory, Ltd., 1988.

Provides information on the judges and their staff members in the Federal courts. Also gives personnel within the Department of Justice. Complete biographies of most of the judges are provided.

Close, Arthur C. & Gregg, John P., Eds. *Washington Representatives 1986.* 11th Edition. Washington, D.C.: Columbia Books, Inc., 1987.

A very complete directory of the representatives in Washington of the major national associations, labor unions and U.S. companies, registered foreign agents, lobbyists, lawyers, law firms and special interest groups, together with their clients and areas of regulatory and legislative concern. Great for pinpointing law-related opportunities in the Washington politicking milieu.

Cook, Betsy, Ed. *Federal Yellow Book.* Vol. XXII, No. 1. Washington, D.C.: Monitor Publishing Co., 1987.

Impressive and exhaustive listing of organizations and the individuals in them. Has complete information on the Executive Office, the Departments, independent agencies (e.g., ACTION, EPA) and regional offices. Includes phone numbers. Updated every three months.

The Council of State Governments. *State Administrative Officials Classified by Functions.* Lexington, KY: The Council of State Governments, 1984.

Just as the title says. This organization, as you can see by the subsequent listings, is the best single source for state governmental information. They also publish a newsletter.

__________________. *State Elective Officials & The Legislatures, 1985-86.* Lexington, KY: The Council of State Governments, 1985.

Lists names and party affiliations of the governor, lt. governor, secretary of state and selected top officials as well as the names and addresses of all legislators for every state.

__________________. *State Legislative Leadership, Committees and Staff, 1985-86.* Lexington, KY: The Council of State Governments, 1985.

A must for the state government job seeker or lobbyist. Most legislative committees and aides have staffers with law degrees. Lists legislators, contact numbers, aides and committees by state. Also has a list of selected committees by area of interest. A new edition should be out soon for 1987-88.

Editors of the National and Federal Legal Employment Report. *1988-1989 Federal Personnel Office Directory.* Washington, D.C.: Federal Reports, Inc., 1988.

A very comprehensive, well-organized list of U.S. Government hiring offices throughout the United States and abroad. Contains detailed information about special recruitment programs for women and minorities, disabled persons, students and veterans. Briefly explains hiring procedures. Organized by department or agency and by geographic region and state. Available for $12.75 by contacting:

Federal Reports, Inc.
1010 Vermont Avenue, Ste. 408
Washington, D.C. 20005
(202) 393-3311

Federal Bar Association. *Lawyers Job Bulletin Board.* 1815 H Street, N.W., Washington, D.C. 20006. (202) 638-0252.

Monthly job postings for Federal Bar Assn. members, primarily in federal jobs. Available to members of the Federal Bar for $20 and to non-members for $30.

The Federal Judicial Center. *The Third Branch.* Washington, D.C.: The Federal Judicial Center.

The newsbulletin of the Federal Courts. Posts job openings in the court system. Available for free. Contact:

The Federal Judicial Center
1520 H Street, N.W.
Washington, D.C. 20005
(202) 633-6011

Federal Reports, Inc. *The National and Federal Legal Employment Report.* Washington, D.C.: Federal Reports, Inc.

A monthly listing of available attorney and law-related professional positions with the federal government and other public and private employers in Washington, the United States and abroad. The tops in government job listings. Subscriptions rates are: $30 for 3 months, $53 for 6 months and $95 for 12 months. Write or call:

Federal Reports, Inc.
1010 Vermont Street, N.W., Ste. 408
Washington, D.C. 20005
(202) 393-3311

The National Directory of State Agencies. Bethesda, MD: National Standards Assn., 1987.

This directory has three components: State elected officials and agency key personnel, state agencies organized by function and an alphabetical listing of all the individuals listed. Particularly helpful for hunting down the persons in each state to whom a resume or inquiry should be sent when you have a particular interest in mind, e.g., agriculture or nuclear energy.

Office of the Federal Register. *The United States Government Manual.* Washington, D.C.: U.S. Govt. Printing Office, 1987/88.

This is the official handbook of the Federal Government. It describes the purposes and the programs of most government agencies and lists their top personnel. Brief statements about quasi-official agencies and some international organizations are also included. Available for $20.

U.S. Government Printing Office. *Official Congressional Directory, 100th Congress.* Washington, D.C.: U.S. Govt. Printing Office, 1987.

Biographies on members, committee assignments, departments, diplomatic offices and representatives, the Executive Office of the President, information on the judiciary . . . ad infinitum. Available in paper for $15.

* * *

Public Interest

The good news is that you will find that people are very helpful when you tell them that you're interested in public interest law. Several law schools mentioned that they are more than willing to cooperate with non-alumni who are looking for careers in public interest law. And, hallelujah, there are beginning to be some excellent guides to the field. Many law schools have developed useful materials about local opportunities. There are many terrific organizations and small firms working in areas of public interest from children's rights to nuclear regulation. You can just about find an organization for any public issue.

Each Legal Services Corporation office is required to submit an annual report which details the year's activities. These can be enormously helpful as background information on what practice at a Legal Service office would be like. All not-for-profit organizations, too, are required to submit annual reports, including financial information, to the state in which they are incorporated. These are available for little or no charge.

* * *

Public Interest—Background

Anzalone, Joan, Ed. *Good Works: A Guide to Careers in Social Change.* 3rd Edition. New York: Dembner Books, 1985.

Includes profiles of people engaged in full-time social change work, listings of such organizations and a compilation of resources and networks. Terrific information presented very thoroughly. Information on organizations gives issues and projects, salaries and who to contact.

Beck, Kirsten. *Cultivating the Wasteland.* New York: Volunteer Lawyers for the Arts, 1983.

Explores the economic and artistic viability of cultural programs, influencing the cable franchising process and the potential of local cable opportunities and programming. Interesting for those interested in the public service aspects of cable television. A joint project of Volunteer Lawyers for the Arts and the American Council for the Arts. For more information, contact:

Volunteer Lawyers for the Arts
1560 Broadway, Suite 711
New York, NY 10036
(212) 575-1150

Howard, Richard Eric. *Guide to Careers in the Public Sector.* Cambridge, MA: The Office of Career Services and Off-Campus Learning, Harvard University, 1982.

Job hunting advice as well as a clear plan for serious career exploration in this area. Designed for Harvard students but the value extends beyond this population.

National Association of Attorneys General. *Biennial Report 1987-1988.* Washington, D.C.: Nat'l Assn. of AGs, 1987.

Lists and gives biographies of member state AGs. Presents legislative stands taken by the Association. NAAG also publishes newsletters: *Antitrust & Commerce Report, Environmental Protection Report, Criminal Justice Report, Consumer Protection Report,* and *Medicaid Fraud Report.* This biennial report is available for $10 from:

NAAG
444 North Capitol Street
Washington, D.C. 20001
(202) 628-0435

U.S. Department of Justice. *Annual Report of the Attorney General of the United States.* Washington, D.C.: U.S. Dept. of Justice, 1988.

Details year's activities in all of the Attorney General's offices (e.g., Office of Legal Policy) and in the divisions (e.g., Criminal Division). Useful to get an understanding of what the AG's office handles. Note: state attorney general offices also publish annual reports which give good information about areas of practice and current issues in these offices. Published annually.

* * *

Public Interest—Investigation

ACCESS, Wesleyan Station, Middletown, CT 06457. (203) 344-7924.

This is one of the best things to happen to public service law. This computerized service provides job listings and pertinent information on public interest organizations. They have a separate law list. Check availability at your law school. For a small fee, an individual can send a letter detailing employment interests and receive appropriate job listings for three months.

Alliance for Justice. *Directory of Public Interest Law Centers.* Washington, D.C.: Alliance for Justice, 1986. (202) 624-8390.

The Alliance, a national association of organizations working for equal justice, compiles the directory from a survey of non-profit, tax-exempt law centers that provide legal representation to otherwise unrepresented interests. The alphabetical listing of groups includes phone numbers, index by interest area and geographical location.

Bundy, Mary Lee & Gilchrist, Irvin, Eds. *The National Civil Rights Directory.* College Park, MD: Urban Information Interpreters, Inc., 1979.

Describes the objectives and activities of national civil rights organizations as well as providing information on local and specially-focussed organizations (e.g., migrant workers, prisoners, etc.). Lists the periodicals published by the groups in the directory with information on how to obtain them. Also provides a short bibliography of civil rights-related organizations. A bit outdated. May only be available in libraries or placement offices.

Brown Burnett, Lolita & Plank, Lynne. *Annotated Bibliography of Public Interest Placement Resources.* National Assn. for Public Interest Law (NAPIL), 215 Pennsylvania Avenue, S.E., Washington, D.C. 20003. (202) 546-4918.

This is it! This is the most complete guide to public interest placement that you could ever find. The information about resources is complete and detailed. This is a critical resource to get. Free.

Connecticut Women's Educational and Legal Fund, Inc. *Organizations Involved in Legal Rights of Women.* CWELF, 22 Maple Avenue, Hartford, CT 06114. (203) 247-6090.

A good, and inexpensive, source on women's rights organizations nationwide. They do not claim to have developed an exhaustive list although it is pretty thorough. To obtain a copy, send $3 to the address above.

The Council of New York Law Associates. *Newsletter.* CNYLA, 99 Hudson Street, New York, NY 10013. (212) 219-1800.

Published every three weeks, provides information on public interest cases available to be taken on, training opportunities, conferences and placement opportunities in the private and public sectors.

D.C. Bar Office of Public Service Activities. *Washington D.C. Organizations Providing Free or Reduced-Fee Legal Representation or Referrals to Volunteer Lawyers.*

This list is available from the D.C. Bar Office as follows:

1426 H Street, N.W.
8th Floor
Washington, D.C. 20005

Foundation for Public Affairs. *Public Interest Profiles Fifth Edition 1986-1987.* Washington, D.C.: FPA, 1986.

Descriptions of 250 leading public interest and public policy organizations chosen on the basis of their influence on national policy, news coverage received and representative nature of the group. In-depth information is presented on purpose, budget, issues, funding sources, publications, contacts and recent press statements. Published biennially.

Fox, Ronald W., Ed. *Public Interest Directory: A Law Student's Guide on How and Where to Find Public Interest/Human Services Jobs.* 2nd Edition. Cambridge, MA: Harvard Law School Placement Office, 1986.

A selected listing of public interest outfits along with career guidance suggestions. Profiles of two HLS graduates who took the public service route. Available for $15 from:

Harvard Law School
Placement Office
1563 Massachusetts Avenue
Cambridge, MA 02138

Gardner, Richard, Ed. *Alternative America.* Cambridge, MA: Resources, 1984.

A listing of alternative businesses (e.g., food coops, small presses, hi-tech businesses). It's worth a look if you're interested in a socially conscious career that isn't traditionally public sector. Address, company name and type of organization are listed alphabetically and geographically.

Kaiser, Geoffrey & Mule, Barbara. *The Public Interest Handbook: A Guide to Legal Careers in Public Interest Organizations.* West Cornwall, CT: Locust Hill Press, 1987.

Gives an overview of the various areas of public interest practice as well as data on hundreds of public interest organizations with employment information. Cross-indexed alphabetically and by area of specialization. Extremely useful.

Legal Services Corporation. *Program Directory.* Washington, D.C.: Legal Services Corp., 1984.

A list of all the offices and support centers by state with contact persons for each.

Martindale-Hubbell Law Directory, Vol. II

Volume II of their megadirectory contains a section on U.S. Government lawyers by agency or employer.

National Association for Public Interest Law. 215 Pennsylvania Avenue, S.E., Washington, D.C. 20003. (202) 546-4918.

This is a wonderful organization that is really helping to organize the field. The newsletter, The NAPIL Connection, is available for $25 to nonmembers. It contains information on placement opportunities as well as useful resources. The NAPIL Fellowships Guide, available for $10 to nonmembers, is for recent graduates who are looking for ways to get into public service law. Year or two year fellowships are one of the best ways to start.

National Clearinghouse for Legal Services. *Clearinghouse Review.* Chicago, IL: Nat'l Clearinghouse for Legal Services, Inc. (312) 939-3830.

This is a big one in the public interest field. This monthly publication has articles, case development news and advance sheet highlights and, in addition, it posts job openings in legal services programs and public interest law. Inside the front cover is a listing of specialized litigation and support centers. Clearinghouse publication lists are available free of charge. Previews of their job postings are listed in a publication, *Job Market Previews,* sent to legal services and law schools.

The National District Attorneys Association. *The 1984 National Directory of Prosecuting Attorneys.* Alexandria, VA: NDAA, 1984.

A guide to state prosecution systems. Gives jurisdiction and authority of state, county and city attorneys. Lists prosecuting attorneys by state and also has an alphabetical index.

The National Jewish Law Students Network. *1987 Guide to Jewish Legal Opportunities.* 3rd Edition. Washington, D.C.: Nat'l Jewish Law Students Network, 1987.

Describes in depth the legal opportunities in American Jewish organizations in the U.S. and Israel. Primarily for law school internship programs but very useful for getting the lay of these organizations.

National Lawyers Guild. *National Referral Directory 1986-1987.* New York: National Lawyers Guild, 1986.

Based on information that Guild members have provided about themselves. Lists legal workers, attorneys, investigators and administrators. Arranged by state. Includes areas of practice. Note: the Massachusetts Chapter of the Guild does annual law office surveys to locate firms, agencies and organizations engaged in public interest law, poverty law and progressive legal and political work. The San Francisco Bay Area Chapter does this and, in addition, lists potential job openings.

National Legal Aid & Defender Association. *The 1987/88 Directory of Legal Aid and Defender Offices in the United States.* Washington, D.C.: NLADA, 1987.

Lists civil legal aid offices, legal services corporation offices and support centers, defender offices, state associations for criminal defense and public defenders and special needs programs. The Directory also has a very thorough bibliography which is worth perusing. Also of interest is their newsletter, which contains job listings, *NLADA Cornerstone.*

New York City Commission on the Status of Women. *Women's Organizations: A New York City Directory.* New York: NY Commn. on the Status of Women, 1986.

Organized by issue (e.g., teen pregnancy, education, etc.). Each organization is described with its address, phone number and contact person. This has a great bibliography. It also has a list entitled "Women's Directories Nationwide" in an appendix.

Available for $5.95 (plus NY tax) and $1.55 for shipping from:

Citibooks
One Center Street
Room 2223
New York, NY 10007
(212) 669-8245

Public Interest Clearinghouse. *Directory.* 2nd Edition. San Francisco, CA: Public Interest Clearinghouse, 1985. (415) 557-4014.

Organizations doing legal work in the public interest presented in alphabetical order. Also provides a list of specializations. Information given on services, phone number and address. Contact persons not listed. Their newsletter, *Impact,* reports on legislation, management, etc. but has little placement information.

________________. *Public Interest Employment Report.* San Francisco, CA 94102. (415) 565-4695.

Lists available positions for California only. Check your law school placement office for a copy.

Renz, Loren, Ed. *The Foundation Directory.* 11th Edition. New York: The Foundation Center, 1987.

Non-governmental grantmakers in the U.S. Begins with a financial analysis of the field as a whole. Information listed by geographical location and cross-indexed by fields of interest. If you think you might be interested in a position as counsel to a philanthropic agency or are interested in non-legal careers in this area, this is an indispensable guide.

Trial Lawyers for Public Justice (a project of the Citizens Legal Clinic). TLPJ, 2000 P Street, N.W., Ste. 611, Washington, D.C. 20036. (202) 463-8600.

TLPJ is a public interest law firm which often functions as an information center and litigation support service in toxic torts, environmental and plaintiff's products liability cases. For an annual report, contact them through the information above.

U.S. Department of Justice. Executive Office for U.S. Attorneys, Washington, D.C. 20530.

Upon request they will send you a list of U.S. Attorneys.

U.S. Environmental Protection Agency, Region I. *Directory of Environmental Groups in New England.* Boston, MA: USEPA, Region I, 1984. (617) 223-7223.

Lists all federal agencies with environmental responsibilities, all New England state environmental agencies, regional voluntary organizations and state-by-state listings of groups. An alphabetical index is provided.

Washington Council of Lawyers. *Directory of Washington, D.C. Area Pro Bono and Public Interest Law Organizations.* 1200 New Hampshire Avenue, N.W., Ste. 700, Washington, D.C. 20036. (202) 659-5964.

Lists over 125 D.C. area non-profit organizations which devote some share of their resources to public interest law or research. Gives address, contact persons, area of law and phone number. Check with the Bar of your locality for similar organizational listings. Available from them for $2.50. A new directory is due in June of 1988.

Wiseberg, Laurie S. & Sirett, Hazel, Eds. *North American Human Rights Directory.* 3rd Edition. Washington, D.C.: Human Rights Internet, 1984.

Describes over 700 organizations in Canada and the U.S. concerned with issues of human rights or social justice. Listed alphabetically. Also has a useful 'dictionary' of acronyms so that you don't get lost in the alphabet soup. Geographic and subject focus lists. Gives phone numbers, contacts, descriptions and background on each.

* * *

International (Public, Private and Non-Legal)

Aulick, Jane L., Ed. *Looking for Employment in Foreign Countries.* 7th Edition. New York: World Trade Academy Press, Inc., 1985.

Hints on hunting for international jobs in government, religious and non-profit organizations, and private business. Sample resumes and cover letters are included. Profiles foreign countries.

Directory of Foreign Firms Operating in the United States. 5th Edition. New York: Uniworld Business Publications, Inc., 1986.

Grouped first by foreign country, then alphabetically, then by list of American affiliates. Lists address, products or services, phone numbers and name of president or other top officer.

Elwood, Robert L., Ed. *Directory of Opportunities in International Law.* Charlottesville, VA: John Bassett Moore Society of International Law, 1977.

Lists potential employers in the categories of law firms, corporations and banks, U.S. Government agencies and offices, United Nations and U.N. specialized agencies, other international organizations, fellowship programs for advanced study, graduate legal study in the US, and volunteer programs. Available for $20 through:

John Bassett Moore Society
University of Virginia School of Law
Charlottesville, VA 22901

The International Corporate 1000. Washington, D.C.: Monitor Publishing Co., 1987.

A listing of who runs the world's 1000 largest corporations. Business description, titles, names of officers and managers.

Kocher, Eric. *International Jobs: Where They Are, How to Get Them.* Revised. Reading, MA: Addison-Wesley Publishing Co., 1983.

An outstanding, comprehensive guide to finding international jobs. Solid information about international positions in Federal Government. The bibliography is excellent.

Powers, Linda, Ed. *Careers in International Affairs.* Revised Edition. Washington, D.C.: School of Foreign Service, Georgetown Univ., 1988.

Good background on options and paths. Available for $11.

TransCentury Recruitment Center. *Job Opportunities Bulletin.* 1724 Kalorama Road, N.W., Washington, D.C. 20009. (202) 328-4400.

TransCentury assists domestic and international development and investment. They provide technical advice on training and development.

Union of International Associations, Ed. *Yearbook of International Organizations, 1985-86.* 22nd Edition. Brussels, Belgium: Union of Int'l Assns., 1985.

Similar to the Encyclopedia of Associations (which also has very comprehensive international information in Volume IV).

U.S. Non-Profit Organizations in Development Assistance Abroad. New York: Technical Assistance Information Clearinghouse, 1983.

Comprehensive directory of information on over 400 non-profit organizations, agencies, missions and foundations with information on their programs and objectives in 124 Third World countries.

Wiseberg, Laurie S., Ed. *Human Rights Internet: Eastern Europe and the USSR.* Cambridge, MA: HRI, 1984.

Describes unofficial human rights organizations existing in Eastern Europe and the USSR as well as official human rights organizations in the area and elsewhere in the world focussing on the area.

__________________. & Scoble, Harry M., Eds. *Human Rights Directory: Latin America, Africa, Asia.* Cambridge, MA: HRI, 1981.

Gives descriptive information on nearly 400 organizations in these regions which are concerned with human rights.

__________________. & Sirett, Hazel, Eds. *Human Rights Directory: Western Europe.* Cambridge, MA: HRI, 1982.

Over 800 organizations listed that are working on human rights and social justice. Cross-indexed by geographical location and by specialty.

Other Sources of Useful Information:

Certain classic stand-bys, such as *Moody's* and *Standard & Poor's*, have information on overseas businesses. Check the reference section in your firm or in your local library.

There are a newsletters in this area, too. Ones to look out for are:

The IDB, monthly newsletter of the Inter-America Development Bank

International Lawyer's Newsletter. Also posts job listings, from Kluwer Academic Publishers, Norwell, MA 02061

Topics, the quarterly publication of the Overseas Private Investment Corp.

* * *

Non-Legal Careers

You have worlds of resources available to you once you step outside of strictly lawyer careers. In addition to career libraries and placement offices in universities and professional schools (e.g. business schools), businesses themselves produce a great deal of informational literature. If you know what area you might be interested in, the larger organizations in the field might have newsletters that you can get copies of. Or, if they are public companies, their annual reports or SEC filings can be good sources of information. Check on Lexis. For investment banks, for example, Goldman, Sachs; Donaldson, Lufkin & Jenrette and Salomon, Inc., all have annual reviews which are highly informative propaganda. Some companies, like Morgan Stanley, have highly polished career information with personal profiles of employees. The periodicals for an industry, such as *Broadcasting* or *Venture,* will often have annual listings of the top performers or best sales or biggest growth companies in their industry. These are great sources of potential employers. Ones to note, aside from the two mentioned:

Buildings
Business Week
Consultants News
Datamation
Financial World
Forbes
Fortune
Inc.
Modern Healthcare
Real Estate Review

* * *

Non-Legal—Background

Anderson, EveLyn G. & Dushoff, Elaine G., Eds. *Legal Careers: Choices & Options.* Volume II. Washington, D.C.: National Assn. for Law Placement, 1983.

An expansion of Volume I, see under "Wayne," below. This volume includes business, hospitals, labor unions and media as well as the categories in Volume I. Also has a list of publications, organizations and positions not requiring bar admission.

Association of Consulting Management Engineers. *How to Select and Use Management Consultants.* ACME, 230 Park Avenue, New York, NY 10017.

Free 33-page booklet. While not exactly an overview of the profession, this gives you the basics of what management consultants do.

Cook, Alberta I. "Lawyers Lured by Other Careers, Lifestyles." *The National Law Journal,* 2/16/87, Vol. 9, No. 23, p. 1.

Useful article not only for information regarding lawyers who are changing jobs but for more background on career planners specializing in law like Celia Paul and Larry R. Richard.

Parker, Penny J., Ed. *Legal Careers in Business.* Volume III. Washington, D.C.: National Assn. for Law Placement, 1984.

Identifies the traditional positions occupied by lawyers in business as well as those areas where a law background would be useful. Information is available for 182 companies from the following industry categories: accounting, banking/finance, energy/oil & gas, insurance, manufacturing, retail, utilities and others.

Prashker, Marti & Valiunas, S. Peter. *Money Jobs! Training Programs Run by Banking, Accounting, Isurance, and Brokerage Firms—and How to Get into Them.* New York: Crown Publishers, Inc., 1984.

Profiles the types of finance jobs and the largest finance and banking houses. Also gives tips on resume writing and interviewing. Oriented to the college crowd but useful for basic background information.

Ranno, Gigi, Ed. *Careers and the MBA, 1988.* 19th Edition. Boston, MA: Bob Adams, Inc., 1987.

Profiles 100 leading MBA recruiters. Articles on issues affecting MBAs. Also analyzes 23 major industries and lists 700 companies that are currently recruiting MBAs. These industries are often happy to hire JD cross-overs.

Utley, Frances with Munneke, Gary. *Nonlegal Careers for Lawyers: In the Private Sector.* Chicago, IL: ABA Press, 1984 (1980).

Offers encouragement and sound advice to the lawyer who isn't interested in law practice. A good survey of the opportunities in business and industry for which legal training is especially useful but where law is not practiced per se. Gives good tips, strategies and resources for finding a nonlegal position. Watch out for Munneke's upcoming *Non-Legal Careers in the Public Sector* which should be published by the ABA soon.

Wayne, Ellen & McCombs, Betsy, Eds. *Legal Careers: Choices & Options.* Volume I. Washington, D.C.: National Assn. for Law Placement, 1982.

Profiles positions held by lawyers in banks/trust companies, consulting, corporations, educational institutions, insurance, law firms, accounting, public service, bar associations, government agencies, trade associations and other areas. Also gives a helpful list of publications and organizations as well as a list of positions not requiring bar admission.

* * *

Non-Legal—Investigation

Association of MBA Executives. *MBA Employment Guide.* 1986-1987 Edition. New York: AMBA Executives Inc., 1986.

Gives in-depth profiles of 100 major MBA employing companies as well as providing a list of 1000 American companies indexed by business function and location. Also has articles on MBA employment trends and job search strategies. The organization might be helpful to contact:

AMBA Executives Inc.
305 Madison Avenue
New York, NY 10165

Close, Arthur C., Ed. *National Directory of Corporate Public Affairs 1986.* 4th Edition. Washington, D.C.: Columbia Books, Inc., 1986.

An alphabetical directory of 1,500 companies with public affairs programs such as political action committees, public information services or corporate giving programs. Summaries of figures on corporate philanthropic activity and PAC donations are here, too. Also has an alphabetical list of the corporate officers engaged in public affairs. Public affairs is an area where a law background would be extremely useful.

Gruber, Katherine, Ed. *Encyclopedia of Associations.* 21st Edition. Detroit, MI: Gale Research, Co., 1987.

Comprehensive guide to national associations indexed alphabetically and by keyword. Includes chief officer, purpose, activities, number of members and publications. A little awkward to use but it has an enormous amount of information. Volume IV contains information on international organizations. Associations are a good way to begin making contacts in a new field.

Kennedy, James H., Ed. *Directory of Management Consultants.* 4th Edition. Fitzwilliam, NH: Consultants News, 1986.

Lists management consulting firms alphabetically and cross-indexed by service, industry and location. Also describes the most reputable professional organizations for management consultants. Gives a good bibliography for the would-be consultant. While you should be able to find a copy in a library, you can buy it for $58.50, prepaid. The 1988 issue will be out in mid-1988. They also publish *Consultants News:*

Templeton Road
Fitzwilliam, NH 03447.

McLean, Janice, Ed. *The Consultants and Consulting Organization Directory.* 8th Edition. Detroit, MI: Gale Research Co., 1988.

Comprehensive guide to the multitudes of consultants. A career education just to look at. Gives areas of specialization, phone numbers, addresses, contacts. Cross-indexed geographically, then by subjects/fields and indexed by officers and principals. Also includes international information.

The National Job Bank. 4th Edition. Boston, MA: Bob Adams, Inc., 1987.

Employment information on 10,000 larger U.S. companies. Includes contact names, telephone numbers, addresses, business descriptions, job categories and educational backgrounds sought. Cross-indexed by industry and state. Note: there are individual job banks for cities (Minneapolis, New York) and regions (Florida, Northwest) which are available in many bookstores, especially those near colleges.

Russell, John J., Ed. *Directory of National Trade and Professional Associations of the United States.* 23rd Edition. Washington, D.C.: Columbia Books, 1988.

Alphabetical listing of 4,300 national trade and professional associations. Includes chief officer, number of members, annual budget and publications. Many of these will hold conferences and have newsletters which may post job listings.

Salzman, Marian L. & Sullivan, Deidre A. *Inside Management Training.* New York: Plume Books, 1985.

Profiles over 100 major companies in more than a dozen career areas. Gives detailed information on compensation, benefits and advancement requirements.

Wade, William A., Ed. *The Corporate 1000.* Washington, D.C.: Monitor Publishing Co., 1987.

Lists names of officers and managers with direct dial phone numbers when available. Gives description of company's business. Heads of subsidiaries and different functions (e.g., DP, personnel, etc.) are listed when possible. Indexed by individual name, company and subsidiary, geographically by state and by industry. This will give you contacts inside the organization for information interviewing or in order to send your resume to the right person.

The Wall Street Journal.

Watch for their Special Reports. For example, the 9/29/86 report contained:

The World's 100 Biggest Public Companies
The 50 Largest Banking Concerns
The 25 Biggest Insurers
The 25 Largest Financial-Services Companies

* * *

Education (Programs and Positions)

Association of American Law Schools. *Placement Bulletin.* Washington, D.C.

Lists positions available as faculty, deans, administrators, researchers and related areas of legal education. Published six times a year. Should be available at any law school placement office.

The Foundation Center. *Foundation Grants to Individuals.* New York: The Foundation Center, 1986.

Principally a list of scholarships, fellowships, internships, awards and prizes given by foundations to students, academics or researchers.

The Graduate Group. *1986 1st Annual Law School Career Opportunities.* West Hartford, CT: The Graduate Group, 1986.

Postings of law teaching positions around the country.

Wayne, Ellen & McCombs, Betsy, Eds. *Graduate Law Study Programs 1982.* 13th Edition Boston, MA: Joint Committee on Law Study Programs, New England School of Law, 1982.

Good guide if you think that re-tooling by schooling could head you in a new and preferred direction. Lists the advanced law programs in the U.S. and abroad with information on how to apply.

Westermeier, Marie & McNett, Kay. *The NAPIL Fellowships Guide.* Washington, D.C.: National Assn. for Public Interest Law, 1987.

Listings of over 200 openings for one or two year fellowships with a variety of public interest organizations. Also lists summer internship programs for students.

Zenoff, Elyce H. & Barron, Jerome, A. "So You Want to Be a Law Professor." *ABA Journal,* Nov. 1983, Vol. 69, pp. 1712-1717.

Tips on how to apply for and how to land a teaching job.

* * *

RESUME WRITING AND INTERVIEWING (Chapters 10 and 11)

Good, Edward C. *Does Your Resume Wear Blue Jeans?* Charlottesville, VA: The Word Store, 1985.

An entertaining, basic book on resume preparation which has some very effective techniques on graphic design and layout. Demonstrates how to use graphic design basics to draw the reader's attention to what is most important to you.

Legal Employment Letter Service.

This service will send word processed job letters and resumes to law firms listed in Martindale-Hubbell. Letters can be sent to all firms of a certain size or those of your choice. Also will send to federal judges and state appellate judges. Reported to be the best national service.

Word Store
1047 Emmet Street
P.O. Box 5628
Charlottesville, VA 22905
(804) 971-4741

Medley, H. Anthony. *Sweaty Palms: The Neglected Art of Being Interviewed.* Belmont, CA: Lifetime Learning Publications, 1978.

This is an easy-to-read, practical guide to the interview. It covers just about everything—from whether or not to tell jokes to how to handle the skeletons in your closet. The format of the book is particularly helpful because it includes checklists and commonly asked questions. Medley is a lawyer who runs videotaped interviewing technique sessions for law firms.

The National Law Journal. New York Law Publishing Co. 111 Eighth Avenue, New York, NY 10011. 1-800-221-8195. (212) 741-8300.

In October, they publish a special section on recruiting with articles on interviewing tips written by search consultants. The 1987 edition included: "Preparation is the Key to a Winning Interview" by Jean Fergus. Also has interviews with firm placement personnel which can be useful for gaining insights into what firms are looking for.

Ryan, Joseph. *Stating Your Case: How to Interview for a Job as a Lawyer.* St. Paul, MN: West Publishing Co., 1982.

Ryan, a partner at O'Melveny & Myers, gives an employer's perspective on interviewing with law firms, corporations and the government. While aimed at law students, both the information on how to make your resume appealing and the resources for various fields make this useful to anyone. This may be the best book of its kind for lawyers.

Yate, Martin. *Knock 'Em Dead.* 2nd Edition. Boston, MA: Bob Adams, Inc., 1987.

A guide to being a successful interviewee. Includes good tips on handling trick questions and stress interviews.

* * *

BUILDING YOUR PRACTICE (Appendix G)

American Bar Association, Economics of Law Practice Section. The ELP specializes in advice on marketing, developing, managing and systematizing your law practice. Recent titles include:

Marketing Your Practice: A Practical Guide to Client Development (1986)
A Lawyer's Checklist for Buying Insurance (1986)
The Art of Managing Your Support Staff (1986)
Practical Planning: A How-To Guide for Solos and Small Law Firms (1985)
A Planning Workbook for Law Firm Management, 2nd Edition (1985)

To receive a complete listing of ELP publications, write or call:

American Bar Association
Order Fulfillment 511
750 N. Lake Shore Drive
Chicago, IL 60611
(312) 988-5555

Attorneys Personnel Report. Professional Publications, Inc., 3690 No. Peachtree Road, Ste. 200, Atlanta, GA 30341. (404) 455-7600.

A monthly newsletter which is written for lawyers, personnel administrators and recruiters. Offers advice on salary and benefits, motivation and recruiting. Tracks the trends in firm personnel management. Also does annual surveys of salaries. Available for $149/year. They offer a full refund guarantee: If you are ever not fully satisfied, they will refund the whole subscription price. This publisher also publishes the following similarly useful management newsletters:

Attorneys Marketing Report ($119/year)
Attorneys Computer Report ($119/year)
Attorneys Office Management Report ($96/year)

Baden, Clifford & Friedman, Dana E., Eds. *New Management Initiatives for Working Parents: Reports from an April 1981 Conference.* Boston, MA: Wheelock College, 1981.

Discusses an array of child care alternatives and gives tips on how to start up the different types of programs. Great for enterprising parents or conscious law firm policy makers. Useful to realize that there are options when in the crunch between personal and professional issues. Note: many states have held similar conferences so check with a local library or college women's studies program for resources for your area.

Brill, Steven & Murray, Lisa C., Eds. *The American Lawyer Management Service.* New York: Am-Law Newspapers Group, Inc., 1988.

This quarterly looseleaf service is in three volumes: Practice Development, Human Resources and Management & Administration. It is a management encyclopedia for managing partners and law firm administrators. A compilation of articles, checklists, forms, surveys and questionnaires that provides practical advice and analysis on topics that range from practice development to partner compensation to support staff to operations and finance. Updates are provided in March, June, September and December. The service costs $475, each update costs $95. (212) 956-3712.

Cash, Capital, and Billing. *The American Lawyer Management Report,* June, 1988.

A review of effective firm financial management practices which includes billing and collecting techniques, loans and profit development. Note: *The American Lawyer* publishes monthly management reports that cover a variety of topics. They are available for $5 from:

The American lawyer
600 Third Avenue
New York, NY 10016
(212) 973-2800

Corporate Clients and Their Lawyers: A Colloquy. LawLetters, Inc., 332 So. Michigan Avenue, Ste. 1460, Chicago, IL 60604. (312) 922-0722.

An interesting collection of insights and essays from corporate counsel about what it is that they want from outside counsel. Also contains dialogue between managing partners and corporate counsel on the issue of service. Available for $25. See below, "The New Balance of Power", for a publication on a similar theme.

Foonberg, Jay G. *How to Get and Keep Good Clients.* Boston, MA: Lawyers Alert Press, 1986.

This is a very clear, basic book on marketing and practice development for the solo or small firm practitioner. He includes such things as a step-by-step guide to an initial client interview, suggestions for personalized license plates and preparing informational mailings. He also discusses how to get clients to leave your existing firm and go with you. Foonberg, a JD and CPA and former chair of the California Bar's Economics of Law Practice Section, is a highly readable and practical source.

Foonberg, Jay G. *How to Start and Build a Law Practice.* 2nd Edition. Chicago, IL: ABA Press, 1984 (1976).

No nonsense, terrific guide for the beginning solo practitioner. Includes samples of forms. Covers all of the basics: From office location to start-up costs to time keeping to malpractice insurance. Clearly written and engaging. A new edition should be available soon.

Jett, Charles and Dory Hollander, "So You Want To Be A CFO? How To Ride The 'Doom Loop' To A Winning Career." *Cashflow* Magazine. December, 1986.

A new way of looking at job burn-out and skill development by analyzing the components of learning and anxiety. Helpful for individuals to assess when a change might be most productive and for persons involved in human resource development.

Lauter, David. "The Thrill of Starting Your Own Firm." *The National Law Journal,* 4/9/84, p. 1 et seq.

Profiles of three young firms along with a ten point checklist for starting up a firm. Note: the *Law Journal* often has articles on law practice development and management. See the "Resume Writing and Interviewing" section for a description of their special recruitment issue.

Lawyer Hiring & Training Report. LawLetters, Inc. 332 So. Michigan Avenue, Ste. 1460, Chicago, IL 60604. (312) 922-0722.

Contains articles on hiring, training and developing lawyers. While this may seem aimed at the larger firm, such management would be great for the forward-thinking small firm. Also lists CLE seminars held nation-wide. While this is expensive, $249/year, individual issues are available to non-subscribers for $20 each. Monica Patton handles these orders.

Lewin, Tamar. "Law Firms Expanding Scope." *The New York Times,* 2/11/87, p. D7.

A discussion of what the author calls the "corporatization" of law firms. Arnold & Porter's subsidiary, APCO Associates, is featured. An interesting discussion of the recent movement of law firms into non-legal areas.

National Association for Law Placement. 440 First Street, N.W., Ste. 302, Washington, D.C. 20001. (202) 783-5171.

NALP has the following titles that would be useful in developing and managing a law firm:

Law Placement Office Forms: A Sampling (1978)
The Lawyer Hiring Handbook (1986)
Managing the Recruitment Process (1982)

NALP also has periodicals, audio cassettes and videotapes which could be very useful in organizing and managing the hiring of lawyers. To obtain further information, write or call to the address above.

"The New Balance of Power." The American Lawyer Management Report, November, 1986.

A report from a conference held for corporate counsel and law firm partners to discuss their changing relationship. Discusses billing, competition for clients, selecting outside counsel and controlling costs. Very interesting forum. Similar to "Corporate Clients, etc." listed above. See above under "Cash, Capital and Billing" for information on how to obtain a copy.

Of Counsel. Prentice Hall Law & Business, 855 Valley Road, Clifton, NJ 07013. 1-800-223-0231. (201) 472-7400.

This is a semimonthly newsletter on developments in legal practice and management. Management trends and strategies, new technology and developments in the profession are featured. While a year's subscription is over $300, you can get the first month on a trial basis.

Oshiro, Carl & Snyder, Harry. *Getting Action: How to Petition State Government.* Mt. Vernon, NY: Consumers Union of the United States, Inc., 1980.

This is an excellent manual for the public interest practitioner or social change lawyer. Gives clear information on how to petition the state to redress grievances such as due process, health regulations and funding. Even includes a petitioner's kit containing checklists, worksheets and a sample petition.

Siconolfi, Michael. "Law Firms Aren't Simply for Law As Attempts to Diversify Begin." *The Wall Street Journal,* 11/18/85, p. 37.

A short discussion of the pros and cons relating to law firm expansion into real estate, investment banking, financial analysis and consulting.

Singer, Gerald M. *How to Go Directly into Your Own Computerized Solo Law Practice Without Missing a Meal (Or a Byte).* Rochester, NY: The Lawyers Co-Operative Publishing Co., 1986.

A solid book for those determined to open a solo shop or for those who are trying to determine whether or not to do so. While he used the Kaypro-10 computer to set up his office, his advice is applicable to any computer system. He covers all of the basics from getting office space to tax advantages and cash flow to expanding one's practice. Get this one and Foonberg's ABA volume. If they thrill you, then you've probably got the stuff to go solo.

Solomon, Burt. "Clout Merchants." *National Journal,* 3/21/87, pp. 662-666.

Discusses the trend among Washington law, public relations, communications and lobbying firms to take on responsibilities that are blurring the distinctions between them. Charts the various fields that these businesses are moving into. Discusses their strategies for growth through merger and expansion. A potentially interesting development for law firms.

The Staff of Catalyst. *The Corporate Guide to Parental Leaves.* New York: Catalyst, 1986.

A planning and implementation guide for up-to-date parental leave policies to meet the needs of men and women. For address, see below.

________________. *Flexible Benefits: How to Set Up a Plan When Your Employees are Complaining, Your Costs are Rising and You're Too Busy to Think About It.* New York: Catalyst, 1986.

A practical manual (including sample plan designs) for developing your own benefit plan. Also provides information on administering the plan. To get more information, write or call:

Catalyst
250 Park Avenue South
New York, NY 10003
(212) 777-8900

Appendices

Appendix A
Job Titles that Have Attracted Attorneys

No list of jobs and niches that have been occupied by attorneys could be complete. And even the most complete list would be so only for a short period of time as attorneys found their collective way into uncharted territory.

Nonetheless, a basic list of well-defined occupational positions has the utility of expanding one's horizons and inducing an ever more creative approach to career planning and job searching.

The listing below was compiled from a variety of sources including publications of the National Association for Law Placement.

PRIVATE PRACTICE

Business Law

- Banking
- Corporations
- Securities Regulation
- Bankruptcy
- Corporate Finance
- Admiralty & Maritime
- Energy
- Investment Banking
- Utilities
- Reorganizations
- Mergers
- Commodities
- Trade Regulation
- Unfair Competition
- Oil & Gas
- Mining
- Natural Resources
- Advertising
- Insurance
- Foreign Trade
- Economic Development
- Interstate Commerce
- Agriculture

Family Law

- Adoption
- Conservatorship
- Foster Parenting
- Guardianship
- Marriage
- Divorce
- Wills, Trusts, Settlement of Estates
- Abuse
- Mother's Rights
- Father's Rights
- Children's Rights
- Surrogate Parenting

Civil Litigation

- Appellate Litigation
- Practice before Administrative Agencies
- Trial Practice
- Malpractice
- Personal Injury and Negligence
- Products Liability

Criminal Justice

- Trials
- Appeals
- Prisoners Rights
- Probation and Parole
- Juvenile Justice
- Rehabilitation

Science and Technology

- Aeronautics
- Engineering
- Genetics
- Patent
- Copyright
- Trademark
- Computers

Health

- Physical Health
- Disabled Persons
- Abused Persons

- Mental Health
- AIDS
- Health Care Systems
- Commitment

Property and Real Estate

- Architecture
- Construction
- Conveyancing
- Cooperatives
- Building Codes
- Condemnation
- Condominium
- Eminent Domain
- Environmental Law
- Land Use
- Shopping Centers
- Tenant Rights
- Urban Development

Taxation

- Income and Other Taxation
- Estate and Gift Taxation
- Practice and Administration
- Federal and State Liaison

Employment

- Worker Safety
- Equal Employment Opportunity
- Collective Bargaining
- Worker's Compensation
- Employee Benefits
- Civil Service
- Labor (Management)
- Labor (Union)
- Unemployment

Consumer Goods and Services

- Purchases Generally
- Debtor's Rights
- Insurance

Transportation

- Corporate Responsibility
- Product Liability
- Energy
- Utilities
- Food
- Drugs

Art, Entertainment and Media

- Motion Pictures
- Sports
- Press
- TV and Radio
- Art and Theatre
- Recreation/Leisure
- Communications
- Music
- Culture
- Libel
- Literary Property
- First Amendment

Public Interest/Human Services

- International Human Rights
- Civil Rights
- Civil Liberties
- Women's Rights
- Elderly
- Minorities
- Gay Power
- Poverty
- Community Organizing/Citizen Action
- Municipal Affairs
- Education
- Welfare
- Rural Residents
- Small Farm Owners
- Military Justice
- Veterans
- Immigration
- Antitrust
- Constitutional
- Government
- Legislation
- Election
- Youth
- Urban Affairs
- Disarmament/Arms Control
- Environment
- Disability Law

Alternate Dispute Resolution

- Mediation
- Negotiation
- Arbitration

Law Practice

- Law Office Economics
- Paralegal Services
- Prepaid Legal Services
- Professional Education
- Specialization
- Law Research Materials
- Advertising
- Ethics
- Legal Clinics
- General Practice
- Recruitment

LAW AND NON-LAW POSITIONS IN BUSINESS

Banks/Trust Companies

- Commercial Loan Officer
- Counseling Officer
- Leasing Contract Administrator
- Loan Workout Officer
- Manager, Employee Benefits Department
- Regulation Analyst
- Trust Officer

Consulting Companies/Firms

- Actuary
- Arbitrator
- Law Firm Consultant
- Counsel
- Pension Administrator/Consultant
- New Business Development
- Principal

Corporations

- Affirmative Action Officer
- Airport Administrator
- Contract Administrator
- Corporate Counsel
- Director of Public Relations
- Director of Real Estate Development
- Foundation Director
- Labor Relations Administrator
- Landman
- Legal Editor
- Natural Gas Purchase Representative
- Real Estate Developer
- Underwriter
- VP, Administration
- VP, Development
- VP, Research

Insurance Industry

- Adjuster
- Attorney-Pension Operations
- Broker
- Field Education Director
- Financial Plans Sales Director
- Pension Profit Sharing Analyst
- Real Estate Manager
- Tax Attorney

Public Accounting Firms

- Counsel
- Pension Planner
- Benefits & Compensation Consulting
- Tax Accountant

Trade Associations

- Counsel
- Industrial Legal Advisor
- Lobbyist
- Prepaid Legal Plan Administrator
- VP, Government Affairs

EDUCATIONAL INSTITUTIONS

- Counsel
- Dean
- Director of Alumni Affairs
- Director of Clinical Programs
- Director of Continuing Legal Education
- Director of Law Center
- Director of Patents and Licensing
- Equal Opportunity Officer
- Librarian
- Professor

GOVERNMENT

Federal

- Agency Counsel
- Committee Counsel

FBI Agent
IRS Agent
Law Clerk
Legislative Aide
Legislation Drafter

State & Local

Agency Counsel
City Manager
City Solicitor
Committee Counsel
Court Administrator
Court Clerk
County Attorney
District Attorney
Hearings Officer
Legislative Aide
School District Attorney
Town Counsel

OTHER

Agent for Athletes
Agent for Entertainers
Public Interest Attorney
Consumer Protection Advocate

Appendix B

IMPUTED CHARACTERISTICS OF FIELDS OF LAW PRACTICE

	Public Service Field	Prestige Score	Intellectual Challenge Score	Rapidity of Change Score	Public Service Score	Ethical Conduct Score	Freedom of Action Score
1.	Securities	68	63	62	44	57	39
2.	Tax	67	67	66	43	55	46
3.	Antitrust (defendants)	65	64	56	40	53	39
4.	Patents	61	56	44	45	62	47
5.	Antitrust (plaintiffs)	60	65	57	46	47	65
6.	Banking	59	47	42	42	58	35
7.	Public utilities	59	55	53	48	56	39
8.	General corporate	59	51	48	44	59	41
9.	Probate	58	45	32	44	57	46
10.	Municipal	56	44	38	45	56	41
11.	Admiralty	56	52	34	42	62	48
12.	Civil litigation	54	52	48	51	45	55
13.	Labor (management)	53	52	53	45	46	38
14.	Real estate	51	45	37	43	48	50
15.	Commercial	49	52	48	46	55	48
16.	Labor (unions)	49	53	53	51	47	42
17.	Environmental (defendants)	49	61	65	47	51	43
18.	Personal injury (defendants)	48	33	42	43	38	46
19.	Environmental (plaintiffs)	47	61	65	72	58	66
20.	Civil rights/civil liberties	46	61	65	77	64	70
21.	Criminal (prosecution)	44	48	56	56	47	53
22.	General family (paying)	42	38	41	52	54	55
23.	Criminal (defense)	41	51	57	57	33	64
24.	Consumer (creditor)	40	50	60	46	43	41
25.	Personal injury (plaintiffs)	38	35	43	43	25	64
26.	Consumer (debtor)	38	52	59	65	50	62
27.	Condemnations	37	35	36	43	39	49
28.	Landlord-tenant	37	43	47	55	41	52
29.	Divorce	35	30	45	50	30	54
30.	General family (poverty)	34	38	51	76	61	64

From: Heinz & Laumann, *Chicago Lawyers: The Social Structure of the Bar* (New York: Russell Sage Foundation, 1982).

Appendix C

Positions Frequently Filled by Persons with Law Degrees

There are many government jobs which do not require a law degree, but which are often filled by persons with such a degree. The following is a list of law-related jobs. To obtain more information regarding how to apply for a particular type of position, contact the Federal Information Center at (202) 653-8468. These positions are in the competitive service and, for most of them you must get your name listed on the appropriate register. For some of these positions an examination (sometimes given only once or twice a year) is required. For others, you will be evaluated based on education and experience. For a few of the positions, you will be instructed to apply directly to the agencies that have the jobs.

Civil Rights Analyst
Equal Opportunity Specialist/Assistant or Manager
Contract Administrator/Negotiator/Specialist
Procurement Analyst
Contract Termination Specialist
Contract Price/Cost Analyst
Contractor Industrial Relations Specialist
Employee Relations Specialist
Labor Relations Specialist
Reemployment Rights Compliance Specialist
Wage and Hour Compliance Specialist
Mediation Specialist
Labor-Management Relations Examiner
Criminal Investigator
Investigator
Game Law Enforcement Officer
Special Agent
Alcohol, Tobacco & Firearms Inspector
Immigration Inspector
Customs Patrol Officer
Customs Inspector
Border Patrol Agent
Legal Instruments Examiner
Hearings and Appeals Officer
Industrial Property Clearance Specialist
Industrial Security Specialist
Insurance Examiner
Intelligence Analyst
Financial Institutions Examiner
Foreign Affairs Officer
Foreign Law Specialist
International Trade Specialist
International Relations Officer
Passport & Visa Examiner
Import Specialist
Realty Specialist
Land Law Specialist

Appendix D

SAMPLE CAREER MATRIX: LITIGATOR, COUNTY ATTORNEY'S OFFICE

SERVICES	Legislation	Appellate Work	Trials	Contracts	Motion Practice	Investigation	Policy Determination Criminal	Policy Determination Civil
CLIENTS								
Environmental Agencies	1. Council 2. 1st Chair 3. Negotiator 4. Admin. 5. Liaison	1. Council 2. 1st Chair 3. Negotiator 4. Admin. 5. Liaison	1. Council 2. 1st Chair 3. Negotiator 4. Admin. 5. Liaison	1. Council 2. 1st Chair 3. Negotiator 4. Admin. 5. Liaison	1. Council 2. 1st Chair 3. Negotiator 4. Admin. 5. Liaison	1. Council 2. 1st Chair 3. Negotiator 4. Admin. 5. Liaison	1. Council 2. 1st Chair 3. Negotiator 4. Admin. 5. Liaison	1. Council 2. 1st Chair 3. Negotiator
County Government	1. Council 2. 1st Chair 3. Negotiator 4. Admin. 5. Liaison	1. Council 2. 1st Chair 3. Negotiator 4. Admin. 5. Liaison	1. Council 2. 1st Chair 3. Negotiator 4. Admin. 5. Liaison	1. Council 2. 1st Chair 3. Negotiator 4. Admin. 5. Liaison	1. Council 2. 1st Chair 3. Negotiator 4. Admin. 5. Liaison	1. Council 2. 1st Chair 3. Negotiator 4. Admin. 5. Liaison	1. Council 2. 1st Chair 3. Negotiator 4. Admin. 5. Liaison	1. Council 2. 1st Chair 3. Negotiator
County Hospital	1. 2. 3. 4.	1. 2. 3. 4.	1. 2. 3. 4.	1. 2. 3. 4.	1. 1st Chair 2. Negotiator 3. Liaison 4.	1. 1st Chair 2. Negotiator 3. Liaison 4.	1. 2. 3. 4.	1. 2. 3. 4.
Highway Department	1. 1st Chair 2. Negotiator 3. Liaison 4.	1. 2. 3. 4.	1. 2. 3. 4.	1. 2. 3. 4.	1. 2. 3. 4.	1. 2. 3. 4.	1. 1st Chair 2. Negotiator 3. Liaison 4.	1. 1st Chair 2. Negotiator 3. Liaison 4.
State's Attorney	1. 2. 3. 4.	1. Council 2. 1st Chair 3. 4.	1. Council 2. 1st Chair 3. 4.	1. 2. 3. 4.	1. Council 2. 1st Chair 3. 4.	1. 2. 3. 4.	1. 2. 3. 4.	1. 2. 3. 4.
Private Clients	1. 2. 3. 4.	1. 2. 3. 4.	1. 1st Chair 2. 3. 4.	1. 1st Chair 2. 3. 4.	1. 2. 3. 4.	1. 1st Chair 2. 3. 4.	1. 2. 3. 4.	1. 2. 3. 4.

SAMPLE CAREER MATRIX: LITIGATION ASSOCIATE

SERVICES	General Corporate	Investing	Lending	Workouts	Regulatory	Loan Default	Tort	Breach of Contract
CLIENTS								
Developers	1. Law 2. Facts 3. 2nd Chair 4.	1. 2. 3. 4.	1. 2. 3. 4.	1. Law 2. Facts 3. 2nd Chair 4.	1. Law 2. Facts 3. 2nd Chair 4.	1. Law 2. Facts 3. 2nd Chair 4.	1. 2. 3. 4.	1. Law 2. Facts 3. Chair 4.
Lenders	1. 2. 3. 4.	1. 2. 3. 4.	1. 2. 3. 4.	1. Law 2. Facts 3. 2nd Chair 4.	1. 2. 3. 4.	1. Law 2. Facts 3. 2nd Chair 4.	1. 2. 3. 4.	1. Law 2. Facts 3. 2nd Chair
Investors	1. 2. 3. 4.	1. 2. 3. 4.	1. 2. 3. 4.	1. Law 2. Facts 3. 2nd Chair 4.	1. 2. 3. 4.	1. Law 2. Facts 3. 2nd Chair 4.	1. 2. 3. 4.	1. Law 2. Facts 3. 2nd Chair 4.
Product Liability Insurers	1. 2. 3. 4.	1. 2. 3. 4.	1. 2. 3. 4.	1. 2. 3. 4.	1. 2. 3. 4.	1. 2. 3. 4.	1. Law/Fact 2. 2nd Chair 3. 1st Chair 4.	1. 2 3. 4.
Professional Liability	1. 2. 3. 4.	1. 2. 3. 4.	1. 2. 3. 4.	1. 2. 3. 4.	1. 2. 3. 4.	1. 2. 3. 4.	1. Law/Fact 2. 2nd Chair 3. 1st Chair 4. Design	1. 2. 3. 4.
Manufacturers	1. Law 2. Facts 3. 2nd Chair 4.	1. 2. 3. 4.	1. Law 2. Facts 3. 2nd Chair 4.	1. 2. 3. 4.	1. 2. 3. 4.	1. Law 2. Facts 3. 2nd Chair 4.	1. Law 2. Facts 3. 2nd Chair 4. 1st Chair	1. Law 2. Facts 3. 2nd Chair 4.

SAMPLE CAREER MATRIX: REAL ESTATE ASSOCIATE

SERVICES	General Corporate	Deal Structure	Work Outs	Syndication	Permanent Loans	Construction Loans	Acquisitions	Zoning
CLIENTS								
Developers	1. Facts 2. 2nd Chair 3. 1st Chair 4. Design	1. Facts 2. 2nd Chair 3. 1st Chair 4. Design	1. Law 2. Facts 3. 2nd Chair 4.	1. Law 2. Facts 3. 2nd Chair 4.	1. Law 2. Facts 3. 4.	1. Law 2. Facts 3. 4.	1. Law 2. Facts 3. 2nd Chair 4.	1. Facts 2. 2nd Chair 3. 1st Chair 4. Design
Municipalities	1. 2. 3. 4.	1. 2. 3. 4.	1. 2. 3. 4.	1. 2. 3. 4.	1. 2. 3. 4.	1. 2. 3. 4.	1. 2. 3. 4.	1. Facts 2. 2nd Chair 3. 1st Chair 4. Design
Investors	1. 2. 3. 4.	1. Law 2. Facts 3. 2nd Chair 4.	1. 2. 3. 4.	1. Law 2. Facts 3. 2nd Chair 4.	1. 2. 3. 4.	1. 2. 3. 4.	1. Law 2. Facts 3. 2nd Chair 4.	1. 2. 3. 4.
Banks Liability Insurers	1. 2. 3. 4.	1. 2. 3. 4.	1. Law 2. Facts 3. 2nd Chair 4.	1. 2. 3. 4.	1. 2. 3. 4.	1. Law 2. Facts 3. 2nd Chair 4.	1. 2. 3. 4.	1. 2 3. 4.
Entrepreneurs	1. Law 2. Facts 3. 4.	1. Law 2. Facts 3. 4.	1. 2. 3. 4.	1. 2. 3. 4.	1. 2. 3. 4.	1. 2. 3. 4.	1. 2. 3. 4.	1. 2. 3. 4.

Appendix E

Sample Statements of Specific Experiences and Skills

Lawyer 1 (Young litigation associate)

Products Liability Case. I served as second chair in a federal products liability action in which the plaintiff received an eye injury when a grinding wheel attached to a grinder manufactured by our client exploded. I drafted all pleadings, responded to discovery requests, and deposed the plaintiff and five witnesses to the accident. I was responsible for conducting the library research which ultimately led to our selection of our expert witness. I then served as the firm's liaison with the expert witness and with the client's employees and executives. The case is currently scheduled for a May trial. I will be responsible for preparing the trial book, and for the direct examination of some of our secondary witnesses.

Real Estate Case. Our client, a former manufacturer and financier of prefabricated homes, instituted a foreclosure by advertisement action against several homeowners who were in default on their mortgage payments. I served as second chair for the client in three actions filed by homeowners to enjoin the foreclosure process. I was responsible for all of the research, pleadings, and briefings related to removal of the cases to Federal Court, and preparation for the direct examination of our witnesses. We succeeded in obtaining a preliminary injunction at the evidentiary hearing. In addition, I prepared an extensive review and summary of the proper procedure for the introduction of business documents. Finally, I successfully prepared and argued a motion for costs and attorneys fees for failure to respond in a timely manner to our discovery requests. I have been thoroughly involved in all of the strategy formulation and business consideration discussions involved in this case.

Lawyer 2 (Senior Associate, International)

Foreign Market Development Project. In connection with a multinational company's strategic plan, I prepared an export marketing survey of several Asian countries. This involved extensive legal and factual research, and several international trips. This investigation covered such issues as the political stability of local governments, the demographics of their consumer populations, customs procedures, import costs, reviews and licenses, and methods for intra-country distribution. I used sources within and outside of both US and foreign governments, and then organized the materials in a manner—briefing books, graphs, sample procedures, pro-formas—so that the company's senior marketing and legal executives were able to recommend a course of action to top management. I was involved in all steps of the project, from its conceptualization and research, through the presentation to top management, to the eventual business decision to proceed with the project.

Foreign Distributorship Agreement. Recently, I revised extensively the foreign distributorship agreement used by a major American manufacturer. This was a client that came to the firm as a result of a presentation I made to an industry trade group. One part of the project involved working with the client's CFO and commercial bank to bring the agreement's financing and warranty provisions into line with the company's expanded export markets and product lines. The second part concerned developing a program to insure the foreign distributors' compliance with the Office of Export Administration's new and stricter regulations governing distributing licenses. This involved the development of a briefing book and seminar series that was used by the company's marketing department in educating foreign distributors on appropriate procedures.

Joint Venture. A few years ago, I assisted a U.S. cast metals company in its preliminary planning regarding a possible joint venture in Mexico. This was a client that I had brought into my first firm and later took with me to my second firm. The company wished to enter into an agreement with Mexican investors to supervise the construction and operation of an iron foundry in Mexico in exchange for a management fee and part of the foundry's production. I surveyed Mexico's investment and import laws applicable to such projects, as well as identified possible sources of financing from the U.S. Export-Import Bank, the Overseas Private Investment Corporation, and the International Finance Corporation, the private lending arm of the World Bank.

U.S. Trade Sanctions. A California export trading company asked for my advice regarding the applicability of U.S. trade sanctions to one of its transactions. The firm was acting as a buying agent for a Dutch energy company in connection with its purchase of a large quantity of steel plate form a South African mill. It suspected that the Dutch company planned to resell the plate to a Middle Eastern country unfriendly to the United States. The California firm did not want to go through with the transaction if its role might constitute a violation of U.S. trade sanctions. After reviewing relevant U.S. statutes, regulations, and administrative orders and consulting informally with staff personnel in the Treasury Department's Office of Foreign Assets Control (the agency administering U.S. trade sanctions), I was able to suggest certain amendments to the agency agreement that allowed the company to proceed.

Import Transaction. A group of entrepreneurs from the U.S. and Hong Kong retained our firm to represent them in connection with a proposed exhibition of Chinese art and handicraft items in various U.S. cities. The merchandise, valued at over $7 million, ranged from $200,000 stone carvings to dime store toys. As the senior associate on the matter, I assisted in negotiating and drafting the various commercial agreements between the show's organizers and the Chinese Government, as well as those between the organizers and their financial backers. The latter work also included negotiating the letters of credit relating to the event. Confronted, in addition, with the problem of how the exhibitors could postpone paying high "column 2" tariffs on the goods until they were resold or until the United States granted "most-favored-nation" status to the PRC, I conceived of structuring the show as an official trade fair. It became the first multi-city trade fair ever chartered by the Commerce Department. I handled the negotiations with Commerce, and later acted as the principal liaison between the exhibition and the U.S. Customs Service during the show's tour. Besides the trade fair concept, the exhibition raised customs law issues ranging from the proper tariff classification of jade bathtubs to some highly unusual uses of bonded warehouses and foreign trade zones. I estimate that my customs counseling efforts saved the show's organizers several million dollars in duties.

Import Relief Proceedings. Latin America's largest iron foundry, another client I brought into the firm, faced two major import relief proceedings in one year. I headed up the firm's defense of the company in both cases. The first concerned a petition filed by the American Pipe Fittings Association seeking the withdrawal of all cast-iron and steel pipe fittings from eligibility under the U.S. Generalized System of Preferences. This type of proceeding involves a hearing before the Office of the U.S. Trade Representative on the merits of the case and another before the U.S. International Trade Commission on the probable effect on the U.S. economy of the proposed action. I represented the company at the two hearings and filed supporting briefs. The decision, which came after a six month period of interagency consultation and lobbying, was extremely favorable: only certain South Korean and Taiwanese fittings were withdrawn from the program. Thus, my client actually gained from the proceeding since South Korea and Taiwan were its chief Third World competitors. The other proceeding involved a countervailing duty petition filed by a U.S. foundry against my client's exports of continuous cast iron bars. The petitioner alleged that the Latin American government was unfairly subsidizing these exports of my client. In this type of proceeding, the Commerce Department investigates the subsidization issue, and the U.S. International Trade Commission determines whether the exports are causing or threatening injury to the U.S. industry. After the first hearing and round of briefs, the ITC issued a preliminary negative injury determination terminating the case. The equivalent of granting a motion to dismiss, such orders are issued in only a handful of import relief proceedings each year.

Lawyer 3 (Senior tax and real estate associate)

Acquisition and Syndication of New Office Project. Our firm represented a major real estate syndicator in connection with its acquisition and syndication of an interest in a 44-story office building. Our client became a partner in the partnership owning the building, then in the early stages of construction, in exchange for a capital contribution of $48 million. I performed tax research and analysis and helped structure and negotiate the transaction by which our client was admitted to the partnership, and drafted the revised partnership agreement. Our client then syndicated its interest in the partnership, raising $90 million in a private offering. In connection with the syndication, I drafted the partnership agreement for the syndicated partnership, the portions of the offering memorandum describing tax consequences and summarizing the terms of the operating partnership agreement and the investment partnership agreement, and the legal opinion included in the offering materials. I also worked with the client's accountants in preparing projections for the offering memorandum.

Corporate Acquisition. Our firm represented ________________ Corporation that franchises fast-food outlets, in connection with the acquisition by ________________ Corporation of a 50% interest in U.S. operations for $10 million plus contingent consideration. I worked with our client's Canadian counsel in structuring the transaction to minimize both U.S. and Canadian income taxes to the corporation and its owners. We achieved an indefinite deferral of both U.S. and Canadian income tax with respect to $8 million of the purchase price. The two companies formed a jointly-owned holding company to own the U.S. subsidiary. The holding company was organized with both common and preferred stock, and provisions requiring contingent additional contributions, buy-outs and redemption. I helped draft subscription and incorporation documents and a shareholders agreement for the holding company, and drafted a legal opinion with regard to certain of the tax consequences of the transaction.

Real Estate Partnerships and Tax-Exempt Financing. Our client was the owner and developer of a suburban office building to be constructed. I helped negotiate and drafted the partnership agreement for a partnership to own the building, having as partners our client and the principal shareholders of the company that had agreed to also be the major tenant in the building. In addition, our firm acted as bond counsel in connection with financing the construction of the building with tax-exempt bonds under the "small-issue" exemption. I was responsible for review and analysis of the project and the documentation to assure qualification for tax-exempt financing, and prepared all IRS filings in connection with the bond issue.

Corporate Recapitalization. Our client was a small family-owned corporation that operated a men's clothing store. Most of the stock of the corporation was owned by the founder and his wife. The founder was approaching retirement age and was passing managing responsibilities to his son and one other key employee. I structured a tax-free recapitalization of the corporation's stock, creating two classes, which allowed the son and the key employee to participate in the growth of the business beyond its current value and granted them increased voting rights on corporate issues. I drafted all of the corporate documentation for the transaction and negotiated and drafted shareholders agreements to which the new stock granted the son and the employee was subject.

Restaurant Syndication. Our client raised funds for two new pizza restaurants through a private offering of partnership interests. I performed tax research and planning in structuring the partnership, and drafted the investment partnership agreement and tax discussions in the offering materials.

Lawyer 4 (Senior litigation associate)

Personal Injury Litigation. From August 1984 through March 1986, I assumed full responsibility for over 150 insurance defense cases. These responsibilities included written discovery, depositions, motions and pre-trials for each file. In addition, I participated in litigation strategy and technique as the cases progressed. I acted as trial attorney on ten cases, three of which concluded in jury verdicts. The cases involved several legal issues, ranging from negligence and products liability to libel and commodities fraud. Since March 1986, I have handled several litigation files on behalf of plaintiffs, and have been solely responsible for pleadings, written discovery, depositions, motions and client counseling. Two of the cases settled in late 1986 for $155,000.

Trademark/Patent Litigation. For the last two years, I have acted as local counsel for an out of state law firm specializing in patent and trademark litigation. I have become involved in three complex patent and trademark cases litigated in the United States District Court. As local counsel, I have been responsible for preparing and presenting several successful motions regarding discovery, attorney-client privilege and summary judgment. In addition, I have assumed responsibility for coordinating documents between the local court and my client firm, and have participated in all status hearings and settlement conferences with District Court judges and magistrates. Two of the cases remain pending, and the third was dismissed pursuant to a judgment entered against the defendant.

Real Estate Management Services. As counsel for a large volume real estate management company, I have been responsible for preparing and presenting well over one hundred eviction proceedings. This has required extensive use of litigation and negotiation skills, and familiarity with lease agreements and landlord/tenant law. Judgment has been entered in favor of the landlord in every complaint presented to the court.

Legal Research Instructor. As a teacher of paralegals at the ____________________
University's ____________________
program for over a year, I have developed research and writing skills as well as strong communication techniques needed to convey these skills to the students. The class meets for eight three hour sessions over five months and covers topics ranging from briefing cases to citations and legal writing. I am responsible for preparing class lectures, reading and writing assignments, correcting assignments and delivering class lectures. Over thirty students are in each class, and their various backgrounds and levels of expertise demand that the lectures be well organized, clear and informative. In addition, I have participated in staff meetings geared toward improving the program to help maintain ABA approval of the program. I have consistently received excellent evaluations from the students at the completion of the course.

Appendix F
Sample Work Evaluations

Lawyer A

During my tenure as an associate with ____________________ I consistently received the highest grades of any associate during our formal reviews. This was reflected in formal evaluations as well as bonuses. ____________________ awarded bonuses based upon number of hours billed and also performance. During the spring of 1985 I was told that I would be asked to become a partner at the end of 1986. I became a partner in January, 1987 after practicing for only four and one-half years. The partners who have worked with me will say that I am aggressive, enjoying accepting responsibility, hardworking and "get the job done." ____________________, an attorney with whom I have worked on cases and whom I have known for twenty-five years, will say that I am a person of intelligence and good character and that I performed well in the cases on which we collaborated.

Lawyer B

1. Professor ____________________ served as Acting Dean of the ____________________ Law School my first year as Lecturer there. He was also one of my teachers when I was a student there. Before coming to ____________________ Law School, he was a partner at the firm of ____________________. Professor ____________________ will provide a very strong reference for my writing ability and intellectual capabilities. He will say that I have a brilliant mind, and a deep sense of concern for others; that I am an independent and creative thinker, a problem solver; that I am diplomatic, and have an ability to see a situation from all perspectives; that I am extremely hard working, and have a very high standard of quality; that I am well liked by those who work with me; and that I am an exceptional lawyer. He will give his unqualified recommendation for my employment.

2. ____________________, Director of ____________________, was the Director during my two years on the staff of that organization. Before coming to that position, she was in private practice in Boston, Massachusetts. She will affirm that I am extremely bright, very self-directed, hard working and diligent. She will also avow to my proficiency for writing, and my ability to learn and assume responsibility quickly. She will say that I am well-liked by colleagues, and am supportive of those with whom I work; and that I have the intellectual capacity to succeed in any area of the law. She will give her unqualified recommendation for my employment.

Lawyer C

1. ____________________ is a partner in municipal finance at the firm of ____________________ in Chicago and 19____________ graduate of Law School. I worked closely with him in a number health care and educational financings over a number of years. He will say that I am a bright and personable lawyer who is analytically quick and a creative problem solver. I am independent in my thinking and practical, rather that overly theoretical, in my approach to problems. I am diplomatic, but I can be quite tough in negotiation. I am very well liked and respected for my ability by those who work with me, both clients and others. I am diligent and hard working, and my legal work is thoughtful, precise and of very high quality. He will highly recommend my employment.

2. ________________________ is a partner in corporate finance, health care and tax exempt finance at the firm of ______________ ________________________ and a 19 ___ graduate of ________________________ Law School. As of March 1, 1987, he will be joining ________________________ the investment banking firm and his largest client, as an investment banking partner. I worked as much with him as with any lawyer at _____ ________________________ . He will say that he has the highest regard for me both professionally and personally. I am a bright, creative and hard working lawyer. I have exceptionally strong abilities as a deal maker and in the process do not sacrifice work quality or the interests of my clients. I have handled, with an extremely high degree of professionalism, a number of complex transactions, both with him and with others, and often in "ground-breaking" areas. I do first rate work. I handle myself in a very professional manner. Clients enjoy working with me and have great confidence in my work and my judgment. He would like to work with me as a client whether I am in [city A] or [city B] and would highly recommend my employment.

Appendix G
Building Your Practice

Overview: The Rationale for Planning

The basics of the practice of law are changing. Fixed expenses are increasing as a percentage of revenue. Client relationships are increasingly transactional, less institutional. Production capacities are uncertain. Law practice owners are vulnerable to the "free agency" of both partners and associates. There is an excess of supply over demand of lawyers competing for the most desirable clients—clients needing customized legal service, insensitive to price, and who pay bills fully and promptly. Law practice is in a state of transition. Whatever turns your career path takes, an entrepreneurial bent is likely to be of great value as that transition gathers momentum.

It is increasingly accepted, if relatively little understood, that "law has to be practiced like a business." But what does this mean? To advance the analysis we must get beyond platitudes and on to specifics.

Is profit to be maximized? Over what period of time? To provide return to owners? To management? To employees? Is there anything to social or pro bono responsibilities? Is a client's interest superior to the economic interest of the lawyer?

The practice of law, however, has much to learn from the practice of business in general, and from service businesses in particular. The learning relates to decision making, organization, productivity, human resources, marketing, and, in general, to surviving and prospering in a competitive marketplace.

The most important lesson that American business has learned in recent years is the significance of the consumer. The American automobile industry for a long time produced the type of car that it wanted to produce—large, expensive to operate and maintain, and with designs that changed as frequently as hemlines. The industry was prosperous and self-satisfied. It was not prepared for the combination of dramatic gasoline price increases, foreign imports, and consumers prepared to vote with their pocketbooks.

At present the American legal industry is in the throes of a transition that resembles that of the automobile industry. Emphasis is still too much on the producer point of view—law review quality documents, high priced manual labor, low cost-consciousness. Too little effort is devoted to determining client preferences and to developing the mechanisms for producing the client-desired services cost-effectively. High cost lawyer labor is still used heavily, sometimes indiscriminately, in producing services. For cost-sensitive clients (an increasing percentage of legal consumers), alternative solutions to producing what were formerly "legal" services are now provided by banks, insurance companies, brokers of all types, accountants, and financial planners.

To prosper in this new environment, law firms will have to "target" clients, determine needs, tailor services to client preferences, and communicate the firm's desire and capacity to provide those services.

The old standbys of law practice marketing (articles and speeches to other lawyers, brochures, etc.) are being replaced by: Market research, market segmentation, product design and positioning, and communications that include newsletters, subject matter seminars, focus group interviews, and individualized presentations to corporate counsel. The emphasis is turning to the clients, their needs, and their desires. Who are they? What do they buy? How much? Guided by what buying influences? Answering such questions is the beginning of planning.

Planning is a process that begins by defining the current status of a law practice . . . be it of a firm, a practice area group within a firm, or a sole practitioner. The planning process then continues with assessment of available market opportunities and the selection of those in which the law practice would like to compete. Said another way:

> Planning is the process of identifying firm-compatible market niches and determining in which ones the firm can capture market share and serve clients competitively, profitably, and well.

Business planning is a relatively straightforward process. It can be learned from the growing literature produced by law firm researchers, consultants, and the ABA Section of Economics of Law Practice. Theoretically, these resources, combined with a good dose of common sense, are sufficient.

However straightforward the planning process is in theory, it often becomes convoluted and complex in actual law practice situations. Practical threshold questions abound. Who should be responsible for gathering the relevant firm and market facts and for leading the planning effort? The Executive Committee? The Planning Committee? A single partner? The legal administrator? Consultants? Who will benefit from this time-consuming, non-revenue-producing activity? Over what period of time? Who should pay for the effort? What is the role and what are the objectives of the individual lawyer in the institutional planning process?

The characteristic structure of most firms—multiple-owner operated, committee-run businesses—makes it difficult for the firm to focus the time, attention, and sophistication that planning issues deserve. In smaller firms and with sole practitioners, even where many of the above issues simplify, there is often a greater problem finding excess lawyer capacity within the practice that can be expended on planning activities.

Even for lawyers who are not yet owners of their practice, planning for growth and to accommodate change in the market are not unimportant. For most lawyers in private practice, then, this chapter addresses how to approach key questions: What are the sources of profit in my current practice? How can I increase and strengthen my revenue stream? What legal services should I offer to secure new sources of revenue? What will it cost to design and produce these services?

* * *

THE PRESENT STATUS OF YOUR PRACTICE

Any plan must begin with the present. An architect cannot design an addition to a house without studying the house as it exists. It is even harder for a lawyer or firm to plan for growth without a firm grasp of the outlines and specifics of the current practice. What kinds of clients do you serve? How are they served? What are the firm's competitive strengths? Weaknesses?

The analysis should be both broad and deep. If substantial professional time within the firm cannot be budgeted for the process, the time and skills of a market analyst may be required.

Creating a Database and Analyzing It

Information should be gathered and analyzed to answer questions such as: What types of clients consume what proportion of the firm's billable time? On what kinds of matters? Which practice areas generate what proportion of the total revenues? At what cost? What trends are evident in the last few years?

An overview of a practice can be accomplished by compiling annual databases (e.g., in a spreadsheet, manual or electronic) of clients, services, revenues, origin of the business, and potential for future business.

1987 SERVICES RENDERED

Client	Service	Revenue	Origin	Potential
ABC, Inc.	Zoning	$8,000	Existing	Many small builders
ABC, Inc.	Financing	$10,000	"	need industry knowledgeable lawyers
ABC, Inc.	Contracts	$3,000	"	
Ace S & L	RE workout	$20,000	Referral	Has lots of workouts. Many S & L's in same situation.
. . .	. . .	. . .	. . .	. . .

INDUSTRY ANALYSIS

Industry	No. of Clients	Notes
Construction	3	Limited to residential.
Retail	16	Clothing (10) Food (3), Misc (3).
Publishing	8	All are in New York.
Universities	2	New clients ('87) brought in by JTB and GRM for Admin. Law.
. . .	. . .	. . .

SERVICE ANALYSIS

Service	No. of Clients	Notes
Labor	3	Old established clients.
Litigation	12	Types A, B, C.
Tax	8	Can expand to other E.B. clients.
Employee Benefits	16	Analyze these for labor need.
. . .	. . .	. . .

The organized collection of information (i.e., database) facilitates content analysis. A facilitation that is augmented when the information is in an electronic spreadsheet. The information then can be quickly and easily grouped by client type, by industry, by the nature of the service, by practice area, by the revenue produced, etc.

After the basic information has been collected and organized, analysis and review is best done with a second person or in a group. Not only does it bring a variety of perspectives and added creativity to the classification and analysis processes, the conversations tend to lead toward the next planning steps: "I didn't realize how much work we did for the construction industry." "The essential elements of our plaintiff's securities work could be applied to the employment discrimination field."

From the database, it will be easy to extract and display information in various ways. A couple of examples are presented above.

Naturally, the more detailed and finely subdivided the information collected, the more subtle can be the analysis.

Internal Audit: The Lawyers' Perspectives

Another practice assessment tool is the internal audit—a collection of the practice percep

WHY CLIENTS CHOOSE OUR FIRM

Client	Timeliness	Reputation	Service	Industry Experience	Cost	Chemistry
A	2	1	3	6	5	4
B	5	3	1	2	4	6
C	1	3	4	5	2	6
-	-	-	-	-	-	-
-	-	-	-	-	-	-
Average	3.2	2.1	3.5	4.7	4.4	5.1

tions and goals of the individual lawyers of the practice area or the firm.

Each lawyer should thoughtfully provide written answers to such practice-defining questions as:

- Why do clients seek out the firm?
- What in the firm reputation attracts clients directly and attracts referrals?
- What skills, competencies, and personalities keep clients?
- What about the firm might be non-attractive to clients?
- What clients have we lost and why?
- What is our major competition?
- What are the future practice opportunities in our practice area?

Internal audits can be of different depths and in different forms (even taped interviews with the busiest lawyers). For each specific situation a decision must be made as to the depth and form most likely to yield a solid effort by all attorneys while avoiding the diminishing returns of taking too much attorney time.

There is a hidden objective of the audit beyond the evident one of accumulating information about the firm or practice. The hidden objective is to begin to get the lawyers thinking in a more entrepreneurial fashion about themselves and the firm from a client's perspective. Do clients really come and stay from a true understanding of the "quality" of the legal work? Do clients even know enough to make distinctions in terms of legal quality? What do clients really want from their lawyer? How is lawyer performance really evaluated by various types of clients?

Client Satisfaction Studies

As is true of most businesses, probably the best source of information is the firm's clientele. Clients should be interviewed to learn of trends in their industries, their anticipated legal service needs, the purchasing influences that cause them to choose your firm, and the state of their current satisfaction with your firm.

Most lawyers seem to assume that clients come to them because of their reputation for delivering quality, technically correct legal services (i.e., a "law review" treatment of a business problem). Surveys, however, suggest that clients choose law firms for a variety of reasons, many remote from quality considerations. This is not to say that a firm may want to consciously lower the quality of its work. It may well, however, in marketing efforts, consciously choose to emphasize firm characteristics beyond technical legal quality.

The purchasing motivation data can be simply collated in a spreadsheet. For example, where clients were asked to rank order six purchasing influences on a 1 to 6 scale, the averages for each influence over all clients (or by client types) can easily be calculated—as shown in the above chart.

As always, varying levels of analysis are possible. For example, if clients are segmented into "New Clients" and "Old Clients", you may be able to determine if the factors that attract clients are different from those that keep them.

STRATEGY DEVELOPMENT

After analyzing your present practice, the next step is to look to the future: evaluating market opportunities, selecting and prioritizing those potential clients for which you want to compete, and organizing and staffing to facilitate that effort.

Lawyer Goals

Statements of interests and aspirations for their individual careers should be collected from the lawyers to establish the goundwork for developing collective goals. This can be a part of the "internal audit" discussed above, can be a separate questionnaire, or can be a retreat topic.

One New York firm introduced its members to the planning process through the circulation of materials describing what planning is and what it is not. Memos accompanying these materials linked planning to relevant client practices and professional literature. Meanwhile, a factual database (similar to the Chart on page 180) covering the firm's practice over a five-year period was assembled. By the time the facts were ready to be reviewed, firm members were prepared to think about the present and future of the firm by department, by service, by client types they wished to serve, and by the revenues they wished to generate.

The partners were canvassed to collect their goals for their own practice and for the collective practice of the firm. The results revealed a theretofore unsuspected broad spectrum of visions of the future. Yet, enough common objectives surfaced to form guidelines for the firm's future development. And the firm benefited from examining and articulating what its members perceived to be its goals and culture.

Market Research

As a tool in the legal profession, to date market research has advanced little beyond the informal networking most lawyers instinctively apply. However, the new Association of Law Firm Marketing Administrators undoubtedly portends rapid change in this area.

Market research is basically a way of testing assumptions. Assumptions about the status of the firm or practice, assumptions about client needs, desires, and trends, and assumptions about the competition. All such assumptions should be tested to the degree practicable before serving as foundations upon which a development strategy will be built.

Market research is often misunderstood and misused. As such, it may be viewed by many attorneys as intrusive or worse. If properly used as a testing tool, however, research provides the best way of minimizing risk in assessing growth opportunities, new ventures, additional offices, adding or eliminating practice areas, etc.

This Appendix is surely not the vehicle for an exposition of the theory and practice of market research in a service industry. The above comments, we hope, will stimulate the entrepreneurially minded to investigate this important matter further. The following two case studies may suggest the spectrum of research tasks from which various law practices might benefit.

Case A. The Washington, D.C. office of a national law firm did market research before adding a new practice area to their array of services. They wanted to develop competence to meet the needs of high-tech companies in the mid-Atlantic corridor. Rather than launching this practice on a hunch, they commissioned a detailed study to test assumptions about: the size of the market, the needs of the market, the degree to which competitor firms were meeting those needs, opportunities to meet currently unmet needs, and alternatives for gaining the competence to serve the market. The Contents page of the study Report shows how these areas of inquiry were addressed:

Executive Summary

Table of Contents

I. Summary of Findings and Recommendations

II. Methodology
   A. Literature Review
   B. Background Interviews

C. Hi-Tech Company Database
D. Hi-Tech Business Survey

III. The Mid-Atlantic Hi-Tech Market
A. Overview
B. Substructure of the Market
C. Infrastructure
D. Specific Institutions

IV. The Demand for Legal Services
A. Overview
B. Study Results
C. Analysis

V. The Supply of Legal Services
A. Overview
B. Study Results
C. Law Firms
D. Analysis

VI. Recommendations
A. Written Business Plan
B. Plan "Outline"
C. Points for Further Study

Appendices

Appendix I:
Background on Greater Washington Business Community

Appendix II:
Directory of Resources in Greater Washington

Appendix III:
Summary of Corporate Questionnaire Responses

Appendix IV:
Bibliography

Appendix V:
Major Washington Area Hi-Tech Law Firms

Appendix VI:
Significant Washington Hi-Tech Practice Groups

Appendix VII:
Secondary Washington Area Hi-Tech Law Firms

Appendix VIII:
Miscellaneous Information

Case B. A small, relatively new, general practice firm based in the Midwest set dual goals of continued growth and refocusing its practice on a local client base. The lawyers were spending up to 80% of their time out of town, but weren't sure how to begin to build a local client base. After identifying, through the assessment process, three distinct client groups as their ideal base, a questionnaire was devised and was used in a telephone survey that reached 50 CEO's and COO's of companies that fit the client profile. The study confirmed certain assumptions about the client base for the firm and generated some useful ideas on what the target clients were looking for in their lawyers and how to market services to those target clients. The result was a foundation of knowledge upon which to build a competitive strategy for continued growth with a growing local client base.

* * *

STRATEGIC CHOICE

A strategic plan is the product of the planning process. It is a set of management decisions about what a firm will do to be successful. For a service business, a typical plan will encompass at least four features:

1. strategic **diagnosis** findings based upon analyses of the firms strengths and weaknesses relative to its competition and of the threats and opportunities presented by the general business environment;
2. a statement of strategic **direction** consisting of a general statement of mission as to what the business will be like in the next 3 to 5 years, concrete and quantifiable goals with specific timetables, actions to be

undertaken (including persons responsible, time-frames, and resources required), and contingency plans;

3. **implementation** considerations relating to organizational structure, policies and procedures, human resources, and resource allocations; and
4. a **financial plan** setting forth anticipated revenues and expenses.

Although the planning process is intended to result in the plan, the process and the product interact. Not only do the mission and goals of the firm affect the actions which the plan dictates should be undertaken, but the actions and opportunities available to a firm affect its perceptions of its mission and goals. That is, strategic planning is both a top-down and a bottom-up process for a law practice. It is also interactive. Thinking about the particulars of implementation, for example, will often foster further assessments of strengths and weaknesses of the firm, and vice versa.

Framework for Choice

The two basic questions of law practice growth are "What?" and "How?".

What growth is the best for this practice to target? Selling more services to existing clients? Selling similar services to new clients? Selling new services?

And *how* is the expanded work to be produced? Through internal development? Via acquisition? A mix?

Insight can be gained from the expansion experiences of corporate America. In "From Competitive Advantage to Corporate Strategy" (*Harvard Business Review,* May-June, 1987), Michael Porter examined the results of the operating company acquisitions of 33 companies from 1950 to 1986. He found that more than 50% of the total acquisitions were divested, and that more than 75% of the acquisitions in unrelated fields were divested.

These facts suggest that as a law practice expands (whether by acquisition of a new practice group or by internal expansion of existing groups) into unrelated legal services and client groups, there will be a greater risk of failure.

Graphically:

	EXISTING SERVICES	NEW SERVICES
EXISTING CLIENTS	LOW RISK	INTERMEDIATE RISK
NEW CLIENTS	INTERMEDIATE RISK	HIGH RISK

The spectrum of risk extends from selling existing services to existing clients (cross-selling) at the low risk end to selling entirely new services to a new set of clients at the high risk end.

Balanced against the risk, of course, must be the reward. If a desired rate of growth can be obtained with low or intermediate risk expansion types, it would be silly to try to sell new services to new clients. On the other hand, sometimes the most rapidly growing service areas are those that involve new services and new clients.

As we have seen above, ever-further layers of analysis are possible. For example, you can distinguish between new clients in currently served industries and new clients in new industries. You can also distinguish between new services within currently provided practice areas and new services in new practice areas. The chart now becomes nine-celled with a finer subdivision of risk levels.

This subtler breakdown yields five risk levels. The "Intermediate Risk" of the prior chart is subdivided into three gradations of intermediate risk

	EXISTING PRACTICE	NEW SERVICE, CURRENT PRACTICE AREA	NEW SERVICE, NEW PRACTICE AREA
EXISTING CLIENT	RISK LEVEL 1	RISK LEVEL 2	RISK LEVEL 3
NEW CLIENT-EXISTING INDUSTRY	RISK LEVEL 2	RISK LEVEL 3	RISK LEVEL 4
NEW CLIENT-NEW INDUST.	RISK LEVEL 3	RISK LEVEL 4	RISK LEVEL 5

(risk levels 2, 3, and 4) as we go from upper left to lower right on the chart.

Not all new practice areas are equally risky when added to an existing practice. The analysis must consider which activities and clients of the total practice will be complementary.

Sharing of relevant skills and activities between current and new undertakings means there is less uncertainty in both production and marketing of the new service. Also, shared activities make it more likely for the law practice as a whole to either provide a better, more valuable service or to produce the service at a lower cost. Either constitutes a significant competitive advantage, of course.

* * *

IMPLEMENTATION ISSUES

Once a choice of new opportunities has been made, the plan must address the production process, the personnel needs, and communication with the marketplace about the new service.

The Production Process

The most successful lawyers and firms will be those who effectively devise systems that produce quality services with a minimum of high-priced lawyer labor. Consideration of organization and of costs of production are thus central to practice development planning. The objective is to use all available resources (forms, systems, prior work product, technological tools, various forms of labor) in the most cost-effective combinations.

The role of the manager of a practice area (which may be just yourself in a sole practice or small firm) is to identify the market, create and maintain production capabilities, and communicate with the marketplace. In the production process itself, the manager's functions typically entail initial client intake and interviews; diagnosis of the problem; design of the strategy or solution; selection and supervision of legal and non-legal staff needed to produce the service; quality control; and client relations.

"Production systems" may sound foreign to many lawyers. But that is mere semantics. Lawyers have always created the needed production systems. It is just that in the current marketplace greater attention to selecting the most efficient production system is needed than was the case formerly. In *Create A System,* Roberta Ramo, former chair of the ABA Section of Economics of Law Practice, defines a system as, " . . . a documented logical method or way of handling transactions, procedures, or work flow in a law office so as to minimize waste, conserve professional time, and optimize productivity."

Personnel

When planning for a new service offering or practice area, the fundamental human resource question becomes: Do we hire young lawyers and train them or should we expand quickly by a merger or acquisition? The issue is easily stated. Its resolution in any given case is less easy.

Hiring laterally can impose serious strains within a previously stable firm. Pecking orders get confused overnight. Compensation levels are debated at length. And, where the lawyer segment (be it one or twenty) brought in is a significant fraction of the new whole, you may effectively have a completely new firm. Despite these problems, many practices find merger or acquisition the only feasible way to take advantage of new opportunities.

Middle grounds, as lawyers know so well, are always possible. An intermediate growth rate can sometimes be attained by the lateral hiring of one or two key lawyers coupled with increased hiring of young associates to fill out the ranks in the new practice area.

* * *

COMMUNICATION

Lawyers have traditionally looked at communication as the entire marketing process, rather than as the final step after assessment, research, analysis, strategy development and choice, and implementation planning. They have also looked at but a narrow slice of available communication ideas.

There is nothing wrong with the traditional triumvirate of speeches, articles, and a firm brochure. But, often, more can and should be done. The objective of any communication program is to convey a message in a cost-effective manner (whether defined as cost-per-contact, cost-per-qualified-lead, cost-per-sale, etc.).

A common fallacy is the assumption that a single communication mode is best (or even suitable) for all of the practice areas that the firm offers. Subject to firm-wide guidelines and standards, each practice group is best positioned to decide what to say to the marketplace and with what medium to say it (newsletters, third-party-sponsored seminars, newspaper columns, or more traditional things).

Prescriptive remedies for a communications program are of marginal usefulness, since the components must be based upon the details of the situation. However, as a minimum, you should have a concise description of each practice area you offer, written from the client's perspective. A perspective best attained with the editing assistance of a particularly close and loyal client.

It is relatively easy for lawyers to direct the by-product of serving one client to others via a subject matter or industry newsletter. Such newsletters might discuss recent developments in the law, governmental regulations being considered, public policy discussions relevant to the industry, or forms of transactions or deal structures that might have particular relevance to these potential clients. To the extent that practice areas are selected on the basis of untapped market potential, a systematic newsletter effort might be the most efficient way of reaching a large group of client prospects with a message. And in an informed and professional manner.

With a large firm, internal communications need attention as well. And with the availability of desktop publishing, virtually any law practice can quickly produce attractive internal or external memos or newsletters.

Any marketing hard copy, however, should be viewed as an introduction to a personal call or visit. The sincere spoken word and eye-to-eye contact remain the very best form of marketing communication.

Whatever communications program is adopted, it should be viewed as part of a process to be reviewed and updated periodically. In an increasingly competitive legal marketplace, where there are 35,000 new lawyers each year, every lawyer should recall the following axiom at least once a week: Marketing is a process, a point of view, not a product to be put on the shelf.

Appendix H
Sample Interview Questions

The following are questions commonly asked by employers during interviews, as collected and developed by Chicago careers consultant Marsha Myerson Smagley:

1. Why did you leave your job before finding a new job?
2. What was your college Grade Point Average?
3. What have been your key personal and career accomplishments?
4. Describe the skills you use in your job.
5. What do you most and least enjoy in your current position?
6. What differentiates you from other candidates?
7. Describe your last performance review. What percent increase did you receive? What suggestions did your supervisor have for improvement?
8. Describe how your co-workers would evaluate your performance.
9. What are your salary expectations?
10. Why do you want to leave your current position?
11. What areas would you like to improve upon?
12. Tell me all you know about this company.
13. What are your short term and long term goals?
14. If you had to change something about yourself, what would it be?
15. What are your family plans? (Improper question still occasionally asked.)
16. Why did you decide on your particular college major?
17. What are you looking for in a job?
18. Why should we hire you?
19. What qualities do you prefer in a manager?
20. Are you willing to travel? Relocate?
21. Why haven't you found a job yet?
22. What interests you most and least about this position?
23. What do you like to do besides work?
24. What references can we call? Can we call your present employer?
25. What other companies are you interviewing?
26. What interests you about this company?
27. Tell me about yourself.
28. What are you bad at?

Appendix I
Lawyer Evaluation Criteria

While not all employers use identical criteria in evaluating the performance of younger attorneys, there is surely much in common to most employers. The listing below contains the criteria used by one private law firm in quality rating its attorneys. The firm used standard letter grades, A through E, for each evaluator to quality-rate each attorney on each criterion.

LAWYERING SKILLS

Written Work

- Writes with clarity, precision, and persuasiveness.
- Final product is well organized and needs only a minor edit.
- Style of writing is appropriate for particular audience.

Analysis/Research

- Spots the relevant business and legal issues.
- Research is accurate and thorough.
- Reasoning is sound.

Oral Skills

- Speaks to/with colleagues, clients, and opposing counsel in a clear, concise, persuasive, and appropriate manner.
- Has ability to "think on his/her feet".
- Substantive Legal Knowledge
- Has acquired sophisticated understanding of law in the major areas in which he/she works.
- Has developed adequate level of knowledge in other areas basic to the firm's practice.
- Keeps up on new developments.

Comments:

WORK HABITS

Disciplined and Organized

- Responds promptly to telephone calls and to letters.
- Uses good judgment in setting priorities and allocating time.
- Plans and prepares for the unexpected.
- Work product is timely and complete, even under high pressure.
- Timesheets are handed in promptly.

Productivity

- Amount of time expended is appropriate to value of the matter.
- Except in special circumstances (e.g., training or supervision, transition from another attorney), time is recorded and billed in full.

Comments:

JUDGMENT

Independence/Coordination

- Knows when to make a decision and when to ask for guidance or assistance from seniors.
- Keeps colleagues regularly informed on status of matters.

Strategy and Tactics

- Has developed ability to evaluate cost vs. benefit of proposed course of action.
- Knows when and how to be aggressive or passive.
- Can distinguish "deal breakers" from "negotiating points" in negotiating an agreement or settling a lawsuit.

Comments:

BUSINESS DEVELOPMENT AND CLIENT RELATIONS

Client Concerns

- Understands and is responsive to client needs and concerns.
- Keeps informed about business developments for particular clients and industries.
- Keeps client informed about client's legal matters and communicates effectively with client.
- Presence and judgment inspire client confidence.

Promotion

- Seeks forums and opportunities to promote the firm to existing and potential clients.
- Demonstrates ability to attract and retain clients.
- Contributes to the firm's public relations efforts.

Community Activities

- Participates actively and effectively in community organizations and activities, bar association activities and the like that tend to reflect credit upon the firm.

Comments:

PERSONAL CHARACTERISTICS

Growth/Maturity

- Learns from experience and seeks opportunities for new challenges.
- Sensitive to other perspectives and viewpoints and flexible enough to handle difficult personalities.
- Personal appearance and attire are appropriate and does not display unpleasant mannerisms or personality quirks that seriously interfere with ability to work with clients and colleagues.

Responsiveness/Persistence

- Willing to pitch in in a crisis situation and functions effectively under pressure.
- Is a "team player".
- Is able and willing to persist on a matter until appropriate result is reached.

Comments:

CONTRIBUTIONS TO FIRM

Training and Supervision

- Effectively trains and supervises junior associates.

Recruiting

- Participates in recruiting program.

Firm Group and Team Participation and Enhancement

- Contributes to functioning of firm, group, and team (e.g., regularly attends meetings, makes presentations, suggests innovative ideas, contributes to organizational development effort, etc.)

Fees

- Contributes to billing and collection efforts regarding clients with whom he/she is actively involved.

Staff Relations

- Works well with others.

Comments: